THE Act OF Marriage
The Beauty of
SEXUAL LOVE

Tim and Beverly LaHaye

Zondervan Books by Tim LaHaye

Anger Is a Choice
How to Win Over Depression
Revelation Unveiled

Zondervan Books by Tim and Beverly LaHaye

The Act of Marriage
The Act of Marriage After 40

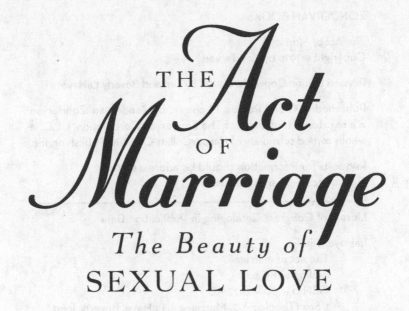

THE Act OF Marriage

The Beauty of
SEXUAL LOVE

Tim and Beverly LaHaye

ZONDERVAN
BOOKS

ZONDERVAN BOOKS

The Act of Marriage
Copyright © 1976 by Zondervan

Revised Edition Copyright © 1998 by Tim and Beverly LaHaye

Published in Grand Rapids, Michigan, by Zondervan. Zondervan
is a registered trademark of The Zondervan Corporation, L.L.C., a
wholly owned subsidiary of HarperCollins Christian Publishing, Inc.

Requests for information should be addressed to
customercare@harpercollins.com.

Library of Congress Cataloging-in-Publication Data

LaHaye, Tim F.
    The act of marriage.
    Bibliography: p.
    ISBN 0 - 310 - 21177 - 8
    1. Sex (Theology). 2. Marriage. I. LaHaye, Beverly, joint
author. II. Title.
BT708.L42
301.41'8
75 - 37742

Published in association with Alive Communications, Inc., 7680
Goddard Street, Suite 200, Colorado Springs, CO 80920.

Illustrations by Jon Post
Interior design by Sue Vandenberg Koppenol

Printed in the United States of America

$PrintCode

To all those who believe married love
can be beautiful, exciting, and fulfilling
and to those who wish
they could believe

Contents

Acknowledgments

We are indebted to a large number of people in the preparation of this book, including the hundreds of counselees who freely shared their problems, hang-ups, and blessings, and our married friends from whom we gained helpful insights as we discussed some of these subjects. Mrs. William (Barrie) Lyons, Family Life Seminar researcher and secretary, prepared the manuscript; Dr. James DeSaegher, head of the English department at Christian Heritage College, edited it; Dr. Ed Wheat, a family physician from Springdale, Arkansas, reviewed the manuscript carefully to assure medical accuracy and supplied a good deal of technical advice; and Dr. Bob Phillips, of Fresno, California, also provided several suggestions. In addition, the seventeen hundred couples who filled out our ninety-two-question sex survey furnished insights we would never have realized otherwise. Finally, we value the information derived from the many authors whose books are listed in the bibliography.

All quotations are used by permission. Grateful appreciation is expressed to the following publishers for permission to use extensive quotations:

Random House, publishers of *The Key to Feminine Response* by Ronald M. Deutsch, illustrations by Philip C. Johnson.

David McKay Co., publishers of *Any Woman Can* and *How to Get More Out of Sex* by David Reuben.

Doubleday & Co., publishers of *The Power of Sexual Surrender* by Marie N. Robinson.

Little, Brown & Co., publishers of *Human Sexual Response* by William H. Masters and Virginia E. Johnson.

The Redbook Publishing Company, publishers of *Redbook*.

Introduction

This book is unlike any other I have ever written. It should be read only by married couples, those immediately contemplating marriage, and those who counsel married couples.

It is deliberately frank. I have long felt a need for a clear and detailed presentation of the intimate relationship that exists between a husband and wife. Most Christian books on this subject skirt the real issues and leave too much to the imagination; such evasiveness is not adequately instructive. Secular books, on the other hand, often go overboard telling it like it is in crude language repulsive to those who need help. In addition, such books usually advocate practices considered improper by biblical standards.

To keep the facts that every couple needs to know from being offensive, I am writing this book with the help of Beverly, my wife of fifty years. In addition to the delicate sense of balance she brings to this work, I have drawn on her extensive counseling experiences as a minister's wife, conference speaker, and registrar of Christian Heritage College.

Both of us have counseled enough married couples to convince us that an enormous number of them are not enjoying all the blessings of which they are capable or for which God has designed them. We have discovered that many others find the intimacies of married love distasteful and unpleasant. Through the years, we have developed several teaching principles that have helped such people in a relatively short period of time.

The requests of counselors, pastors, and others persuaded us that these same principles could help thousands of people if presented in book form.

Before we had had time to begin the project, Dr. Robert K. DeVries, then executive vice president of Zondervan Publishing House, invited us to lunch to present us with the first printed copy of my previous book, *How to Win Over Depression*. "A book that is sorely needed today, written by a Christian couple, would concern sexual adjustment in marriage," he remarked, "and we would like to ask you two to write it." We thanked him and promised to pray about it.

At first Bev was reluctant to get heavily involved with the endeavor until the Lord gave her a specific sign. Within the next two months she counseled at least ten wives who were averse to sexual intercourse. The success those women soon achieved in their love lives convinced her that God required her active participation in the project.

As we began to read current literature on the subject, convinced that God meant lovemaking to be enjoyed by both partners, we prayed that He would lead us to make this work fully biblical and highly practical. He provided many counseling illustrations and pertinent suggestions from pastors, doctors, and friends, among them Dr. Ed Wheat, a family physician who has prepared a superb series of lectures on the subject. When we met him at our Family Life Seminar in Tulsa, Oklahoma, he presented us with a complete set of his cassettes and graciously offered us the freedom to use anything in them. We recommend these cassettes to every married couple and those planning to be married in the near future; they are unquestionably the finest we have ever reviewed. In fact, Dr. Wheat includes information in them that we have not found in the fifty or more books we have scrutinized on this subject.

Inasmuch as most of the people we counsel are Christians, we concluded through our reading that Christians generally experience a higher degree of sexual enjoyment than non-Christians. However, there was no way to prove our assumption. We then prepared an intimate survey for married couples and offered it to those who have attended our Family Life Seminars. By comparing the responses with those of secular sex surveys, our conclusions were confirmed and other interesting and valuable facts were discovered. The results of our survey appear in chapter 13, and parts of it are scattered through the book.

While we were writing the last chapter of this book, *Redbook* magazine published a Sexual Pleasure Survey showing the preferences of 100,000 women. The survey was taken by the magazine and written by Robert J. Levin (coauthor with Masters and Johnson of *The Pleasure Bond*). The most significant finding of *Redbook*'s survey and the one listed first was that "sexual satisfaction is related significantly to religious belief. With notable consistency, the greater the intensity of a woman's religious convictions, the likelier she is to be highly satisfied with the sexual pleasures of marriage."[1] Naturally we were delighted to find that *Redbook*'s survey revealed results quite similar to those of our survey. On the strength of his research Mr. Levin emphatically confirmed that "strongly religious women (over 25) seem to be more responsive ... [and] she is more likely than the nonreligious woman to be orgasmic almost every time she engages in sex."[2] This further convinces us that our presupposition is accurate.

No single book by human beings will ever become the last word on any subject; therefore we don't claim this manual on married love to be final. But we do believe it contains much valuable information helpful to almost any married couple, and several of its insights are not currently found in any other book of its kind. We therefore send it out with our prayers that God will use it to enrich both the love and the love lives of those who read it.

1998 Update

Little did we dream twenty-two years ago when we sent the first manuscript of this book to the publisher that it would become a Christian best-seller, not only in this country but also in several countries in South America, Europe, and Asia. To date there are over two and a half million copies in print in English alone.

Nor did we dream that it would be given or recommended by more ministers than any other on this subject to the young couples they marry. Scores of pastors have told me that they make this book required reading for couples before they begin their premarital counseling sessions. In fact, many young pastors have told me that their pastor had given it to them prior to their own marriage, and because it was such a blessing to them, they now give it to all the couples they marry. Several reported that they keep extra copies on hand to give to newlyweds or to those counselees who are having trouble in this area. One pastor said, "Your publisher should sell me copies at a discount. I have given at least three hundred copies to premarrieds or couples in need."

One pastor in his mid-thirties showed me a picture he and his wife had taken on their honeymoon with a time-delayed camera. They were lying in bed, with the covers up around their necks. Around them were twelve copies of *The Act of Marriage*—wedding gifts from some of the many young couples in the church whom he had compelled to read the book before they were married.

I cannot tell you how many parents have proudly told me they gave it to their son or daughter just before marriage. Some even said, "Our marriage got off to a rocky start in this area, and your book helped us so much we knew it would help them." And many young married women have thanked us for writing the book (sometimes blushing as they talked); they wanted us to know they would have been totally unprepared if they had not read it before their wedding.

The amazing thing is that the book came very close to not being published in the first place. It took us two and a half years to write the original version, including research, testing and talking with many doctors, counselors, and married couples. During this process the word got around to some of my minister friends. Nine of them came to me with great concern. They were concerned that I would likely ruin my reputation if I published a book like this, because "ministers don't write books on sex."

Such comments from respected friends in the ministry drove us to our knees as we inquired of the Lord what we should do. We certainly did not want to jeopardize our ministry. In quite a vivid way the Lord caused us to search our motives: Were we more interested in helping people or protecting our ministry? That was an easy decision to make, so we sent the book in, and every year it continues to minister to thousands of couples. Yes, even more than we ever dreamed.

So you may well ask, why then a new edition with updated and expanded concepts? After all, sex doesn't change. The biblical principles on the subject haven't changed. True, but our culture has. Not only is it almost universally acceptable to talk about sex in marriage today, it is also acknowledged by most Christian leaders that it is necessary to do so. Teens today know more about sex than those of any other generation in the history of the world, thanks to humanistic educators and amoral movie and TV producers. Some of the subjects we discreetly touched on in passing can be expanded on today. In addition, some of the latest discoveries in the field of medicine and social practice confirm the very principles we teach. And more important, these past twenty-two years have given us even greater proof and more illustrations that the true beauty of sexual love is best found in a Christian marriage. In fact, we will prove in this version that Spirit-controlled Christians enjoy the beauty of sexual lovemaking more than anyone else in our society. They don't have an obsession with sex nor read pornographic literature to be stimulated properly, they just go on year after year enjoying it—just as our heavenly Father intended. We also include the answers to some of the questions some readers have sent in.

We are convinced that with the publication of this version, *The Act of Marriage* just got better. After you have read it, we hope you agree.

Tim and Beverly LaHaye
Washington, D.C.

16

Notes

1. Robert J. Levin and Amy Levin, "Sexual Pleasure: The Surprising Preferences in 100,000 Women," *Redbook* 145 (September 1970), 52.

2. Ibid., 53.

One

The Sanctity of Sex

The act of marriage is that beautiful and intimate relationship shared uniquely by a husband and wife in the privacy of their love—and it is sacred. In a real sense, God designed them for that relationship.

Proof that it is a sacred experience appears in God's first commandment to humankind: "Be fruitful and increase in number; fill the earth and subdue it" (Gen. 1:28). That charge was given before sin entered the world; therefore lovemaking and procreation were ordained and enjoyed while the man and the woman continued in their original state of innocence.

This necessarily includes the strong and beautiful mating urge a husband and wife feel for each other. Doubtless Adam and Eve felt that urge in the Garden of Eden, just as God intended, and although we lack any written report for proof, it is reasonable to conclude that

Adam and Eve made love before sin entered the garden (see Gen. 2:25).

The idea that God designed our sex organs for our enjoyment comes almost as a surprise to some people. But Dr. Henry Brandt, a Christian psychologist, reminds us, "God created all parts of the human body. He did not create some parts good and some bad; He created them all good, for when He had finished His creation, He looked at it and said, 'It is all very good'" (Gen. 1:31, paraphrased). Again, this occurred before sin marred the perfection of Paradise.

After forty years of counseling hundreds of couples in the intimate areas of their marital lives, we are convinced that many have the erroneous idea lurking in their minds that something is wrong or dirty about the act of marriage. Admittedly, the unwillingness of many Christian leaders through the years to talk frankly about it has called into question the beauty of this necessary part of married life; but man's distortions of God's plans are always exposed when we resort to the Word of God.

To dispel this false notion we note that all three members of the Holy Trinity are on record in the Bible as endorsing the relationship. We have already cited God the Father's stamp of approval as recorded in Genesis 1:28. Anyone attending a Christian wedding has probably been reminded that the Lord Jesus Christ chose a wedding at which to perform His first miracle; ministers almost universally interpret that as His divine sign of approval. In addition, Christ clearly states in Matthew 19:5 that "the two will become one flesh." The wedding ceremony in itself is not the act that really unites a couple in holy matrimony in the eyes of God; it merely grants them the public license to retreat privately to some romantic spot and experience the "one flesh" relationship that truly unites them as husband and wife.

God the Holy Spirit is certainly not silent on the subject either, for He endorsed this sacred experience on many occasions in Scripture. In subsequent chapters we will consider most of them, but we cite one here to indicate His approval. In Hebrews 13:4 He inspired His writer to record this principle: "Marriage should be honored by all, and the marriage bed kept pure." Nothing could be clearer than this statement. Anyone who suggests anything amiss between husband and wife in regard to the act of marriage simply does not understand the Scriptures. The Author could have merely stated, "Marriage should be honored by all," which would be sufficient; but just to be certain that no one missed His point, He amplified it with another phrase, "and the marriage bed kept pure." It is pure because it remains a sacred experience.

Subconsciously I was reluctant until recently to use the word *coitus* to describe lovemaking, even though I knew it to be an accurate term. That changed when I discovered that the Holy Spirit's word for *bed* in Hebrews 13:4 was the Greek *koite* (pronounced koy'-tay), meaning "cohabitation by implanting the male sperm."[1] *Koite* comes from the root word *keimai* meaning "to lie" and is akin to *koimao,* which means "to cause to sleep."[2] Although our word *coitus* has come from the Latin *coitio,* the Greek word *koite* has the same meaning and signifies the relationship a married couple experiences in the bed that they "cohabit." Based on this meaning of the word, Hebrews 13:4 could be translated, "Coitus in marriage should be honored by all and kept pure." Partners in coitus avail themselves of the possibility of the God-given privilege of creating a new life, another human being, as a result of the expression of their love.

For More Than Propagation

My first sex counseling experience was a complete wipeout. As a junior ministerial student, I was stopped one day by a soccer teammate as we left the practice field for the shower room. I had noticed that this big, athletic young man was not himself. We had both been married for little more than a year, but he didn't seem to be happy. By nature he was an easygoing fellow, but after some months of marriage he became tense, irritable, and generally uptight. Finally he blurted out, "How long do you think I should go along with married celibacy?" His young wife apparently believed that sexual relations were "only for the propagation of the race." Since they had agreed to delay having a family until after graduation, he had become a rather frustrated young bridegroom. Very seriously he asked, "Tim, is there anything in the Bible that teaches sex is for enjoyment?"

Unfortunately I was too uninformed to provide an answer. I had been blessed with a bride who didn't entertain such notions, and I had given no thought to such a problem. Since that experience, however, I have endeavored to collect a number of Scripture references during my Bible study to determine what God's Word teaches on the subject. I have found many passages that touch on married lovemaking; some speak primarily about propagation, but many others prove that God intended the act of marriage for mutual pleasure. In fact, if the truth were known, it has probably provided men and women with the greatest single source of married enjoyment since the days of Adam and Eve, just as God intended.

Unfortunately, the opposite is also true. When a couple's sexual love life is unsatisfactory, it produces much stress in their relationship. Men who are disinterested and women who are averse to sex increase tension in the home, and this tension is often followed by unkind and selfish expressions or conduct that can be disastrous to a marriage. In many cases an unfulfilled sex life leads to infidelity or divorce.

About five years after the first edition of this book had been published, I spotted a lonely looking woman in her early forties coming into our Sunday evening service. Somehow I was not surprised that she was waiting for me when the service was over. Thinking I had never met her before, she introduced herself—the former wife of my college athlete friend mentioned above. In the twenty years they were married she had borne him four sons, all of whom were separated from their father most of the time now since he had divorced her. Apparently the day came when he could no longer tolerate her self-imposed abstinence or celibacy, and he became attracted to someone who was more responsive to his sexual needs. While his decision to leave his family cannot be condoned in a Christian, I am confident, knowing the youthful character of the man and his commitment to Christ, that it would not have happened if his wife had not been afflicted with an unbiblical mental attitude toward married lovemaking. For as we shall discover later in this book, the most important organ either partner brings to their wedding bed is their brain. It controls all other organs.

The Bible on Sex

Because the Bible clearly and repeatedly speaks out against the misuse or abuse of sex, labeling it "adultery" or "fornication," many people—either innocently or as a means of trying to justify their immorality—have misinterpreted the teaching and concluded that God condemns all sex. However, the contrary is true. The Bible always speaks approvingly of this relationship—as long as it is confined to married partners. The only prohibition on sex in the Scripture relates to extramarital or premarital activity. Without question, the Bible is abundantly clear on that subject, condemning all such conduct.

God is the creator of sex. He set our human drives in motion, not to torture men and women, but to bring them enjoyment and fulfillment. Keep in mind how it all came about. Adam was unfulfilled in the Garden of Eden. Although he lived in the world's most beautiful garden, surrounded by tame animals of every sort, he had no companionship with his own kind. God then took some flesh from Adam and performed another creative miracle—woman—similar to man in every respect except her physical reproductive system. Instead of being opposites, they were complementary to each other. What kind of God would go out of His way to equip His special creatures for an activity, give them the necessary drives to consummate it, and then forbid its use? Certainly not the loving God presented so clearly in the Bible. Romans 8:32 assures us, "He who did not spare his own Son, but gave him up for us all—how will he not also, along with him, graciously give us all things?" When we look at it objectively, we realize that sex was given at least in part for marital enjoyment.

For further proof that God approves lovemaking between married partners, consider the beautiful story that explains its origin. Of all God's creations only the human being was made "in the image of God" (Gen. 1:27). This in itself makes humans the unique living creatures on the earth. The next verse further states, "God *blessed them* and said to them, 'Be fruitful and increase in number'" (v. 28). Then He delivered His personal comment regarding all His creation: "God saw *all* that he had made, and it was *very good*" (v. 31).

Genesis 2 affords a more detailed description of God's creation of Adam and Eve, including the statement that God Himself brought Eve to Adam (v. 22), evidently to introduce them formally and give them the command to be fruitful. Then it beautifully describes their innocence in these words: "The man and his wife were both naked, and they felt no shame" (v. 25). Adam and Eve knew no embarrassment or shame on that occasion for three reasons: they were introduced by a holy and righteous God who commanded them to make love; their minds were not preconditioned to guilt, for no prohibitions concerning the act of marriage had yet been given; and no other people were around to observe their intimate relations.

Interestingly enough, the best lovemaking in the world is not limited to beautiful people or two with perfectly sculpted bodies. It is at its best when two healthy lovers, more interested in satisfying their partner's needs than their own, approach their marriage bed without guilt. That is why virtue is the best preparation for marriage, and why faithfulness throughout the relationship is so enriching. God's plan was for one man and one woman to share the ecstasy of that experience only with each other.

Adam "Knew" His Wife

Additional evidence of God's blessing on this sacred relationship appears in the charming expression used in Genesis 4:1 to describe the act of marriage between Adam and Eve: "And Adam knew his wife Eve; and she conceived . . ." (literal translation). What better way is there to describe the sublime, intimate interlocking of mind, heart, emotions, and body in a passionately eruptive climax that engulfs the participants in a wave of innocent relaxation that thoroughly expresses their love? The experience is a mutual "knowledge" of each other that is sacred, personal, and intimate. Such encounters were designed by God for mutual blessing and enjoyment.

Some people have the strange idea that anything spiritually acceptable to God cannot be enjoyable. In recent years we have found great success in counseling married couples to pray together regularly. The book *How to Be Happy Though Married*[3] describes a particular method of conversational prayer that we have found most helpful, and we frequently suggest this procedure because of its variety and practicality. Through the years many couples have tried it and reported remarkable results.

One emotional, outgoing young wife who exclaimed that it had changed their relationship also confided, "The main reason I was reluctant to pray with my husband before going to bed was that I feared it would hinder lovemaking. But to my amazement, I found we were so emotionally close after prayer that it set the stage for loving." Her experience is not rare; in fact, we have found no reason why a couple cannot pray before or after a spirited time of loving. However, most couples find themselves so relaxed afterward that all they want to do is sleep—the sleep of contentment.

A Ravishing Lover

At the risk of shocking some people, we would point out that the Bible doesn't mince any words on the subject. The Song of Songs is notoriously frank in this respect (consider 2:3–17 and 4:1–7).

The book of Proverbs warns against taking up with the "strange woman" (a prostitute) but by contrast challenges a husband: "may you *rejoice* in the wife of your youth." How? By letting "her breasts satisfy you always, may you ever be captivated by her love" (Prov. 5:18–19). It is obvious that this ravishing lovemaking experience should make a man rejoice, conferring on him ecstatic pleasure. The context plainly signifies an experience intended for mutual enjoyment. This passage also indicates that such lovemaking was not designed solely for the propagation of the race, but also for sheer enjoyment by the partners. If we understand it correctly, and we think we do, it isn't to be a hurried or endured experience. Modern experts tell us that "foreplay" before entrance is essential to a mutually satisfying experience. We find no fault with that; we would, however, point out that Solomon made the same suggestion three thousand years ago!

All Bible passages should be studied in the light of their purpose in order to avoid wresting or twisting their meaning. The above concept is strong enough as we have presented it, but it becomes even more powerful when we understand its setting. The inspired words of Proverbs 1–9 record the instructions of Solomon, the world's wisest man, to his son, teaching him to handle the tremendous sex drive within himself and to avoid being tempted by its improper use. Solomon wanted his son to enjoy a lifetime of the legitimate use of that drive by confining it to the act of marriage. Since this entire passage concerns wisdom, it is obvious that enjoyable, satisfying married love is the course of wisdom. Extramarital love is presented as the way of folly, offering short-term pleasure by bringing "destruction" (heartache, guilt, sorrow) in the end.

We would be remiss if we failed to point out Proverbs 5:21: "For a man's ways are in full view of the LORD, and he examines all his paths." This text includes lovemaking: God sees the intimacy practiced by married partners and approves it. His judgment is reserved only for those who violate His plan and desecrate themselves by engaging in sex outside of marriage.

"Caressing" in the Old Testament

It may be hard for us to think of Old Testament saints as being good lovers, but they were. In fact, one may never hear a sermon on Isaac's relation with his wife, Rebekah, recorded in Genesis 26:6–11. This man, who made it into God's "Who's Who" of faith in Hebrews 11, was observed by King Abimelech "caressing" his wife. We are not told how far his advances went, but he obviously was sufficiently intimate to make the king conclude that she was Isaac's wife, not his sister, as he had at first falsely declared. Isaac erred, not in engaging in foreplay with his wife, but in not restricting it to the privacy of their bedroom. The fact that he was caught, however, suggests that it was common and permissible in their day for husbands and wives to "caress." God planned it that way.

Further insight into God's approval of the act of marriage appears in the commandments and ordinances of God to Moses for the children of Israel. He instructed that a man was to be exempt from military service and all business responsibilities for one year after his marriage (Deut. 24:5) so that these two people could get to "know" each other at a time when their sex drives were strongest and under circumstances that would provide ample opportunity for experimentation and enjoyment. Admittedly, this provision was also given to make it possible for a young man to "propagate" before he faced the risk of death on the battlefield. Contraceptives were not used at that time, and since the couple had so much time to be with each other, it is easy to see why children usually came early in the marriage.

Another verse displays how thoroughly God understands the sexual drive He created in human beings— 1 Corinthians 7:9: "It is better to marry than to burn with passion." Why? Because there is one legitimate, God-ordained method for releasing the natural pressure He has created in human beings—the act of marriage. It is God's primary method for release of the sex drive. He intended that husband and wife be totally dependent on each other for sexual satisfaction.

The New Testament on Lovemaking

The Bible is the best manual ever written on human behavior. It covers all kinds of interpersonal relationships, including sexual love. Some examples have already been given, but one of the most outstanding passages follows. This is probably the clearest passage on the subject in the Bible:

> But since there is so much immorality, each man should have his own wife, and each woman her own husband. The husband should fulfill his marital duty to his wife, and likewise the wife to her husband. The wife's body does not

belong to her alone but also to her husband. In the same way, the husband's body does not belong to him alone but also to his wife. Do not deprive each other except by mutual consent and for a time, so that you may devote yourselves to prayer. Then come together again so that Satan will not tempt you because of your lack of self-control. (1 Corinthians 7:2–5)

These concepts will be explained more fully later in this book, but here we will merely delineate the four central principles taught in this passage concerning lovemaking.

1. Both husband and wife have sexual needs and drives that should be fulfilled in marriage.
2. When a person marries, he forfeits control of his body to his partner.
3. Both partners are forbidden to refuse the meeting of their mate's sexual needs.
4. The act of marriage is approved by God.

A young mother of three came to ask me to recommend a psychiatrist to her. When I inquired why she needed one, she hesitatingly explained that her husband felt she must be harboring some deep-rooted psychological problem about sex. She had never experienced an orgasm, could not relax during lovemaking, and felt guilty about it all. When asked when she first had these guilt feelings, she admitted to heavy petting before marriage that violated her Christian principles and the warning of her parents. She finally conceded, "Our whole four-year courtship seemed to be a continuous scene of Tom trying to seduce me and my fighting him off. I made too many compromises and am honestly amazed that we didn't go the whole route before our wedding. After we were married, it just seemed to be more of the same. Why did God include this sex business in marriage anyway?"

That young woman did not require a battery of psychological tests and years of counseling therapy. She simply needed to confess her premarital sins and then learn what the Bible teaches about marital love. Once her guilt had been removed, she quickly perceived that her mental picture of the act of marriage was entirely wrong. After studying the Bible and reading several books on the subject, with her pastor's assurances that love-making is a beautiful part of God's divine plan for married couples, she became a new wife. Her husband, who had always been a lukewarm Christian, met me between services one Sunday. "I don't know what you've been telling my wife, but it has changed our marriage!" His spiritual growth since then has been exciting to watch— all because a wife caught the big picture that God planned lovemaking to be a mutually enjoyable experience.

Have you wondered why we are bombarded by sex exploitation on every hand today? Most best-selling books, top-draw movies, and magazines reek with sex, and no one will deny that sex is without question the most popular international sport. The "tell it like it is" craze has simply brought into the open what has been paramount in people's minds since Adam and Eve.

Admittedly God never intended the cheap, perverted, publicly displayed sex we see today. This is the result of man's depraved nature, destroying the good things God has imparted to man. God intended the act of marriage to be the most sublime experience two people could share on earth.

We believe that even though Spirit-filled Christians do not have an obsession with sex, do not corrupt their minds with warped distortions of it, and do not speak of it incessantly, they enjoy it more on a permanent lifetime basis than any other group of people. We have reached this conclusion not only from the hundreds of people whom we have counseled on these intimate subjects, the many letters and questions we have received during more than forty years in the ministry, and the more than eight hundred Family Life Seminars we have conducted, but also from the fact that mutual pleasure and enjoyment are God's purpose in designing us as He did. He has made that clear in His Word.

Notes

1. James Strong, "Dictionary of the Words in the Greek Testament" in *Strong's Exhaustive Concordance of Words in the Greek Testament* (New York: Abingdon-Cokesbury, 1890), 42.

2. Joseph Henry Thayer, *Thayer's Greek-English Lexicon of the New Testament*, rev. ed. (Marshalltown, Del.: National Foundation for Christian Education, 1899), 352.

3. Tim LaHaye (Wheaton, Ill.: Tyndale House, 1968).

TWO

What Lovemaking Means to a Man

Viewing life through someone else's eyes is a key to communication on any level. The failure of many wives to understand what lovemaking really means to a man often leads to an erroneous conclusion that stifles her natural ability to respond to his advances.

Susie began our counseling interview by grumbling, "Our problem is—Bill is a beast! All he ever thinks of is sex, sex, sex! Ever since I met him it seems I've been fighting him off. Maybe he's oversexed!" What kind of man do you envision after hearing her description of Bill? Probably a copper-skinned giant with virility exuding from every pore of his body and elevator eyes that flirt with every pretty girl who comes along. Nothing could be further from the truth! Bill is a quiet, dependable, hardworking, affectionate family man in his late twenties who is still a little insecure. When I asked how often they made love, she replied, "Three or four times a week." (We have discovered that wives usually report more frequent lovemaking experiences than their husbands, and a dissatisfied husband usually underestimates the frequency of their experiences. By averaging their reports, we gain a more accurate figure.) Actually Bill is not abnormal; in fact, our survey and others find that he is functioning well within the range of the average husband at his age.

Susie had three problems: she did not like sexual relations, she did not understand Bill's needs, and she was more interested in herself than in her husband. When she confessed her sin of selfishness and learned what loving really meant to him, it changed their bedroom life. Today she enjoys lovemaking, and recently she dropped us a thank-you note for the time we had spent with her, concluding, "Would you believe the other night Bill said, 'Honey, what's come over you? For years I chased you around the bed, and now you're chasing me!'" Doubtless, she did not have to chase him very far.

The act of marriage is vitally significant to the husband for at least five different reasons:

1. *It satisfies his sex drive.* It is usually agreed that the male in all species of living creatures has the stronger sex drive, and Homo sapiens is no exception. That does not suggest that women lack a strong sex drive, but as we will see in the next chapter, hers is sporadic whereas his is almost continual.

God designed man to be the aggressor, provider, and leader of his family. Somehow that is tied to his sex drive. The woman who resents her husband's sex drive while enjoying his aggressive leadership had better face the fact that she cannot have one without the other.

To illustrate the physical cause of the male sex drive, let us introduce the scientific evidence that "each drop of [seminal] fluid is said to contain as many as 300 million sperm."[1] Since it is possible for a man to have two to five ejaculations a day, depending upon his age, it is obvious that his reproductive system manufactures a supply of semen and many millions of tiny sperm daily. If unreleased through coitus, this can be very frustrating to his mental and physical well-being. One writer has said, "A normal and healthy man has a semen build-up every 42 to 78 hours that produces a pressure that needs to be released." A variety of conditions will determine the frequency of that pressure. For example, if psychological work or family problems weigh on his mind, he will not be as vitally conscious of that pressure as when he is relaxed. Studies have indicated that men from rural areas consistently desire coitus more frequently than do men from urban areas in the same age brackets. Researchers explain that this occurs because urbanites tend to undergo more psychological pressures than their rural counterparts. One other possibility, however, is that rural men of all ages tend to work harder physically and thus are probably in better physical condition than their urban counterparts, who may enjoy a more sedentary life.

One of the most common misconceptions in the minds of young married women pertains to the sexual needs of their husbands. Because of their lack of experience, preconceived notions, and most of all their fear of pregnancy, many young wives do not share their husbands' enthusiasm for lovemaking. This trend seems to reverse itself later in the marriage, but in the earlier years the frequency of sex is often cause for conflict and disagreement. Young wives may equate their husbands' youthful passion with bestiality, not realizing that their husbands' drives are not unique, but characteristic of most normal men. These drives are the gift of God to produce the motivation for procreation, which is still the primary social purpose of humankind. That gift influences not only a man's sexual behavior but also his personality, work, motivation, and almost every other characteristic in his life. Without it he would not be the man she fell in love with. It is a wise woman who cooperates with that need rather than fights against it.

In human relations, attitude is everything. This is certainly true of lovemaking. If either person looks on it as a duty to perform, that attitude will soon be perceived by his or her mate; and it will gradually deteriorate until the passion of their love is lost. Unless they read a book like this or receive Christian counseling to change their mental attitude toward the experience, it will not be long before their love is gone.

2. *It fulfills his manhood.* A man usually possesses a stronger ego than a woman. If he is not a man in his own eyes, he is nothing; and somehow his sex drive seems to be intricately linked to his ego. I have never met an impotent or sexually frustrated man who enjoyed a strong self-image. A sexually satisfied husband is a man who will rapidly develop self-confidence in other areas of his life.

Most men do not blame their insecurities on sexual frustration, because they are either too proud or do not realize the connection; but I have observed it so often that whenever I find a fractured male ego, I look for sexual frustration. A man can endure academic, occupational, and social failure as long as he and his wife relate well together in the bedroom; but success in other fields becomes a hollow mockery if he strikes out in bed. To the man, being unsuccessful in his bedroom signals failure in life.

One loving wife asked what she could do for her husband whose business had just collapsed. He was more depressed than she had ever seen him before, and she felt incapable of reaching him. "I'm confident he will bounce back," she said. "He's too dynamic a man to let this one failure ruin his whole life." Since she had already prayed with him and they had committed their economic future to God, I suggested that she make aggressive love to him, that she dress provocatively and use her feminine charm to seduce him. She spontaneously asked, "Don't you think he'll get suspicious? He's always been the aggressor in that department." Her response gave me an opportunity to explain that his fractured ego needed the reassurance of her love during a time of defeat. Many husbands subconsciously fear that their wives endure lovemaking out of a sense of duty or some lesser motivation. What every man needs, especially during a period of defeat, is to be convinced that his wife loves him for himself, not for anything he does for her. I knew her dynamic, choleric husband well enough to perceive that he was not complicated enough to get suspicious; any surprise would give way to ecstasy. Later his wife reported that he not only lacked suspicion but, within five minutes after lovemaking, began to share a new business idea with her. Although that idea never materialized, it started him upward. He soon found his niche and today is enjoying a successful career.

One instructive aspect of this case is the fact that her husband now credits his wife with helping him "bounce back." He never refers to their lovemaking experience, of course, but says such things as "My wife is quite a gal! When I was down and out, she still had faith in me. It was her confidence that sparked my own." Actually, before she ever came to me, she had verbalized her confidence in him many times by such expressions as "Don't let it get you down; you can start over again." But not until she made love to him did she communicate her confidence in terms that he could understand. Much later she offered a rather interesting comment to me: she could not remember her husband ever holding her so tightly during lovemaking. But that is not really difficult to understand. Men are just boys grown tall, and this man's failure had shaken his manhood and accentuated the boy that lurks in the heart of every man. But love once again succeeded when all else failed.

Some women will probably take exception to this use of lovemaking as another example of the "exploitation of sex." We prefer to think of it as the expression of unselfish love. Because of her love for her husband, this wife created an atmosphere on the basis of her husband's need, not his feelings—nor hers, for that matter. It is a beautiful fulfillment of the Bible's description of love: "Each of you should look not only to your own interests [needs], but also to the interests [needs] of others" (Phil. 2:4).

One woman told us, "No matter what our love life consists of, there is one time each month when I always try to get my husband to make love to me—the night after he has paid the family bills. It seems to be the only thing that gets him back to normal." Her husband gets an *F* for failing to commit his problems to God and learning to rejoice by faith (1 Thess. 5:18), but she rates an *A* for being a wise and loving wife.

These stories appear in stark contrast to what usually goes on when hubby's ego is flattened by failure, debt, or problems. Most self-centered wives are so "shaken" by the sight of an insecure husband during a period of testing that they are ill-prepared to be a husband's "help-meet" during the time of his distress. Do not be deceived by that thin coating of tough masculinity most men wear; underneath are many emotional needs that only a loving wife can supply.

The old Victorian nonsense that a "nice lady doesn't act as if she enjoys sex" conflicts with a good husband's need to know that his wife thoroughly enjoys his lovemaking. It seems that the Victorians did not distinguish between their premarital and their marital taboos. Naturally a good, wholesome Christian woman will not flaunt her enjoyment of sex; that is a personal matter. Far too many insecure women are tricked into thinking that they should look and act sexy in public. That is distorted sex appeal! A truly secure woman will convey her sex appeal and satisfaction only to her husband. It gives him great pleasure and, in fact, makes his own sexual pleasure much more satisfying when he is assured that it has been mutually enjoyed. A wise and considerate woman goes out of her way to let her man know that he is a good lover and that she enjoys their relations together. It is good for his ego and promotes honest communication between them. Only a false and insincere modesty would hide such vital knowledge from a partner. Genuine love flourishes in giving. That is why a devoted husband finds great delight in knowing his wife enjoys his lovemaking.

The benefits of such love not only intensify the solidarity of the lovers, but also spill over and bless the children. A secure man becomes a better father, uses better judgment, and has an improved capacity to love the entire family.

3. *It enhances his love for his wife.* We are familiar with the word *syndrome,* but we usually associate it with negative things like illness, depression, anger, or fear. However, it is appropriately used in conjunction with love. A love syndrome never hurt anyone, and such a syndrome is created between married partners when their lovemaking is mutually satisfying.

Because a man has been endowed by God with an intense sex drive and a conscience, the satisfactory release of that drive without provoking his conscience will enhance his love for the person who makes that possible. But only one person on earth can do that—his wife.

Follow our reasoning. A man's sex drive can be relieved only by ejaculation. This can be achieved by (1) intercourse, (2) masturbation, (3) nocturnal emission, or (4) homosexuality. Intercourse is beyond comparison the most satisfying means of ejaculation, but this in turn can be accomplished by the act of marriage, by prostitution, or by adultery. Only one of these, however, is accompanied by a clear conscience—married love. Our chapter of questions and answers (chapter 15) will deal with illegitimate sexual experiences, but here it must be pointed out that they all have one factor in common: although they provide biological release, they do not guarantee lasting enjoyment, because the conscience God has given to every man "accuses" him when he violates divine standards of morality (read Rom. 1; 2:14–15). When sex provides only gratification and is followed by guilt, it makes a mockery of what God intended to be a very satisfying experience. By contrast, the act of marriage when properly performed is followed by physical relaxation based on innocence. Because sex is such a necessary part of a man's life and married love preserves the innocence of his conscience, the woman who provides these for him will increasingly become the object of his love.

Bobbie was a typical southern belle who came for counseling because she felt Joe didn't love her any more. Although she couldn't prove it, she charged, "I'm sure he's seeing another woman." It seemed incredible that any man would look elsewhere when he had such a beautiful wife with so charming an accent. But under questioning, it turned out that she had been using sex as a reward, rationing it out only on Joe's good behavior. Like any normal man, Joe found that intolerable. We may never know whether he was actually unfaithful, for after some straightforward talk in the counseling room, Bobbie went home to love her husband unconditionally. At first he was stunned to find his wife sexually aggressive, but in typically masculine fashion he made the necessary adjustment. He found legitimate, enjoyable lovemaking with his wife so satisfying that he was no longer tempted to look elsewhere.

One satisfied husband summed it up rather graphically when asked if he had ever been tempted to try extramarital experiences: "When you have a Cadillac in the garage, how can you be tempted to steal a Volkswagen off the street?"

Female attitudes have been changing for the good in this area in recent years. Formerly it was common for many wives to look upon the sex act as a "necessary part of marriage" or a "wifely duty to perform." Now an increasing number of women view it as a God-given means of enriching their relationships for a lifetime.

4. *It reduces friction in the home.* Another result of a satisfying relationship between a couple is that it tends to reduce minor irritations in the home. A sexually satisfied man is usually a contented man. This will not solve major problems—it will not repair a bent fender or compensate for overcharging the budget—but it does reduce minor irritations. Many a wife has commented, "My husband is easier to get along with when our love life is what it should be. The children's jangling does not get on his nerves so much, and he finds it easier to be patient with other people."

Most men do not realize that some of their unexplained irritations can often be traced to an unsatisfied sex drive, but a wise wife will remain alert to this possibility. Somehow the world looks better to a man and his difficulties shrink to life size when sexual harmony prevails. It is as though his hard work and the pressures of life are worth it all when he and his wife consummate their love properly.

More is involved in this than just the satisfaction of the glands. A man sacrifices a great deal when he gets married—or at least he thinks so. As a single man, he is rather carefree and unpressured. If he wishes to spend a night out with the boys, he doesn't have to give an account of his whereabouts or satisfy another person's interests. If he sees something he wants, he just buys it whether he can afford it or not. That all changes with marriage.

Furthermore, his carefree spirit must give way to the increasing weight of responsibility marriage uniquely places on him. A woman thinks about economics occasionally, but usually with limited, short-range deliberation.

The husband, however, must go to bed with the mental awareness that he is the supporter of his family. He awakens in the morning with the thought, *I'd better do a good job today; my wife and kids are depending on me.* Unless he learns early in life to commit his way to the Lord, that can be a heavy load to carry.

A husband of weak character came home one evening and announced to his wife, "I'm moving out tonight; I don't want to be married any more." Our investigation revealed that he was not interested in anyone else, but he confessed, "I'd rather spend my evenings working on my racing car than on a second job to support a family." His wife admitted that their physical relationship had been minimal and that she had never shown any appreciation for the sacrifices he had made for the family. Realizing that her indifference may have contributed to his dissatisfaction and irritation, she pleaded with him, "Give me another chance, and I'll prove to you that marriage is worth whatever sacrifices we both have to make." Some women get that second chance and prove it—this one didn't. The husband went his own selfish way into irresponsibility, and both remained miserable.

5. *It provides life's most exciting experience.* The titanic emotional and physical explosion that culminates the act of marriage for the husband is easily the most exciting experience he ever enjoys, at least on a repeatable basis. At that moment all other thoughts are obliterated from his mind; every gland and organ of his body seems to reach a fevered pitch. He feels as if his blood pressure and temperature soar nearly to the point of losing control. By this time his breathing accelerates and he groans in ecstasy as the pressure breaks forth with the

release of semen into the object of his love. Words are inadequate to describe this fantastic experience. Although the aggressive nature of men finds them engaging in various exciting activities (we know ski jumpers, motorcycle racers, jet pilots, sky divers, and pro football players), they all agree that lovemaking heads the list.

A heart patient provided the best description that we have heard of what the act of marriage means to a man. Warned by his doctor that any unnecessary physical exertion could kill him, he continued love relations with his wife. At times he endured a body-rending experience of shock afterward—his heart palpitating, his face losing its color, and his extremities turning cold and clammy. Sometimes it took one or two hours before he could even get off the bed. When I suggested he might kill himself some day in making love to his wife, he quickly responded, "I can't think of a better way to go!"

The most beautiful aspect of all this is that God created the experience for man to share only with his wife. If he loves and cherishes her the way God commands him, a warm and affectionate relationship will develop to enrich their entire married life; the exciting and pleasurable experience of mutual lovemaking will be shared several thousand times during their marriage.

Napoleon Hill, in his very practical book for businessmen, *Think and Grow Rich,* betrays a common misunderstanding of the male sex drive when he cautions salesmen to limit the expression of their sex drive because it will tend to demotivate them.[2] Nothing could be further from the truth. A sexually satisfied husband is a motivated man. Hill was probably a victim of the false notion characteristic of the past generation that held that sex demanded such a great expenditure of energy that it certainly must sap a man's strength. Unless he is speaking of an abnormal frequency of several times a day, his advice is simply not valid. A sexually frustrated man has a hard time concentrating, is prone to be edgy and harder to work with, and, more important, finds it difficult to retain lasting goals. By contrast, the truly satisfied husband refuses to waste his business day on trivia; he wants each moment to count so he can get home to the wife and family who give all his hard work real purpose and meaning.

Two letters sent to "Dear Abby" less than ten days apart bring a chuckle but well illustrate our point. The first one, from an irate husband who complained about his wife's lousy housekeeping, admitted to one positive trait he liked: "She'll go to bed with me whenever I want." The second letter came from a salesman who asked Abby to tell the first man to be grateful for his marital blessings: "If I had a wife like that, I'd be motivated to make enough money to hire her a maid to clean the house!"

Marabel Morgan, author of *The Total Woman*,[3] suggests that a man has two things on his mind when he gets home at night—food and sex—and not always in that order.

Sex Drive and Thought Life

The most consistent spiritual problem faced by the average red-blooded Christian man relates to his thought life. The male sex drive is so powerful that sex often seems to be uppermost in his mind. Any man in military service can testify that 95 percent of a serviceman's off-duty conversation revolves around sex. Dirty jokes and stories punctuated by four-letter words become a constant verbal bombardment.

Shortly after he becomes a Christian, such a man is convicted by the Word of God and the Holy Spirit to change his thought patterns. Our Lord, of course, knew this universal male problem, for He admonished, "I tell you that anyone who looks at a woman lustfully has already committed adultery with her in his heart" (Matt. 5:28). Such mental adultery has probably brought more sincere men to spiritual defeat than any other single sin.

Many Christian women fail to understand this male problem, and this is one reason why they often adopt such scanty dress. If they realized the thought problems that their indecent exposure causes the average man, many of them would dress more modestly; but since they are not so sexually stimulated at the sight of a male body, they do not readily perceive the male response. I caught this message as a G.I. stationed at the Las Vegas Army Air Base. After nineteen days on K.P. I received what I anticipated to be the greatest duty assignment possible—sweeping out the Wacs' barracks. To my dismay, after checking out the smallest whisk broom I could find, I found the barracks empty; all the women were working. I returned to the quartermaster for a regular-sized broom, but during the cleanup I became aware of something rather startling: not one nude male pinup picture appeared in the two decks of that facility. By contrast, the 197 men in our barracks sported 193 pinup pictures of girls! Not until the recent overemphasis on sex have women reflected an increasing problem in this area. But they apparently have to cultivate it; men get it by nature.

Another illustration of the fact that women seem to lack the visual lust problem occurred recently in our home. Looking through *Sports Illustrated*, I came upon a picture of Mr. America. As I was admiring his bulging biceps and rippling muscles, Bev came up behind me, saw what I was looking at, and spontaneously responded, "Ugh, how grotesque!" Women have their own brand of spiritual problems, but mental-attitude lust is seldom one of them.

We have reviewed all this to make an important point. A loving, sexually responsive wife can be a great asset to her husband in keeping his thought life pleasing to God. That is not to suggest that his victory in Christ is dependent on his wife's behavior—that is never the case. In fact, God has promised to give a warm-blooded, affectionate man the grace to live with a cold, indifferent woman. But many a carnal Christian husband has used his wife's sexual rejection as an excuse to compound his spiritual defeat further by periods of mental-attitude lust.

A loving wife who understands her husband's temptations in this regard will restrain the desire to squelch his advances and, because she thinks more of his needs than of her own tiredness, will give her love freely to him. Her reward will be his ready response to her mood, and together they can share the rapturous experience of married love.

Notes

1. Catherine Parker Anthony, *Textbook of Anatomy and Physiology* (St. Louis: Mosby, 1963), 46.

2. Napoleon Hill, *Think and Grow Rich* (Cleveland: Ralston, 1956), 274.

3. Published by Revell, Old Tappan, N.J., 1973.

T h r e e

What Lovemaking
Means to a Woman

Fortunately for women, men and cultures are changing! It is reported that a generation ago many men appeared to be selfish lovers, and society helped contribute to the "he-man" self-images that made them seem like animals in the bedroom. Sexual pleasure from the little woman was assumed to be their divine right, and their relations were usually one-sided experiences that left an affectionate wife with the frustrated feeling that she had been used, not loved.

Such men were (and some still are) sexual illiterates, totally failing to comprehend a woman's emotional or physical needs. Assuming that he had the gift of intuitive knowledge in this department, a man took his innocent bride to their love nest and taught her only what she needed to know to satisfy *his* sex drive.

It is no wonder that many wives began to lose a desire for sexual intercourse and lovemaking turned into a chore. Even worse, some frustrated wives became evangelists of coolness toward sex. Consequently young brides went into marriage dutifully warned that homemaking, motherhood, and a good reputation were wonderful—but the one drawback to marriage was the "bedroom scene."

The modern Christian husband has been challenged by the Word of God and his pastor, "Husbands, love your wives, just as Christ loved the church. . . . Husbands ought to love their wives as their own bodies" (Eph. 5:25, 28). Thus a Christian man today enters marriage more sensitive to the love needs of his bride and more concerned with her satisfaction. He respects her as a special creation of God who should be accepted and understood. During the past decade several books on marriage dealing quite frankly with the subject have given men a greater understanding of women. Unless a man's head remains in the sand, he can learn many things about her. And the more he knows about her, the more he can tailor his affectionate passions to her emotional needs.

A sage once said, "A woman is the most complex creature on earth." Certainly no reasonable man would claim to understand her fully. However, after dealing with hundreds of these delicate creatures in the privacy of the counseling room, my wife and I have discovered to a greater extent what the act of marriage means to a woman. Every man can profit from reading this chapter; the more a husband knows about his wife's erotic needs and what the act of marriage truly means to her, the more he and his wife can enjoy each other, not only physically but in every other area of life.

Let us consider these five significant areas that show what lovemaking means to a woman:

1. *It fulfills her womanhood.* Self-image psychology is the rage today. Every bookstand carries several self-help publications, and many are best-sellers. We Christians do not agree with all their humanistic conclusions, but we certainly cannot deny the important truth that lasting happiness is impossible until we learn to accept ourselves. Surely this is true of a married woman. If she considers herself unsuccessful in bed, she will have a difficult time accepting her total womanhood.

It should not come as a surprise that almost every bride feels insecure when she marries. From ages eighteen to twenty-five few people are secure. It often takes from one-third to one-half of a lifetime for people to accept themselves. Naturally, being a Spirit-filled Christian contributes to a good self-image, but marriage is one of the most important decisions a person makes in life; consequently any normal person will face it with a degree of trepidation. If a major part of married life proves unsatisfactory, it complicates one's self-image. Not incidentally, we have yet to counsel a woman who has a good self-image if she has no desire for sexual intercourse.

One way to understand the function of the female mind is to contrast it with the male thought system. A man has the God-given mandate to be the provider of the family. Consequently his mental psyche is so oriented that he gains much of his self-image from successful occupational pursuits. That is the reason a man's goals and dreams take a vocational tack early in life. Ask a junior-age boy what he wants to be when he grows up and he will usually reply that he wants to be a fireman, a policeman, a doctor, a baseball player, or a jet pilot. Although he changes that goal several times as he matures, it does indicate his vocational psyche. Ask a little girl what she wants to be when she becomes a woman and she will usually answer "a mother" or "a housewife." In adulthood and even after thorough vocational training, many women still list the role of homemaker as their main vocational objective.

When in Jackson, Mississippi, for a Family Life Seminar, I was interviewed by a young woman reporter. It took only a moment to detect her hostility arising from the humiliation of having to interview a minister. Most newspapers assign cub reporters to the religion desk, as in her case. Obviously she would rather have been assigned to someone "important." Accepting her hostility as a challenge, I decided to break through her tough veneer of professionalism by asking her the question I have presented to scores of people as I travel around the country. I had previously learned that she was a journalism major in college, determined to be the "best reporter in the state." I also discovered that because of an unfortunate love affair at the age of twenty-two, she "hated" men. When she finally became a little friendlier, I began, "I'm taking an informal survey. Would you mind if I ask you a personal question?"

Every curious woman responds affirmatively to that approach. I continued, "What is the one thing you want most out of life?"

She deliberated a moment and replied, "A home and a family."

Somewhat teasingly I asked, "And a husband?"

She blushed a little and said softly, "I guess so."

Even I was a bit surprised to find a woman who seemed to be a card-carrying member of the feminist movement confessing the natural longing of every woman's heart—to be a homemaker.

This intuitive tendency is, in our opinion, the primary drive in a woman. She should never be ashamed of this psychical phenomenon; God made her this way. The most frustrated women in the world are those who stifle or substitute that tendency for a lesser priority. If our assumption is true, and we believe it is, then her rating as a wife is all-important to a woman.

You may be asking, "What relation does that have to the act of marriage?" Everything! A wife is more than a mother and homemaker. She is also a sexual partner to her mate. Like the male, if she does not succeed in the bedroom, she fails also in other areas—for two reasons: first, few men accept bedroom failure without being carnal, nasty, and insulting; second and more important, if her husband doesn't enjoy her lovemaking, he will make his disapproval obvious by blaming her. A woman receives major portions of her self-esteem from her husband. In fact, we have yet to find a woman with a good self-image who disapproves of herself as a wife. This, in our opinion, is one reason divorcées often marry beneath themselves the second time—they have been beaten down by their husbands and forfeited the self-acceptance that is vital to everyone.

An anxious woman came for counseling to ask my opinion as to whether she or her husband was right. "I think sex is unnecessary in a Christian marriage. My husband doesn't agree." Sexually well-adjusted women and all men would side with her husband, but our research indicates that some sexually frustrated women would agree with her. This lady dogmatically announced, "I can live the rest of my life without sex!" Is it any wonder that she ranks as the married woman with the lowest self-image we have ever counseled? When confronted with the challenge that she would never learn to accept herself as a woman unless her husband accepted her as a wife, she returned to her marriage bed with a new motivation. In time, and with God's help, that new attitude transformed both their relationship and her personality. Today she is a mature woman with a reasonably good self-image.

2. *It reassures her of her husband's love.* The one point on which psychologists agree is that all people have a basic need to be loved. This is generally more true of women than men. Women have a tremendous capacity for love, both giving and receiving. Hundreds of illustrations could be given of "mother-love," "wife-love," or "sister-love," but the reader is doubtlessly familiar with these already. However, many are unaware of the five kinds of love required by a woman.

(a) *Companionship love.* Few women enjoy solitude for long periods of time. Have you noticed how few hermits and recluses are women? A few exceptions may be found among the aged, of course, when women become senile or have outlived all their loved ones. But a woman looks upon marriage as perpetual companionship, which explains why so many marital problems occur when a man's job takes him out of the home for long periods of time. Too often he does not understand his wife's need for companionship. When he is regularly surrounded by people, he usually can't wait to get away for a while and be alone. When he arrives home, he may find his wife craving his attention and company.

If men realized this need in their wives, they would spend less time in front of the television set when they are at home and learn to enjoy wifely companionship. It is also true that many women would do well to improve their companionship appeal by talking about things that interest men instead of making small talk. It is unwise for a wife to direct all the conversation toward her interests when her husband comes home. It is a good rule to accompany his arrival home with pleasant conversation that is interesting to him and conveys a message of love and welcome. This usually involves allowing him to share his thoughts with her and showing her interest in his activities. This gives her opportunities to build him up with her positive comments.

Couples seldom have problems being good companions before marriage, but if they fail to cultivate that relationship, they seem to lose it. In a letter to his mother nine months after he was married, our son wrote, "Kathy is my best friend." He didn't realize it, but he was claiming companionship love for his bride.

It is often hard for a woman to give physical love to a man who does not return her companionship love. It is always easier to give love when it is needed and appreciated by the receiver. A good wife must know that her husband needs her companionship just as she requires his, no matter how successful or busy he may be. In fact, the more prosperous he is in his vocation, the more she needs his companionship.

(b) *Compassionate love.* A woman has a natural bedside manner, but only a few men display that kind of compassion. When a child or husband hurts, who runs to his aid? Who jumps out of bed at 2:30 A.M. at the slightest whimper of the baby? Rarely the baby's father! A mother does not manifest compassionate love because she is a mother, but because she is a woman.

Men need to learn that a woman's capacity for compassionate love testifies to her need to receive it also. That is especially true when she is suffering emotionally or physically. It is regrettable that the man who enjoys her compassionate love when he hurts is often slow to return it to his loving wife. The Golden Rule is quite applicable here.

(c) *Romantic love.* Women are romantics! Lurking in the heart of every girl (even when she is grown up) is the image of prince charming on his white horse coming to wake up the beautiful princess with her first kiss of love. For that reason she needs romance, flowers, music, soft lights, dinner out, and a host of other things. Unfortunately many a man fails to understand that, primarily because his need for romantic love is either nonexistent or minimal. But he is married to a creature with an extraordinary need for romance. Some men misjudge their wives, deeming them more practical-minded than other women. To be truthful, these wives have likely tried to overcome that "dream" by becoming practical; to these women it seems better to suppress that desire than to become disappointed over the lack of romanticism in their husbands. However, an occasional night out without the children, some little unexpected gift, or another expression of "romance" can be very rewarding to her.

This difference between men and women may contribute to feelings of incompatibility after marriage. A woman never loses the need to be romanced, whereas a man doesn't even possess that need. His emotions are near the surface and easily ignited; hers are deep and burn slowly. It is this romantic love that makes a woman respond to her husband's little expressions of thoughtfulness like opening the car door, taking her arm as she crosses the street, or expressing the "Sir Walter Raleigh routine." He may sometimes feel a bit foolish, but her response is worth the abashment.

I remember driving up in front of the church one Sunday. Five men were watching as I walked around the car and opened the door for Beverly. Frankly, I felt self-conscious, but she made it all worthwhile, not only by the little squeeze on my hand as we walked into church, but also later that night. After preaching five times that day, I was exhausted as we pulled into the driveway. It was about eleven o'clock and it was raining lightly. As I put the car in park, I was amazed to hear her door open and see her run around in front of the headlights to lift the double garage door. What made her do it? At five o'clock she had a romantic need to be honored and preferred in front of our friends; at eleven o'clock she showed her appreciation and responded to my need.

Don't be tricked into thinking that today's "mod" women are any different, just because some of them wear frumpy clothes and sometimes act as if they care little about manners and etiquette. Something deep down in a woman's heart cries out for romantic love.

Jeri is a case in point. At twenty-one she was led to Christ by a young woman in our church with whom she had gone to high school. When she first started attending services, she wore blue jeans and a white T-shirt. Outwardly she was somewhat coarse and very independent. As she grew in her faith in the Lord, she began to dress up and fix her hair. Surprisingly she proved to be a very attractive young woman. Before long Roy met her, asked to meet her parents, and started dating her. About a year later Jeri came into my office to discuss wedding plans. When I asked what she liked about Roy, she replied, "He treats me like a lady. He's the first fellow who ever came up to the door to pick me up for a date or opened the car door or seated me at the table." When I asked how she liked that kind of treatment, her eyes filled with tears as she whispered, "I love it!" She had dated boys for about seven years, but the first one to treat her like a lady won her heart. The reason is simple: women need romantic love.

(d) *Affectionate love.* Most women crave kisses of appreciation. You perhaps are acquainted with some exceptions—so are we—but if you look deeper you will find that such lack of affection has been learned. It is sometimes caused by a husband who demands quick sex instead of slow lovemaking. Some inconsiderate men can be satisfied with that, but almost all women are not. To them a tender touch, a warm embrace, and the closeness of the one they love is almost as enjoyable as the more intimate contact. In fact, many wives respond to an approving look and words of commendation. It is a wise husband who breaks out of the routine frequently to voice approval of his wife. Such men do not testify to sexual starvation, for they have learned that their wives are ignited by the little expressions of affection that often seem meaningless to a man.

Personally I don't care for flowers. If we never had them in our home, I wouldn't miss them. But almost every time I return from a seminar on a Saturday night, I pick up a bouquet of roses for Bev in the airport. Why? Because I like the response they create in her. Frankly, it took several years to learn the rewards of conforming my behavior to her need for affection. She not only likes yellow roses but is grateful that I was thinking of her as I came into town.

(e) *Passionate love.* Impassioned love comes naturally to a man because of his stronger sex drive. Most women have to cultivate the appetite for passionate loving, but be sure of this—they have the capacity to learn. The husband who confers affectionate love upon his mate can teach her passionate love. And any man who has done so will testify that it is time well invested.

As we will see, a woman's passions are more periodic than a man's. On occasions, given the right place, privacy, and quality of affection, she can thoroughly enjoy passionate love. But remember one thing: it is easier for a woman to express passionate love after the other four needs for love have been satisfied.

When these love needs in a woman's heart have been properly fulfilled, their fulfillment will give assurance of her husband's love, which is becoming increasingly important in an era when men and women mingle together day after day in the business world. Many a married man is surrounded by secretaries or other employees whose physical allurements are on display during working hours. When a husband is confronted by another woman who happens to be on his wavelength, the best safeguard against moral problems is a warm love relationship with his wife. "Male eroticism, fulfilled within the home, does not hunger for more outside."[1] That is also true of the wife. Since she needs to know that her husband needs her, lovemaking becomes a necessary means of reassuring her of that love.

This yearning for reassurance was beautifully shared by a close friend, whose lovely wife had incurred a crippling disease that gradually diminished her bodily movement. Because he loved her dearly and knew she suffered great pain, he restrained himself valiantly from making love to her. One night he was lying beside her, trying to go to sleep, when he felt the bed shaking. Listening for a moment, he heard muffled sobs. "Honey, why are you crying?" She hesitantly replied, "Because I don't think you love me any more."

Naturally he was amazed. "What have I done?"

"It's what you haven't done," she wailed. "You don't make love to me anymore."

At first he inwardly responded, "Good grief! What greater affirmation of my love than to deny myself what every organ in my body is crying out for?" But then he realized that his suffering wife desperately needed the reassurance of his love through the act of marriage. All women do.

3. *It satisfies her sex drive.* Although a woman may not possess as strong or consistent a sex drive as a man, she does have a sex drive. Research indicates that almost all women are more passionate just before, during, or after their monthly menstruation and, of course, in the middle of her month at the time of highest fertility. Moreover, her sexual pleasure grows through the years. As she learns to be uninhibited in her responses to her husband and increasingly learns to experience orgasms, her appreciation and desire for the experience grows.

A woman does not seem so readily tempted to fantasize as does her husband. However, she does have the capacity to remember romantically those exciting experiences of the past. Consequently each thrilling lovemaking event increases her sex drive in the same way that each frustrating experience stifles it. Such a growing sex drive needs an outlet, and married love is God's ordained plan for its expression.

4. *It relaxes her nervous system.* We have consistently noted that women who have no desire for sexual intercourse are nervous women. Note that we did *not* say that every nervous woman is sexually indifferent or negative. Some women are simply nervous by nature. But a lack of desire for sex almost invariably produces nervousness. It is important, therefore, that a wife learn a healthy sexual expression toward her husband.

As with a man, the female nervous system is intrinsically tied to the reproductive organs. God has made it possible for wives from all walks of life to enjoy a hygienically relaxing experience on their marriage bed. It is true that the act of marriage exists for the propagation of the race and personal enjoyment, and it does promote fidelity and fulfillment; but it also contributes a much-needed relaxant for the nervous system.

5. *The ultimate experience.* When properly consummated to orgasm, married love provides a woman with life's most exciting experience. One young mother took exception to that statement, insisting that childbearing offered greater excitement. But we refer to a feminine experience on a regular and frequent basis. There is simply no experience comparable to the act of marriage— for both the wife and the husband, who need each other to gain its ultimate rewards.

The Most Beautiful Meaning of All

An important meaning of the act of marriage is purposely presented last. We think it is the most beautiful of all. Simply stated, it is the provision of one ongoing life experience that a husband and wife share uniquely with each other. In all life's other activities we are compelled to share each other. If the husband is a teacher or mechanic, other persons share in the fruits of his skills. If the wife is a good cook or an attractive woman, the husband is not the only one who enjoys those gifts. But behind their closed bedroom door, a couple experiences oneness—a sublime moment uniting them in an exclusively intimate union unshared by anyone else on earth. That is a major reason why the act of marriage is such a binding, uniting, and enriching influence on a couple.

The meaning of oneness resulting from mutual lovemaking is far more important than the time spent in the experience. If a typical couple spends about thirty minutes in a single lovemaking experience an average of three times a week, the act of love would account for only one and a half hours per week, or nine-tenths of 1 percent of their time. Yet no other repeatable experience is more important to that couple. The partners who relate enjoyably to each other spend many hours in emotional and mental harmony in anticipation of the experience and follow it with many hours of mutual contentment and closeness because of their love. Probably no powerful human encounter cements their relationship more firmly than the act of marriage.

Notes

1. Jerome Rainer and Julie Rainer, *Sexual Pleasure in Marriage* (New York: Pocket Books, 1959), 30.

Four

Why God Created Sex

The most thrilling, exciting, and fulfilling experience in the world (if done properly) is the "act of marriage." God designed it that way. And it is nearly universal, for everywhere you go on planet Earth you see its results—children.

Unfortunately, the experience is not always confined to marriage and therein is the problem—for the sex act, which God intended for marriage as a blessing to both men and women, has become one of the greatest social problems of our day. This problem is not unique to the twenty-first century. If you recall, the misuse of the sex drive so polluted the earth in the days of Noah that God destroyed all but eight people and started the population over again. History shows that nothing has changed. The Bosnian Serbs didn't invent mass rapes; it has been practiced on almost every continent in the world, leaving behind incalculable personal suffering and tragedy.

Our own culture, by the misuse of the God-given gift of sexual expression, has created an unbelievable upsurge of unwed teenage mothers. One American woman is reported to be a grandmother at the age of twenty-four! Social tolerance of this behavior has produced a wave of sexual vice from incest to homosexuality and the murder of over four thousand unborn babies every day. The current wave of sexual permissivism cultivated by the media and humanistic educators is destroying the conscience of America and producing a generation of youth and adults who seem not to know right from wrong. The wanton exercise of the sex drive has produced an unprecedented rise in sexually transmitted diseases (STD) and AIDS-related plagues that, even in this day of advanced medical research, have no cure. The medical profession can only advise "safe sex" (which is far from safe) and abstinence.

This widespread misuse of the sex drive, of course, does not include the untold suffering caused by the rampant violation of wedding vows that recent surveys indicate has affected as much as 30 percent of the married population. Every reader of this book is acquainted with couples whose marriage was either destroyed by one partner having sex with another person or by the sexual attraction of one person to another. And we cannot say Christians don't have that problem. They do! Not as frequently as non-Christians, but sexual sins have invaded even the church at an alarming rate. We have all been shocked by church leaders who have fallen into sexual sin.

Like all pastors, I regret to say I saw it in my own congregation, even in some couples whom I married after giving careful premarital counseling. One beautiful young woman brought her thirty-year-old husband to me and angrily said, "He gave me herpes!" Recently, a young forty-two-year-old grandmother had an "affair" with her boss, a leader in a Christian organization. I was, of course, heartbroken. I had married the woman years ago to her childhood sweetheart.

I cannot begin to convey the emotional trauma and heartache that these experiences and others like them cause many people—particularly the people they love most in this world, their mate, children, parents, and many other friends and relatives. Can you imagine going to the first big family holiday dinner after it has become known that as an act of passion or alienation of affection you violated your wedding vows? Or maybe worse, *not* going for the same reason?

Having counseled hundreds of people who made this terrible mistake, I can tell you, on their behalf, it isn't worth it! It is true, God can and does forgive even adultery and fornication, when truly repented of and confessed, but the relationship is never the same. For many the suffering never really goes away. Unfaithful individuals may never be able to forgive themselves. Their spouses, because of love and obedience to God, may try, but it often takes years before sexual trust is restored between such couples. The suffering experienced before that injury heals is impossible to imagine. It is something you would not wish on anyone, particularly someone you love.

Sexual Sins Are Number One!

This abuse of sex is not new. The apostle Paul addressed the problem already in the first century. Twice he catalogued the most common sins of humankind, both in Romans 1 and Galatians 5. In both instances he listed sexual sins first. Why? Because they are first! In the Romans passage he listed sexual impurity even before envy, greed, and murder. In Galatians 5:19 he listed sexual immorality, impurity, and debauchery ahead of fifteen other sinful practices such as idolatry, witchcraft, hatred, jealousy, and murder.

One of my favorite ministries is speaking at Maximum Man Conferences. I do about five to ten each year. At such conferences I point out to the men that if they have a problem with sexual fantasies or sexual temptation, they are not weird or oversexed as some think; they are very normal. That doesn't mean that this universal temptation is a license to sin; God has promised to judge such sinful practice. I then show them how to have victory over such temptation, and victory is very well possible, witnessed by the fact that most Christian men (as high as 70 percent in some surveys) do not violate their sexual commitment to their wives, even though it is tempting, particularly in this day when sex is used to advertise and sell almost everything. Merchants use the most powerful force in human nature to sell their products, and today they have access to our minds in our own homes via television.

All of this brings us full circle to our question: Why would a loving God introduce the "act of marriage" in the first place? Obviously He had to precede it with a strong sex drive, and that drive, although providing billions of married couples four to six thousand ecstatic experiences over a fifty-year marriage, has also caused billions of others untold heartache and misery beyond description. The truth is, our Creator had several things in mind when giving this beautiful and sacred experience, or "blessing," to married couples. Consider the following:

1. *To propagate the race.* Immediately after creating Adam and Eve, God blessed them and commanded them to "be fruitful and increase in number; fill the earth and subdue it" (Gen. 1:28). For reasons known only to Him, God intended Adam and Eve to propagate the race from the Garden of Eden. We have already seen that this command was given before their sin of rebellion to His will had reared its ugly head as we see in chapter 3. Therefore, He was commanding them to fulfill a righteous act and populate the earth. From that humble beginning of two individuals, God set in motion a replicating power that has produced almost six billion people at the present time, and some suggest that another six billion preceded us, not even factoring in the enormous population that lived before the Flood.

All of this tells us that the principal reason God gave us our incredible sex drive is to propagate the race, not just with living bodies such as Adam had when he was created, but with living souls, such as God breathed into him: and he "became a living being." The eternal soul, with which all people are born, is the most significant part of the nature of humans and the unique feature that distinguishes us from the animal kingdom. It is this spiritual nature that God's Son, Jesus, later came to emancipate by His death on the cross. A second reason God gave humankind a strong sex drive and the "act of marriage" to fulfill it is . . .

2. *To provide mutual pleasure in marriage.* One of the most misleading concepts about God's plan for sexual expression is that He is against it. As I have already tried

to make clear, the truth is that He has given this marvelous gift to married couples of all generations for mutual happiness and pleasure. Solomon makes that point in his Song of Songs that even suggests intimate techniques in the "act of marriage." But the most obvious passage I am familiar with is Proverbs 5:18–20, where in warning his son to restrain himself from having sex with his neighbor's wife no matter how enticing she makes herself, he should enjoy sexual expression only with his wife. Consider this admonition, "May your fountain be blessed [the use of his sexual creativity], and may you rejoice in the wife of your youth . . . may her breasts satisfy you always; may you ever be captivated by her love."

You must admit that this is rather explicit for a book written three thousand years ago. Yet the message is timeless. Couples get married in their youth and should bring sexual and emotional pleasure to each other. This has been the time-honored purpose of marriage, to provide sexual pleasure. And as Solomon said, it "captivated" them in love. The more they provide sexual expression for each other, the more it enriches their love for each other. Only a loving God who has humankind's best interests at heart could have invented such a marvelously pleasurable experience that would bind two people together in love.

And it is interesting that it is equally beneficial to primitive tribespeople as well as those who dwell in kings' palaces. You don't have to be rich and famous to enjoy pleasurable sex in marriage and to experience the enrichment of love that it produces. I have met many people in my world travels who married people they did not even know before they met them at the wedding altar. Their marriage had been arranged by their parents according to the custom in their culture. Yet it was obvious by their body language and treatment of each other that they had built a warm, loving relationship. How? They were "captivated," as Solomon said, by their love. If it works in countries where the individuals do not choose the mate with whom they make love, how much more should it apply in the Western cultures, where we select our own mates.

3. *To reduce sexual temptation.* Even the apostle Paul, who was a single man as far as we know, believed that it is better to marry than to burn with passion. In 1 Corinthians 7:1–4 he also said that because there is so much immorality, each man should have his own wife, and each woman her own husband. Notice that he said nothing about children here; he is talking about relieving the natural sexual passions that build up in both men and women. The reason is that it usually takes only one sexual experience for a wife to get pregnant, yet the average couple will have approximately 150 such experiences a year. Obviously then, God has given couples this wonderful experience to share to make it easier for them to keep their wedding vows.

That is particularly important in our day when the advertising and entertainment industries seem to function under the philosophy that sex sells. They bombard us with it in advertising everything from tires to beer. Hollywood insists on breaking every moral code in movies today, so much so that it is becoming increasingly difficult to watch TV in your own home without having every moral value taught by the church and your parents challenged. In essence, today's producers are convinced that no matter how bad their story is, it will sell if they include enough explicit sex scenes.

In such a sexually surcharged climate, God has given married couples a gift to reduce those temptations to manageable size. It is called the "act of marriage." As already indicated in chapter 2, when properly consummated, this act should strengthen a couple's self-control (as the apostle calls it), which makes them less vulnerable to Satan's temptations (1 Cor. 7:5) by the reduction of their normal sex drive. This obviously would tend to improve their spiritual life as a result.

Very honestly, one of our major purposes in writing this book originally was our anticipation of what we could foresee in the wake of the sexual revolution that promoted promiscuity without regard to consequences, conscience, or the commands of God. We determined that we would provide a manual on sexual behavior for married lovers, most of whom came to their marriage bed as virgins with only a minimum knowledge of this subject, that would not only help them enjoy to the maximum this sublime gift of God but also help them reduce their normal passions to manageable proportions. This can be achieved—even in the twenty-first century!

4. *To produce mutual ownership.* When a couple marry, they promise to give themselves to each other totally. They merge their earthly possessions, the man gives his bride his name, and they give each other their bodies for companionship, for mutual protection, and for mutual sexual expression. As Paul said in 1 Corinthians 7:3–4, "The husband should fulfill his marital duty to his wife, and likewise the wife to her husband. The wife's body does not belong to her alone but also to her husband. In the same way the husband's body does not

belong to him alone but also to his wife." Essentially he is saying that a marriage is giving one's body to the other, and it is sealed by the sexual experience. Each time a couple surrenders to each other for sexual fulfillment, they are demonstrating that mutual ownership contract they made at the wedding altar.

Marriage really is a sexual contract exclusively between two people of the opposite sex who have made this promise: "to keep you only unto me so long as we both shall live." That is why it is not something to be done hurriedly or without careful consideration but deliberately and in the will of God. For it involves giving your body to another person as long as you both shall live. This exchange of ownership of one's body with another is a decision that should last a lifetime.

5. *To produce a unique union and means of communion that is not possible on any other level.* One of the most beautiful teachings on the marvelous relationship of a couple in marriage came from our Lord Jesus Himself when He said, "For this reason a man will leave his father and mother and be united to his wife, and the two will become one flesh" (Matt. 19:5).

Marriage, then, is to be a "union" of two people of the opposite sex. The Creator designed it to be so. They leave the protection of their parents' homes and are united together to begin their own. No longer are they under the primary obligation to obey their parents; they are now united together by the "act of marriage," which Jesus calls the "one flesh" experience. We know He had the sexual union of the couple in mind here because Paul in 1 Corinthians 6:16 warns that he who unites himself with a prostitute is one with her in body. Instead, a couple is uniquely united or joined together by the "act of marriage." By this "act" of exclusive and unique union, which binds a couple together through the years and serves as a constant means of expressing their commitment to one another, the couple communicates their love to each other in a manner not shared with any other person on earth. Such a relationship is not achievable on any other level. And it is approved by God.

In Summary

God obviously had many purposes in mind when He deliberately created our sexual capabilities, from reproduction to pleasure to unique union. Like all things He created, it is all very good. As with many of his wonderful gifts to humankind, it is only when we distort it and misuse it that it becomes twisted and ugly. Sex in marriage is beautiful, enriching, and fulfilling when practiced as He directed—*but only in marriage.* Adultery, fornication, homosexuality, promiscuity, and other forms of sexual abuse become ugly, harmful, and life-shortening. All people have the same choice about the use of their sex drive. They can obey God and confine its expression to marriage, which He calls sacred, or they can adopt the standards of the world and have an affair or become promiscuous.

The results are already determined by God. As He, through Moses, told the children of Israel,

> *I have set before you life and death, blessings and curses.*
> *Now choose life, so that you and your children may live.*
> Deuteronomy 30:19

Five

Sex Education

God has never put a premium on ignorance, and that includes the matter of sex education. His statement "My people are destroyed from lack of knowledge" (Hos. 4:6) is as true in this area of life as in the spiritual. Millions of married couples accept a second-rate experience because they don't know much about the reproductive organs and sexual functions and are unwilling to learn.

Many who have come for counseling because of sexual dysfunction have never read a book on the subject or had proper counseling. Such persistent ignorance has given self-styled sexologists the opportunity to swing to the other extreme and inundate children from kindergarten through twelfth grade with adult doses of sex education. Both extremes lead to unhappiness and frustration.

The public school has rendered itself incompetent in the field of sex education by making two fallacious assumptions:

1. They insist on teaching sex education without moral safeguards, excusing their omission by asserting that the separation of church and state requires that they exclude moral guidelines. That is not only ridiculous, but dangerous! Teaching sex education without moral principles is like pouring gasoline on a fire. Research shows that the male experiences his strongest sex drive between the ages of sixteen and twenty-one. The last thing he needs at that age is exposure to sexually igniting information that he will not use for several years. Moreover, he requires a moral rationale for controlling those drives until he is old enough to accept responsibility for them.

2. These "sexperts" erroneously assume that education will naturally produce sexual happiness. Such an assumption emanates from the humanistic concept that humans are animals and as such should live like them. This philosophy has promoted promiscuity before and after marriage, which in turn has made venereal disease one of the nation's greatest health problems for persons under twenty-four years of age and has heightened the incidence of guilt neurosis after marriage. We predict unparalleled anguish and heartache for the next generation because of this wanton mental destruction of our youth.

Reading that last sentence again reminds me that two years after this book was first published, our local community was in turmoil as the Board of Education insisted on bringing in an even more explicit form of sex education, and it was made compulsory that all students take it whether parents approved of it or not. Along with other ministers, I appeared before the board and warned that if they brought in this new curriculum, totally void of moral values, they would create a wave of unprecedented promiscuity and teenage pregnancy, sexually transmitted diseases, and a decline in learning. They mocked my warning, yet today those are the very social problems facing our nation's youth across the country.

Personally, I lay the drastic decline in the SAT test scores and the increase in school dropouts to the overemphasis on sex in the life of our youth. True, the entertainment industry is also to blame, but these young people received their sex education and moral mistraining in those same valueless explicit classes on sex. Consequently, they have created an obsession with sex during an age when young people really need an obsession on learning. As an educator, I do not believe the average student can maintain an obsession on two subjects at the same time, particularly when one is sex. Girls maybe, but hot-blooded, undisciplined teenage boys? Never!

Educators get what they emphasize. If they emphasize reading, they will get good readers, or if they emphasize math, they will produce good mathematicians. Instead, they have emphasized explicit sex education and have produced the most sexually permissive generation in the history of America. Recent reports indicate that 57 percent of girls and 67 percent of boys have had sex before graduating from high school. According to surveys, this form of public education is not producing responsible sex but is disillusioning many.

It is no wonder that learning has suffered drastically and millions of our youth are not really being prepared for life. And like so many promises of the antimoral humanists, who control most of our nation's public schools, their educational programs have not produced safe sex or even better sex. Instead, they have produced untold suffering by exacerbating the spread of STDs.

Sexual ignorance, however, is not the alternative. Young people need to be instructed that sex is sacred, an experience God has reserved for marriage. Certainly they need to be taught the high cost of promiscuity and the dangers of venereal diseases, and when dating, they must be very conscious of the fact that the bodies of both persons are the temples of the Holy Spirit. Most Bible-believing churches, of course, teach such values unequivocally at youth camps and many youth meetings.

Fortunately for today's Christian young people, the church has responded to their needs by producing many morally based programs that confront them with the need to maintain God's standards of virtue and that teach them how to make sexual love beautiful by saving it for marriage. Josh MacDowell's *True Love Waits* program has been a rich blessing to Christian teens, parents, and church leaders. The Southern Baptists pioneered a program of challenging over a hundred thousand teens to make a written commitment to virtue before marriage. This was picked up by Lutherans, Catholics, and others; now millions of young people have gone on record that they are going to save their first sexual experience for marriage. They will not regret it.

My wife, Beverly, and I were so concerned about this problem that we collaborated on a book for parents so they could be the principal teachers of their own children about sex. We titled it *Against the Tide: How to Raise Sexually Pure Kids in an "Anything Goes" World.*[1] The book instructs parents to teach their own moral values along with the facts of sexuality to their teens. We included a suggestion to parents to take their emerging teenagers out for a special dinner-date and challenge them to a commitment to virtue until marriage. Then we propose that parents be prepared to present their teen with a "virtue ring," which they may wear proudly until their wedding night, at which time they may give it to their new spouse as a token of this important commitment.

I cannot tell you how many parents and even teens have contacted us to thank us for this suggestion. Everywhere I go to speak, some teenager comes up to proudly show me his or her virtue ring. This practice has been promoted on Dr. James Dobson's radio program and also by other agencies. One youth counselor called to tell me he was setting up a whole ministry dedicated to this cause. It won't be long until our dream really comes true—many Christian newlyweds exchanging virtue rings on their wedding night. In anticipation of that, a beautiful senior student at a Christian high school where I spoke showed me her ring with pride and volunteered a new dimension: "I plan to pass this virtue ring on to my daughter someday!"

Learning by Doing

An in-depth study of sex is best pursued just prior to marriage. Let's face it—the material is simply not that complicated. God didn't give Adam and Eve a manual on sexual behavior; they learned by doing. We are convinced that modern Adams and Eves can do the same, provided they are unselfish enough to consider their partner's satisfaction more than their own. A few good books on the subject studied carefully two or three weeks before marriage, a frank discussion with their family doctor, and pastoral counseling usually are adequate preparation.

Another source of help is an honest discussion with the parent of the same sex. As parents, we enjoyed sharing our insights with two of our offspring. With both this discussion and the suggested reading, they seem to have made a beautiful adjustment. The following material includes some of the things we discussed with them about themselves and their partners. When studied by married couples or those about to be married, it proves exceedingly fascinating. When this information is considered in the light of the intended purposes of marriage—conception, pleasure, and marital communication—the reader can hardly escape the fact that God has ingeniously created human beings. No wonder the psalmist declared that we are "fearfully [awesomely] and wonderfully made" (Ps. 139:14). You would do well to study these next few pages carefully. Each organ is listed in the order of its reproductive function, as labeled on the following diagram.

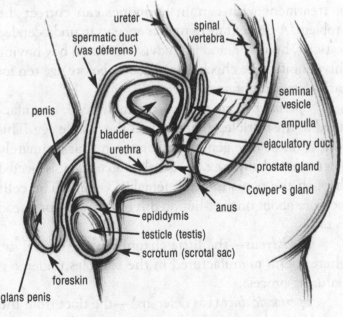

Fig. 1. The male reproductive organs.

It is important to know the basic parts of your reproductive system and your partner's. You should also understand their basic purpose and function.

Scrotum or scrotal sac—the small sac, containing the testicles, that hangs between a man's legs.

Testicles—the sensitive, egg-shaped, sperm-producing organs that hang in the scrotal sac. They are the size and shape of a large nut, approximately 1-1/2 inches long; contain a long tube approximately one one-thousandth of an inch in diameter and about one thousand feet long; and are able to produce 500 million sperm every day. Usually the left testicle hangs lower than the right, but this should cause no alarm—it is quite natural. Sometimes only one testicle drops even after puberty. This is no cause for concern sexually, since a healthy male can be virile with only one functioning testicle. Surgery or treatment with certain hormones can correct the problem. A higher rate of tumors appears in undescended testicles, however, and it is advisable that a boy having this condition be checked by a doctor before age ten for early detection of any difficulty.

Sperm or spermatozoa—the male seed, manufactured in the testicles, that fertilizes the female egg. This seed contains the genetic information that ultimately determines a baby's sex. In sexual intercourse it is ejected through the penis into the female's vagina. The cells measure about one six-hundredth of an inch from head to tail.

Epididymis—the little channel in the scrotal sac where sperm manufactured in the testicles undergo a maturing process.

Spermatic duct (vas deferens)—the duct from the epididymis that carries the sperm into the ampulla chamber. In a vasectomy for sterilization of the husband, a one-inch section of each vas deferens is removed. This surgery can usually be performed under a local anesthetic in a doctor's office and incapacitates a man for perhaps one or two days. The operation will in no way affect his sex life—it merely stops the sperm from entering the penis.

Ampulla chamber—the storage chamber for sperm that have left the epididymis and traveled through the spermatic duct.

Seminal vesicle—the organ producing the seminal fluid that carries the sperm to the prostate gland.

Ejaculatory duct—the organ that expels the sperm and seminal fluid through the penis into the female.

Prostate gland—an important gland, shaped like a large walnut, which contracts and aids in the ejaculation. It produces additional seminal fluid and contains the nerves that control the erection of the penis. It is located between the urinary bladder and the base of the penis surrounding the passage from the bladder. The prostate may become enlarged and block the flow of urine in an older man; this may necessitate a prostatectomy—that is, removal of the prostate—or a simpler operation to enlarge the channel. After either of these operations, the semen in ejaculation enters the bladder and does not leave the body at the time of ejaculation. This does not change the physical sensation of orgasm, but special instructions may need to be followed if the wife wishes to become pregnant. Currently many have resorted to nutritional means to avoid surgery.

The prostate is the only gland in the human body that tends to enlarge after a man reaches forty-five to fifty years of age. It is estimated that at least 65 percent of men in their sixties and seventies have the problems that emanate from an enlarged prostate: urinary drip, difficulty in urinating, and difficulty maintaining an erection. Because it is so important that men be informed of this potential problem, we have addressed the method of avoiding that enlargement in the final chapter under "prostate." Every man over forty-five should read it carefully!

Cowper's gland—the first gland to function when a man is sexually aroused. It sends a few drops of slippery fluid into the urethra, thus preparing it for the safe passage of sperm by neutralizing the acids of the urine that would otherwise kill the sperm.

Urethra—the tube that carries urine from the bladder through the penis for elimination. It also carries the sperm and semen from the prostate gland through the penis.

Penis—the male sex organ through which both the urine and the sperm are released. It can be distended with blood under mental or physical stimulus so that it becomes stiff or erect. The penis is made up of three columns of spongy, erectile tissue, the middle one containing the urethra. The length of the nonstimulated penis varies greatly, but the length of the erect penis is almost always six to seven inches. The crown or rim of the glans becomes harder than the tip during erection, helping to arouse excitement in the female during friction. Circumcision also enables this rim to stand out more from the adjacent tissue of the penis.

Glans penis—the head of the penis; the very sensitive part of the organ that under friction stimulates ejaculation of the sperm and seminal fluid.

Foreskin—the loose skin that covers the glans penis for protection. A substance called smegma often gathers under the foreskin, producing an offensive odor. For this reason the penis should be washed daily. Circumcision is recommended for hygienic reasons but has little effect on stimulating the glans penis.

Areas of sexual sensitivity—the male genital organs—comprising the penis, the scrotal sac, and the area around them—that are exceptionally sensitive to touch. When caressed affectionately by the wife, they produce a pleasurable sexual excitement that prepares the husband for intercourse, usually in a very few minutes.

Nocturnal emission (wet dream)—a natural occurrence that can be an unsettling experience for a boy who is unprepared for it. If he awakens to find his pajamas wet and sticky or hardened to a starchy consistency, he may be needlessly alarmed. What has happened is that pressure has built up because of the increasing rate at which sperm are manufactured. The seminal vesicles and the prostate gland are filled to capacity with fluid, so that the entire reproductive system is waiting for an explosion. Sometimes under these conditions a dream during the night will cause the penis to fill with blood, thus producing an erection. Cowper's gland puts forth its neutralizing drops of fluid into the urethra, and then the ejaculatory muscles, or ducts, and the sperm and seminal fluids are merged and spurt forth through the urethra and the penis. Throughout a boy's teen years there will be many such nocturnal explosions. The constant production of sperm and seminal fluid is one of the factors that causes the man to be the usual initiator for the act of marriage. His aggressiveness should not be looked upon merely as a means of satisfying the male sex urge but as the fulfillment of the God-ordained plan of mutual sexual fellowship between a husband and wife.

Ejaculation—the sexual climax when the fluid is forced from the storeroom through small tubes that meet in the ejaculatory duct just before entering the base of the penis. The muscular contractions that take place at the base of the penis force the seminal fluid past the prostate gland, where it picks up more secretions, then through the urethral canal and out the urethra to aid in the work of impregnating the female. This fluid can be projected forcefully for a distance of twelve to twenty-four inches. It is generally agreed that the half-teaspoonful of semen ejaculated during a normal sexual contact after a two- or three-day abstinence will contain about 250 to 500 million sperm cells. The semen is primarily protein, similar to egg white, and is not dirty or unsanitary, though it has a distinctive odor. A wife need not remove this material by douching unless she wishes.

The ingenious creative work of God can be seen in the beautiful compatibility of the male and female reproductive systems. A woman's genitalia (or sex organs, from a Latin word that means "to give birth") fall into two categories. The external group, located outside the body and easily visible, are the gateway to the second group, the internal, located inside the body; this second, internal group comprises two ovaries, two oviducts or tubes, the uterus, and the vagina.

The reproductive organs are formed several months before birth, but remain inactive until puberty (usually age twelve to fifteen), when they receive the signal to come to sexual maturity. This important signal is given by the pituitary, a small gland situated at the base of the brain.

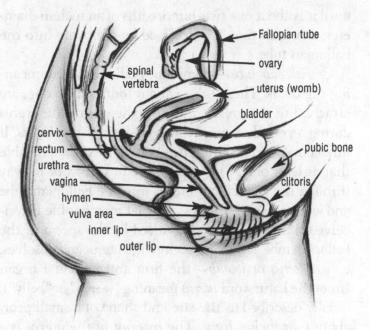

Fig. 2. The female reproductive organs.

Ovaries—organs so called from the Latin word *ova*, which means "eggs." A woman has two ovaries, each about the size of a robin's egg, one on each side of her abdomen. These ovaries, corresponding to the male testicles, produce the female egg. When a girl is born, her ovaries contain between 300,000 and 400,000 little follicles called ova. Only about three or four hundred will ever reach maturity and be released from the ovary. As a girl matures, her ovaries begin to secrete the female sex hormones that cause her to develop. Her breasts begin to enlarge, hair grows under her arms and on her genital organs, her hips start to broaden, and she begins to take on a curvaceous, feminine appearance. At approximately one-month intervals, an egg matures until it is about one two-hundredths of an inch in diameter, at which time it is released by the ovary into the Fallopian tube.

Fallopian tubes—sometimes called oviducts, meaning egg ducts. These tubes, about four inches long, are attached to the uterus and take the egg to the uterus during a period of approximately seventy-two hours. If intercourse occurs during this period, it is very probable that at least one of the active sperm will work its way through the vagina and uterus into the Fallopian tube and will unite with the egg. At that moment life is conceived. If the egg is not fertilized by the sperm in the Fallopian tube, it then passes into the uterus and dissolves.

Uterus or womb—the firm and muscular organ (from the Latin word *uterus* meaning "womb" or "belly"), usually described as the size and shape of a small pear, about four inches long. The interior of the uterus is a narrow, triangular-shaped cavity surrounded by thick muscular walls. The two Fallopian tubes enter at the top. The lower part of the uterine cavity that forms the narrow base of it is called the cervical canal. The uterus, which can be greatly expanded, is the area in which the baby grows during pregnancy.

Cervix—the neck of the uterus, from the Latin word *cervix*, meaning "neck." The cervix surrounds the cervical canal and forms the narrow, lower end of the uterus. About one-half of the cervix projects into the vagina and therefore can be examined by the physician almost as easily as he can look into the ear or nose. Before pregnancy, the cervix feels like the tip of the nose; after childbirth it feels like the point of the chin. The opening of the cervix into the vagina is called the "cervical os" (meaning "cervical mouth or opening" in Latin).

This passageway is so narrow that nothing larger than the lead in a pencil can pass through it easily. The normally tight passage helps to keep the interior of the uterus virtually germ-free, especially since there is a constant, slight current of cleansing moisture that flows outward.

Vagina—the primary female organ for intercourse, comparable to the male penis and designed to receive it. Deriving its name from the Latin word *vagina*, meaning "sheath," it is a very elastic, sheathlike canal that serves as a passage to and from the organs sheltered inside the body. It is three to five inches long, and its inner walls of delicate muscle tissue tend to lie in contact, their smooth surface "draped" in folds.

The walls of the vagina contain many tiny glands that continuously produce a cleansing and lubricating film of moisture so that the vagina is self-cleansing (similar, in this regard, to the eye). In its upper reaches, the vagina forms a curving vault that encloses the tip of the cervix.

Near the external opening of the vagina is a concentration of sensory nerves. This opening is encircled by a constrictor muscle that responds to the communications from these sensory nerves. This muscle can be tightened and relaxed at will. Implanted in the constrictor muscle are two glands called Bartholin's glands; the size of the letter *O* or slightly larger, they produce a very small amount of additional lubricant, mainly upon sexual stimulation.

The first response to sexual stimulation in a woman involves lubrication of the vagina, which occurs usually within ten to thirty seconds. Recently it has been found that this excitation causes the walls of the vagina to be covered with beads of lubricant, much like moisture on cold glass, which has a very practical application at the time of actual insertion of the penis in intercourse. The husband may need to reach gently into the vagina for some of this lubricant, or in many cases he may wish to apply some form of water-soluble artificial lubricant, such as Johnson & Johnson K-Y jelly, obtainable at drugstores. Only a small amount may be needed, applied just to the head of the penis or to the outside of the vagina, for usually enough natural lubrication exists inside the vagina.

Vulva area—the external opening to the vagina, containing several organs including the outer lips called "labia majora." The lips are formed from the same kind of coarse skin as the scrotal sac of the male. Under sexual excitement these lips swell or thicken. When they are opened, they reveal the inner lips, called "labia minora," which are very delicate membranes at the front of the vulva structure. These inner lips are made of skin very similar to the skin of the glans penis.

Hymen—deriving its name from the mythical god of marriage, a membrane at the back part of the outside opening of the vagina that may be relatively tough. The hymen, however, may be absent from birth and therefore its absence is not necessarily an indication of loss of virginity. The opening in the hymen of a virgin is about one inch in diameter, but must be about one and one-half inches in diameter for comfortable intercourse. Fifty percent of brides admit to experiencing some pain at first intercourse; 20 percent have no pain at all; and 30 percent have rather severe pain.

Before marriage every young woman should be examined by a doctor; at his discretion and with her consent, the hymen can be broken to avoid unnecessary delay in intercourse after the wedding. If the young woman has serious objections to this procedure, a physical examination can be scheduled for the day after the wedding. If she chooses to have her husband stretch the hymen on her wedding night, it is very important that lubricating jelly be generously applied to the penis and around the vaginal outlet. Then, with whatever intercourse position is chosen, preferably one so that the penis is directed downward and toward the back of the vaginal opening, she should be the one to do the thrusting in order to control better the amount of pressure she can tolerate. It may take several trials to penetrate the hymen; if she is not successful after a few attempts, she should not keep bruising this area, lest it become so painful that she cannot enjoy the time with her husband. Rather, the couple should just gently and slowly caress each other's genitalia until they are sexually satisfied.

Avoiding Pain

With generous amounts of lubricant on his fingers and with fingernails filed short and smooth, the husband can manually dilate the vaginal opening. He must gently insert one finger into the vagina, then two fingers, using a gradual, firm, downward pressure toward the anus until there is definite pain and until both these fingers can be easily inserted all the way to the base of the fingers. If this is too painful, it is usually better to be patient until the next day before again attempting well-lubricated introduction of the penis. Most of the pain comes from entering too quickly, giving the muscles around the vagina insufficient time to relax. Sometimes an overanxious bridegroom can produce physical pain because of the presence of the hymen. Although this does not produce lasting damage physically, it can leave psychological scars if the bride associates pain with the entrance of the penis into the vagina. In this case, her fear will shut off the natural flow of body fluids in the vaginal area and cause painful intercourse that is most unsatisfactory to both partners.

When the hymen is stretched or torn, there may be bleeding, but usually no more than one or two teaspoonfuls. If this bleeding continues or if there is as much as one tablespoon of blood, the wife should not be afraid, but just look carefully for the exact spot that is bleeding and hold a clean tissue on that spot with firm pressure. There is no bleeding that cannot be stopped by this method. The tissue may be left in place about twelve hours and then loosened by soaking in a warm bath to avoid new bleeding. The couple may resume intercourse the next day. If bleeding recurs, repeat the local pressure.

Urethra—the outlet for the urine from the bladder. The urethral opening is about one-half inch above the vaginal opening and entirely separate from it. It resembles a rounded dimple containing a tiny slit.

The urethra is a tube that runs just beneath the pubic bone and is easily bruised in the first few days after marriage unless plenty of lubrication is provided for the penis in the vagina. This bruising produces what is commonly called "newlywed cystitis" or "honeymoon cystitis." Characterized by pain in the bladder area, blood in the urine, and rather severe burning when the urine passes, it is a symptom that injury to the urethra has allowed bacteria to grow. This may ascend to produce a severe bladder infection called cystitis. It clears up and the pain subsides much faster with medication prescribed by a physician and with drinking extra fluids. It is very important that every couple, regardless of previous sexual experiences, have a surgical lubricant such as K-Y jelly available for use to help prevent the painful condition caused by bruising. This is especially essential during the first few weeks of marriage.

Clitoris—deriving its name from the Latin word *clitoris*, meaning "that which is closed in," the most keenly sensitive organ in a woman's body. As such it is called "the trigger of female desire." Its shaft, approximately one-half to an inch long, is closed by the peak of the labia about two inches above the entrance to the vagina and over the urinary opening, or urethra. At its outer end is a small, rounded body about the size of a pea, called its glans—from a Latin word meaning "acorn."

As far as is presently known, the *only function* of the clitoris is sexual arousal. Stimulation of the clitoris alone will produce an orgasm in nearly all women. It usually enlarges somewhat when caressed, but there is no cause for concern if it does not. In a study of hundreds of women able to reach orgasm, more than half showed no visible enlargement of the clitoris at all, and in many others, this enlargement was only barely discernible, even to touch, as most of the enlargement is in diameter, not in length. The size of the clitoris or its degree of enlargement has nothing to do with sexual satisfaction or sexual capacity. *The clitoris must be stimulated directly or indirectly for the wife to achieve orgasm.*

Labia minora—named from the Latin words for "small lips," the two parallel folds of smooth, hairless, soft tissue that connect to the hood over the clitoris and end just below the entrance to the vagina. Sexual arousal causes these lips to swell to two or three times their normal thickness. At times the gentle stroking of these small lips gives a more pleasant sensation than stroking the clitoris. Because they are connected directly above the clitoris, the friction of the penis's moving against them inside the vagina carries sensation to the clitoris. Thus direct stimulation of the clitoris is not always necessary to increase the intensity of sexual feelings.

Each wife needs to tell her husband specifically and lovingly, verbally or by subtle signals, what type of stimulation in this area gives her most pleasure at any given point in foreplay or in achieving orgasm.

Labia majora—the "major lips" lying outside and parallel to the labia minora, but not nearly so sensitive.

Areas of sensitivity—both the breasts and the genitalia, a woman having a greater number of sensitive areas than a man. This is probably God's means of compensating for the fact that the husband is ordinarily the initiator of intercourse. A woman's breasts are often very sensitive, and thus affectionate caressing helps to prepare her for the act of marriage. When she is aroused, her nipples will often become firm and protrude slightly, indicating proper stimulation. The larger outer lips of the vulva area also become increasingly sensitive as they enlarge under sexual excitement. As we have noted, the vagina and particularly the clitoris are sensitive areas. When a woman is sexually stimulated, several glands begin to secrete a lubrication that bathes the vulva area and the vagina in a slippery mucus, easing the entrance of the penis. This has nothing to do with fertility but is God's ingenious design for making the entrance of the dry penis a pleasurable experience to both husband and wife.

Orgasm—the climax of both women and men in intercourse, followed by a gradual decline in sexual stimulation and producing a warm sense of gratification and satisfaction. A woman never ejaculates or expels fluid as does a man; instead he is the instigator and she the receiver, not only of the male organ, but also of the sperm. Modern research indicates that a woman's orgasmic experience is every bit as titanic as a man's. A major difference is that a man's ejaculation is almost ensured without benefit of prior experience; a woman's is an art that must be learned by two loving, considerate, and cooperating partners.

"Aside from ejaculation, there are two major areas of physiologic difference between female and male orgasmic expression. First, the female is capable of rapid return to orgasm immediately following an orgasmic experience if restimulated before tensions have dropped below plateau-phase response levels. Second, the female is capable of maintaining an orgasmic experience for a relatively long period of time."[2]

Another significant difference between men and women is that a man's orgasm leaves his sex drive almost totally depleted for anywhere from twenty to forty-five minutes. In his youth he may experience as many as three or four ejaculations in a single day, although not usually for more than one or two days in a row. The male sexual reservoir takes time to rejuvenate, depending on age, health, and other factors. This rejuvenating process tends to take longer with age. Thus the frequency of sexual intercourse usually declines from an average of three times a week in a man's forties to twice in his fifties and approximately once in the seventies.

Similarity of male and female anatomies. A good way to summarize the female and the male sexual parts is to remember that the different organs in the two sexes develop out of the same basic structures. The most obvious of these originally similar, or homologous, structures are the clitoris and the penis. The clitoris embodies, in a reduced and modified manner, the chief elements of the male penis, including the spongy tissues that engorge with blood and the glans at the tip with its numerous nerve endings and great sensitivity. The muscles at the base of the penis are paralleled in the pubococcygeus muscles (frequently called the P.C. muscles) surrounding the vagina. The outer lips are the counterpart of the male scrotum. To a slight degree, the meeting of the outer folds of the inner lips over the clitoris corresponds to the foreskin over the glans penis.

It is clear that both male and female sexual organs have other functions besides procreation. Even before the human being is fully mature and able to reproduce, the sexual glands (the ovaries in the female and the testes in the male) have begun their work of making the girl a woman and the boy a man. They manufacture some of the hormones that encourage and control the rate of physical development as well as mental and psychological growth.

Notes

1. Portland Ore.: Multnomah Press, 1993.
2. William H. Masters and Virginia E. Johnson, *Human Sexual Response* (Boston: Little, Brown and Co., 1966), 131.

Six

The Art of Lovemaking

Every significant physical activity in life is learned by practice; why should lovemaking be different? Adult human beings possess the desire and necessary equipment to make love, but the art of lovemaking is learned—it is not innate.

Dr. Ed Wheat of Springdale, Arkansas, told a group of men in a seminar, "If you do what comes naturally in lovemaking, almost every time you will be wrong." In reality he was cautioning his male audience that each "natural" or self-satisfying step in gaining sexual gratification for a man would probably be incompatible with his wife's needs. For that reason, a couple must seriously study this subject just prior to marriage, and then after their marriage they can begin their practice to learn the most satisfying techniques.

It is unrealistic to expect two virgins to reach simultaneous climaxes on the first night of their honeymoon. Research indicates that nine out of ten brides do not experience orgasm in intercourse on the first attempt. Obviously it would be ridiculous for a couple to feel they had failed each other because they happened to be in the ninety percentile. It is much more realistic for a couple to recognize that they must "learn by doing." Isn't that the primary purpose of a honeymoon—for two lovebirds to get away to a romantic spot and learn about each other and their sexual natures?

When intercourse is an expression of love, it can be enjoyable even when one or both partners do not experience an orgasm. The tenderness and intimate relationship may prove to give sufficient satisfaction in themselves. Naturally one must expect intense stimulation ultimately to culminate in orgasm for both, but that goal is not usually achieved immediately. Such a rewarding skill is learned after study, experimentation, and open communication between husband and wife.

The art of love that exists well within the capabilities of every couple reading this book will be presented in this chapter for honeymooners, even though it will probably be read by more married veterans than newlyweds. After all, the difference in lovemaking between virgins and experienced married partners is minor. One marriage counselor has advised, "If couples would treat each other all through marriage as they do on their honeymoon, they would have very few sex problems. But most experienced couples try to take shortcuts, and that is what spoils their potential satisfaction."

The Ultimate Goal

Many pleasurable side effects arise from lovemaking, but we should not lose sight of the fact that the ultimate objective is orgasm for both the husband and wife. For the man this is usually quite simple and easily detected. When sufficient stimulation is applied to the nerve endings in the glans penis, a chain reaction is begun by creating muscular contractions in the prostrate gland, forcing the milky seminal fluid and sperm cells through the urethra with a force strong enough to ejaculate as far as twenty-four inches. Only then does the man realize that almost every organ and gland in his body has been brought into action, for after orgasm they all start to relax, and he becomes overwhelmed with a feeling of contentment.

The woman's orgasm is much more complex, and since she seems to be capable of several levels of climax, it is less obvious. For that reason, many young wives aren't sure whether they have reached an orgasm or not. Just as the gentle art of love has to be learned, so must she discern by personal experience what to expect of an orgasm. Once she has achieved a high-level orgasm, she no longer doubts what it is or when it occurs.

With the goal of mutual orgasm before them, a couple is advised to take whatever time and steps are necessary to achieve that objective. Love, patience, unselfishness, concentration, and persistence place that goal well within the capability of every married couple!

Preparation for Love

One young bride-to-be interrupted me during my usual talk on intimate relationships before marrying the couple. "Pastor LaHaye, do we have to talk about this? It embarrasses me. It will work out by itself." No wonder that naive young lady became pregnant during the first month of marriage, and I would be surprised if she has yet learned sexual satisfaction.

Fortunately most brides expect to enjoy lovemaking and realistically face the fact that some preparation is necessary before they begin the actual experience. All such young people would be advised to consider the following minimal steps in that preparation:

1. Learn as much as you can before the wedding night. The previous chapter on sex education should be read several times to make sure both the bride and groom understand the functions of the male and female reproductive systems. We feel that the reading of this book and others listed at the close of the chapter should not be reviewed together until after the wedding. But both bride and groom should read the basic material separately beforehand and then study it together on their honeymoon. This book is intended to be a help to such a couple on their wedding trip.

2. All prospective brides should visit their doctor several weeks before the wedding, discussing with him the advisability of breaking the hymen in the privacy of his office. If the doctor's examination shows that the hymen is thick and may obstruct sexual intercourse, she should consider letting him stretch it or cut it to avoid unnecessary pain and bleeding during intercourse. However, if the doctor feels she will have no serious difficulty and if the bride chooses, she may wish to leave it intact for her wedding night. In this enlightened age a bridegroom would rather have the hymen surgically removed in advance to reduce the possibility of causing pain to his virtuous young bride. Another alternative is digital stretching, which the husband can do on their wedding night, but this will require instructions from their

doctor. In today's active world many virgins have broken the hymen in accidents while bicycling or horseback riding, or doctors may have had to dilate it because of menstrual difficulties.

The bride should discuss the matter of contraceptives with her doctor. We consider this in greater detail in chapter 12, but it is important for the bride and groom to realize that the fear of pregnancy can seriously detract from the joy of a honeymoon. The young couple should know each other's feelings and decide whether they are prepared to start a family right after marriage or not. If they plan on a short delay, the doctor can advise them on a good, safe contraceptive.

3. It is a rare bride who will be able to provide sufficient natural vaginal lubricant on her honeymoon to avoid painful sensations during the act of love. This possibility can be eliminated by securing a tube of surgical jelly from the druggist, or she may wish to discuss this with her doctor, who can prescribe an adequate preparation for her. She would be advised to have it handy for her husband to use at the proper time.

4. The vaginal exercise program designed by Dr. Arnold Kegel is described in chapter 10. All brides-to-be should become aware of the muscles used and should practice Dr. Kegel's exercises several weeks before the wedding. The program will acquaint her with muscle control, about which most women know nothing, and in addition will magnify her potential sexual feeling during lovemaking. It will also provide her with a means of exciting her husband beyond his fondest dreams. Learning these exercises will further assist them in learning to reach simultaneous orgasms. The bride should carefully study chapter 10 on feminine response.

Preliminary Considerations

We have noted that most women are more romantic than men. "Women are incurably romantic" came the comment from one analyst. Instead of fighting against that fact, the wise husband will cooperate with this need in his wife's heart. Because the honeymoon is the culmination of a girl's lifetime dreams, a loving husband will make every effort to fulfill them.

When I look back on our honeymoon, I have to admit that I planned everything wrong. Bev and I were married on a Saturday night in her home church. An old friend and his wife who came to the wedding decided to join us at our apartment while he gave me a one-hour lecture on the "facts of life." This took place after the reception, pictures, and packing of our car. We went to bed at 1:45 A.M.! Our first married day was spent driving for twelve hours, then stopping about 8 P.M. in a motel room somewhere in the mountains of Kentucky. The next day we arrived in Greenville, South Carolina, where another ministerial student and I were building a trailer court for married students. I promptly went back to work. About the only clear lesson Bev learned from that hectic trip was to begin adjusting immediately to the insane pace to which I have subjected her for over forty exciting years.

If I had known then what I know now, I would have planned those few days after the wedding differently. First, we would have been married in the afternoon. Then we would have slipped away from our friends to be alone, planning at least a week to get acquainted before my bride was confronted with her new lifestyle as a wife.

One of the chief advantages of an afternoon wedding is having an entire first night without the fomenting turmoil that inevitably awaits a young couple after the reception. They need to get away to a hotel room to retire, unpack, freshen up, and leisurely enjoy a snack or dinner together. Most young people eat and sleep erratically before their wedding and, due to the frenzy of preparations, leave the ceremony totally exhausted. They need to sit down quietly, relax from all the excitement, and eat enough to lift their blood sugar level for added energy.

Upon returning to the room, the bridegroom may wish to carry his bride over the threshold in the traditional manner. From this point on, the two of them will be alone and should feel free to become as intimately acquainted as possible. The husband should proceed slowly and very gently with tender caresses and verbal expressions of love. There is a thin line at this stage between a husband's love and a man's passion. The husband who hurries this first encounter may unconsciously convey the thought to his new wife that he is being driven by passion more than love and concern for her. A slow, gentle approach will reveal his love for her through self-control.

It is important to add here that all lovemaking should proceed in circumstances where the couple can be guaranteed absolute privacy. Men are so single-minded that this is not so important to them as to their wives, but modest women need the assurance that no one will accidentally interrupt them. In a motel room it is easy to fasten the night lock. In their bedroom at home, they should install a lock on the door. Such a precaution is a necessary investment for successful lovemaking.

The romantic-minded husband will see to it that lights are turned low, thus ensuring visibility without excessive brightness, and if possible provide soft music.

The Great Unveiling

At this point the husband must be very sensitive to the romantic fantasies of his wife. Some brides will succumb to the lingerie industry's commercials and wear a sexy nightie bought especially for the honeymoon. If so, she may want to slip into the bathroom to make the change. However, the couple may wish to stir sexual excitement for love by undressing one another. The lover finds it terribly exciting and stimulating to be gently undressed by his or her loved one. Although one may experience some embarrassment at being fully unclothed before one's partner the first time, such a feeling will be minimal and will soon dissolve if the undressing proceeds slowly, even in stages, with tender, compassionate expressions of love. When the husband assures his modest bride that she is truly the most beautiful creature he has ever seen, she will most likely respond with a warm embrace.

Foreplay

Almost every sex manual emphasizes the need for an adequate period of foreplay, or loveplay. This is true not only on the first night, but all through marriage. Most men have learned that foreplay is essential to their wives' enjoyment of lovemaking, but they generally minimize their own need for foreplay because they are fully aroused for lovemaking at the sight of their beloved's nude body. Yet current research has revealed that it is easier for a man to retard his ejaculation after a long period of foreplay than after sudden arousal.

Besides, as he learns how to affectionately arouse his wife, he will attain intense excitement in her response himself, and it will enrich his own climax.

How long the couple should spend in foreplay may vary with each couple's need, depending somewhat on their temperaments and cultural background. But it is never wise to be in a hurry. A modest, inexperienced bride may require thirty or more minutes in preparation for lovemaking. After she becomes more experienced, the preparatory time may be reduced to ten or fifteen minutes; occasional exceptions during her emotional cycle when she is particularly amorous may reduce the time even further.

There is no universal pattern for arousing a woman to lovemaking. Some women are stimulated by having their breasts caressed, others are not. Furthermore, a woman's emotional cycle may make it enjoyable for her on some occasions, but not on others. For this reason, a wife should freely instruct her husband through verbal responses and by placing his hands where she wants him to caress her tenderly. Generally a thoughtful husband may gently massage his wife's neck, shoulders, and breasts to arouse her until blood rushes to the nipples and they become firm and erect, though care should be taken not to irritate the nipples by too vigorous action. Any tender fondling and kissing on the upper body will help to arouse her. Gradually the husband should move his hands gently down his wife's body until he contacts the vulva region, mindful to keep his fingernails smoothly filed to avoid producing any discomfort (which could cause her heating emotions to become suddenly chilled).

As the husband is tenderly caressing the clitoris or vaginal area with his hand, the couple will probably be lying on the bed with the wife on her back. If she will spread her legs, keeping her feet flat on the bed, and pull them up toward her body, it will be helpful for them both. The husband finds this voluntary act of coopera- tion very exciting, and it makes her most sensitive areas accessible to his caressing fingers. It is best for the husband to fondle the area around the clitoris, but he should not start foreplay there at first because of poten- tial irritation. As the area starts to engorge with blood, it becomes the primary source of excitement to the wife and is then ready for direct stimulation.

On first arousal the husband will be able to feel the clitoris with his fingers, but his wife will go through several physiological changes as her excitement mounts. Her heart will palpitate, her skin becomes warm, and almost every part of her body becomes sensitive to the touch. Her breathing will be more rapid, her face may grimace as if in pain, and she may groan audibly—and her husband finds this all very exhilarating. The most noticeable change will take place in the vaginal area, where she becomes very moist and the inner lips (labia minora) begin to swell several times their normal size until they form a hood over the clitoris, which may no longer be felt by his fingers. At this point it usually becomes unnecessary to maintain direct contact with the clitoris, for any motion in the vaginal region will vibrate against the thick layers of the swollen hood and transmit the movements to the clitoris indirectly. This will further amplify passion in the wife.

The vigor with which the husband massages this vital area should be determined by the wife. Some prefer it slow and easy, while others enjoy vigorous motion. Some wives like to vary the motion within one lovemaking experience; others may choose to modify it according to their mood. Most important, the husband should be extremely gentle and sensitive to his wife's needs at this point.

The mounting passions and tensions in a wife at this stage can be likened to pushing a cart uphill. As one gradually approaches the top, the peak seems to become steeper; then with a final thrust, the cart can be pushed over the top. Just as one would never stop the cart on the uphill side, so a thoughtful husband will not suspend his motion in the midst of their loveplay. If he does, her emotional cart will *immediately* descend and he will have to regain the emotional loss. This explains why many women cool somewhat during the time it takes a husband to remove his fingers from her vaginal area and place his penis inside, particularly if he has any clothing to remove. With practice he can learn to continue the massaging loveplay while putting the penis into place. This will help his wife continue her climb toward a high emotional peak. After the husband learns more self-control, he may stimulate his wife's clitoris with a lubricated penis. Some wives may prefer this to the husband's fingers. Then it is easily slipped into the vagina when she is ready.

The Culmination

Many an inexperienced husband misunderstands a very important signal from his wife. When his fingers are caressing the vaginal area and he finds it well lubricated, he may consider that to be the signal that she is ready for coitus. This is not true! Until her labia minora are heavily swollen by the influx of an ample supply of blood, the sensitive areas of her vagina will not even be included in their lovemaking. If he proceeds before that, he will probably reach orgasm just as this swelling takes place, and she will be left unfulfilled. His relaxing penis will then be unable to continue the motion on the sides of the vagina and the clitoris necessary to bring her to climax. This common misunderstanding probably has kept more loving partners from learning to reach simultaneous orgasms than anything else.

The husband must also remember when massaging the area of the vagina and clitoris that at first touch with dry fingers his wife might experience some discomfort. If he moistens his finger with vaginal lubrication, she will find clitoral stimulation much more enjoyable. Free and honest communication is essential in this phase of loveplay to maximize the enjoyment of this necessary preparation for the act of marriage.

Several writers in this field, both Christian and secular, suggest that a couple gently massage each other to orgasm on their wedding night for two reasons: (1) it increases the possibility for both to experience an orgasm the first night, and (2) it helps to acquaint them with their partner's bodily functions. We believe this might be a little too much to expect from two inhibited virgins their first night together. We suggest, however, that they arouse each other as outlined above, and when the wife thinks she is ready for entrance, she should take the groom's penis in her hand and place it in her vagina. Upon his wife's signal and while continuing to massage her clitoral area, the husband should use his free hand to take a lubricating jelly (which should be placed on the nightstand in advance) and lubricate the head and shaft of his penis before entrance. He should be careful to support the weight of his body with his elbows and slowly push his penis into her vagina.

Once inside, the husband should try to remain motionless or he may ejaculate in a matter of seconds, abruptly terminating their lovemaking. Even though all his instincts cry out within him to begin his thrusting motion, he must gain self-control for at least one or two minutes. To avoid the loss of his wife's mounting tension, he should continue to massage her clitoral area or the swollen lips of the vulva. The wife can help to increase her passion by slightly rotating her hips as she lies beneath her husband. This helps to maintain motion and friction on her clitoris and bring her vagina into contact with the shaft of his penis without overstimulating him. When she feels her passions mounting beyond control, she should put her legs around her husband's hips and begin her own thrusting movements back and forth on the penis. If she has practiced contracting the vaginal (P.C.) muscle several weeks before marriage as described in chapter 10, she will find more pleasure in the experience and can help her husband by squeezing his penis with the muscle each time he retracts. A squeezing action upon first entry is also helpful to both husband and wife—while the husband is waiting one to two minutes for ejaculatory control, his wife's squeezing can maintain her excitement. Once the husband begins his thrusting motion, the wife should concentrate on the sensations she is experiencing in her clitoris and vaginal area, continuing as much motion as possible that contributes to that feeling.

The husband, no matter how inexperienced, will intuitively recognize his wife's accelerated motion as the signal for him to begin his thrusting motion, and he will likely expel his mixture of seminal fluid and sperm cells into her vagina within just a few thrusts. He should continue thrusting after his ejaculation as long as he can in case his wife's orgasm is all but seconds behind his.

Shortly after ejaculation, his penis will lose its rigidity and will no longer maintain sufficient friction on the vaginal walls and labia minora to increase his wife's excitement. If she has not reached an orgasm during their first coitus, the young lovers should not feel discouraged. The husband can immediately begin manual stimulation of his wife's clitoris and vulval area, as he did in foreplay, to help bring her to orgasm. Although it is possible for a bride to experience orgasm during the couple's first encounter, it is unusual, especially for a virgin.

The Afterglow

Most brides find their initial lovemaking, when preceded by sufficient loveplay, a delightfully exciting experience even without orgasm. The free experimentation with their beloved's nude body is stimulating, unsurpassed by any previous experience. Even such pain as she may have felt in the breaking of her hymen or the possible stretching of the vagina will usually be eclipsed by the stimulation of areas she has never used before. Many wives have indicated that the blast of their lover's warm seminal fluid inside the vagina is also thrilling. Coupled with the intimate closeness of their entwined bodies, this makes it a most enjoyable expression of love. If her orgasm was not achieved, her emotional tension will gradually subside and her reproductive organs, like those of her husband, will slowly return to normal.

There is no need for lovers to withdraw immediately after completion of intercourse. We advise that they remain in each other's embrace for several minutes and continue to exchange caresses. Many couples fall asleep in this position or learn to roll onto their sides, the limp penis gradually sliding out the vagina. Their physical and emotional exhaustion generally produces a deep, satisfying slumber.

It usually takes the husband forty-five minutes to an hour or more before he can be ready for lovemaking again. This is not true of the wife. Research by Masters and Johnson indicates that a woman can experience several orgasms, one right after another.[1] For that reason, whenever a wife is brought to orgasm by her husband's hand during foreplay, he should continue to massage her vaginal and clitoral area, for she will soon regain the feeling of mounting excitement and can repeat the orgasmic experience. It may be difficult for a man to understand how his wife can immediately be ready for more when he is powerless to regain his sex drive without a period of rest, but she is surprisingly capable of continuing orgasms. In fact, some women have reported that their most powerful climaxes are sometimes their fourth or fifth in a lovemaking session. However, if the husband stops his stimulation of the clitoris and vaginal area immediately after the first orgasm, she will gradually lose her mounting passion and retreat to a state of emotional and physical exhaustion similar to that of her husband.

Honeymoon Experimentation

Honeymoons exist not only to provide a special time for companionship, but to promote sexual learning and experimentation. For that reason, couples should try various methods of stimulation, positions (see pages 90–91), times of day, and whatever they both find enjoyable. We recommend that sometime during their honeymoon, in order to understand fully their partner's physiological function during lovemaking, they bring each other to orgasm by hand. This experiment should be carried out in a lighted room where they may be free from any interruptions. Unclothed, they should maintain the same romantic atmosphere and unhurried preparation as for any other period of lovemaking.

It is advisable that the husband try to bring his wife to orgasm first, because after his climax it is usually difficult for him to be vitally interested in lovemaking for some time. Proceeding in the manner outlined above, he should lie on his side next to and slightly above his wife while he tenderly caresses the clitoris and the vaginal area with his hand. When the labia minora are sufficiently swollen, indicating that she is responding properly and her vagina is well lubricated, he will feel that the protective hood has covered the clitoris area, and he can create friction in both places at once. She may want him to insert one finger very gently into the vagina, making slow rhythmic movements inside while his other fingers continue contact with the outer vulval area. This will usually give her a delightful sensation and help to increase her excitement. She should feel free to use her hand to guide her husband's to the most responsive areas and create the most stimulating motions. Then she should concentrate with abandon on those vital areas of friction and let herself go completely, so that if she wishes to groan, cry, wiggle, rotate, or thrust, she may do so.

To fully realize her capability after her first orgasm, the wife should encourage her husband to slacken his motions, but not discontinue them. As her excitement begins to mount again, she can signal him to speed up his motion and increase its vigor to her satisfaction until she reaches another orgasm. Twice will probably be sufficient at this state of their marriage.

After her climax, the wife should turn on her side while the husband lies on his back. Gently massaging the genital region, she should run her fingers over his penis, pubic hair, scrotum, and inner thighs. She should be very careful not to put pressure on his testicles located inside his scrotal sac, as this can be quite uncomfortable. With her hand around the shaft of the penis, she should begin massaging up and down. As her motion becomes more rapid, her husband's body will grow more rigid, and she will be able to verify his response to her touch. This motion should be continued until he ejaculates. Before beginning this exercise, the wife should have several tissues on hand to absorb the discharge.

Dr. Herbert J. Miles, in his excellent book *Sexual Happiness in Marriage*, tells the following story:

> One couple in the research sample had this experience. They attempted intercourse on their wedding night and the wife did not have an orgasm, but the husband did. After intercourse, they attempted to bring her to an orgasm by direct stimulation. In the process she gradually became tense, nervous, and just could not continue the arousal effort, although she tried and wanted to do so. She had to ask her husband to stop the stimulation. They lay there, relaxed, and talked for over three hours, on into the night. Finally, long after midnight she said, "I want us to try that again." They repeated the process of direct stimulation and after about seventeen minutes she reached her first orgasm. What actually happened, in her case, was that she learned much in her first effort and after becoming relaxed and

more confident, she was able to give herself fully
to sexual arousal and thus succeeded.[2]

Some Christians might object to this form of
experimentation. We recommend it for newlyweds,
because they are building a lifetime relationship together
in which lovemaking will play a permanent role for up
to sixty years. The more they know about each other
by personal experience, the more they will enjoy each
other and more likely experience what we consider the
ultimate in lovemaking: simultaneous orgasms most of
the time. This form of "learning by doing" will increase
the likelihood that they will learn the art early in marriage and go on to enjoy it for many years. Part of the
therapy recommended by many experts for sexual dysfunction is this same experimentation. Couples married
for years have been helped to a better understanding of
each other and a better sexual relationship through this
kind of learning process.

Dr. Miles suggests, "There are three steps in sexual adjustment that couples need to learn. They are as
follows: first step—orgasms, second step—orgasms in
intercourse, third step—orgasms together or close
together in intercourse."[3]

A couple should not be discouraged if they do not
achieve the second or third step right away. It may take
several weeks or longer before they can experience
simultaneous orgasms on a regular basis. However, it
should be a goal for which every couple strives.

Another area in which a couple will want to
experiment is positions for most effective sexual arousal.
One of the most convenient has the wife lying on her
back with knees bent and feet pulled up to her hips and

her husband lying on her right side. Dr. Miles explains what the Bible says about a married couple's position for lovemaking.

> This position of sexual arousal is described in the Bible in the Song of Solomon 2:6 and 8:3. These two verses are identical. They read as follows: "Let his left hand be under my head and his right hand embrace me." The word "embrace" could be translated "fondle" or "stimulate." Here in the Bible, in a book dealing with pure married love, a married woman expresses herself with longing that her husband put his left arm under her head and that he use his right hand to stimulate her clitoris.
>
> This position of sexual arousal seems to have been the position used by many people back through the centuries. We do not hesitate to say that the general arousal procedure described here is a part of the plan of God as He created man and woman. Therefore, mankind has used this procedure because it is the plan of God and because it is efficient.[4]

Dr. Miles further gives some sound advice regarding the extent of intimacy between the husband and wife.

> In interpersonal relationships in the community and society, modesty is a queen among virtues, but in the privacy of the marriage bedroom, behind locked doors, and in the presence of pure married love, there is no such thing as modesty. A couple should feel free to do whatever they both enjoy which moves them into a full expression of their mutual love and in a sexual experience.

At this point it is well to give a word of caution. *All sex experiences should be those which both husband and wife want.* Neither, at any time, should force the other to do anything that he does not want to do. Love does not force.[5]

One characteristic of the Holy Spirit is love, and a dominant trait of love is kindness. The intimacy of lovemaking should always be performed with kindness. At times vigorous activity is required, but it will always be expressed in kindness to the other person—a vital evidence that the act of marriage is in reality an act of love.

Clitoral Stimulation

The reluctance of many loving partners to incorporate clitoral stimulation as a necessary and meaningful part of their foreplay has probably cheated more women out of the exciting experience of orgasmic fulfillment than any other one thing. Because it has often been associated with self-stimulation, even some husbands are unaware of how essential a part of the lovemaking process it is.

To highlight the significance of the clitoris to the woman's sexual enjoyment, many researchers have compared it with the penis. It has been called the "most keenly sexual part of a woman's body" and is still regarded by many as "the seat of all sexual satisfaction."[6]

R. M. Deutsch has stated that "stimulation of the clitoris alone will produce an orgasm in nearly all women.... direct clitoral stimulation alone [will] produce the climax."[7] He further indicates that "most researchers agree that the clitoris, unlike any male organ, has only one purpose—sexual stimulation."[8]

Another researcher indicates that the clitoris has the same number of nerve endings as does the penis, but is only one-tenth the size. Therefore it is the culmination in feminine sexual capability. To disregard it is to guarantee feminine orgasmic malfunction or incapability.

From a practical standpoint it has no bearing on reproduction and is unnecessary for any other female function. Thus it is safe to conclude that God designed it to be used in lovemaking. It could well be that the thrilling response of the wife referred to in the Song of Songs 5:4 may allude to the husband's use of clitoral manipulation. Such foreplay is not only acceptable behavior by married partners, but also was designed by God as one of the most delightful aspects of the act of marriage.

The Four Phases of Sexual Arousal

Modern research, particularly that of Masters and Johnson, acquaints us with four distinct phases of sexual arousal for both male and female: (1) the excitement phase, (2) the plateau phase, (3) the orgasmic phase, and (4) the resolution phase. Admittedly, reducing all human responses to a single chart does not allow for individual variation, and from that standpoint such a chart oversimplifies the matter, but it does provide a basic pattern on which to establish a norm. As noted in the following diagrams, only one characteristic response of men is indicated, whereas three are listed for women. The male response is more prone to be basic, whereas women tend to reflect more individual variation. In addition, because of the greater complexity of a woman's orgasmic function, she may experience each of these responses throughout her married life as she is learning the art of love expression.

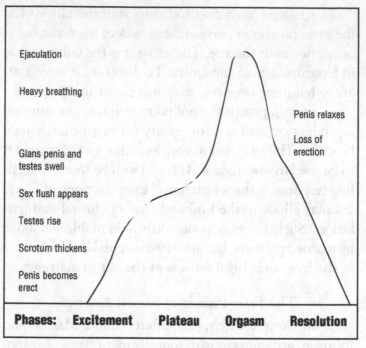

Fig. 3. Sexual response of the husband.

On the wife's chart we have distinguished the three responses as (A) the multiple orgasm, the ideal she would like to achieve; (B) the orgasmic failure, the sexual response that far too many settle for (a failure that often can be changed by a little more understanding, added foreplay, and increased tenderness on the part of her companion); and (C) the single orgasm, probably the most frequent expression of the well-adjusted married woman who may reserve the multiple experience for special occasions when her mood, time allotted for love-making, and other factors fall into place.

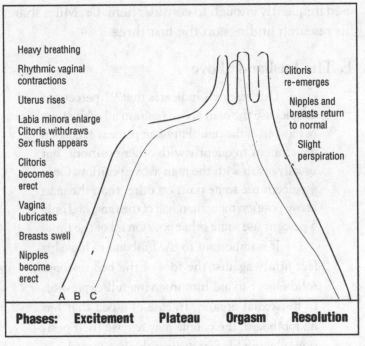

Heavy breathing

Rhythmic vaginal contractions

Uterus rises

Labia minora enlarge
Clitoris withdraws
Sex flush appears

Clitoris becomes erect

Vagina lubricates

Breasts swell

Nipples become erect

A B C

Clitoris re-emerges

Nipples and breasts return to normal

Slight perspiration

Phases: **Excitement**   **Plateau**   **Orgasm**   **Resolution**

Fig. 4. Sexual response of the wife.

As the chart indicates, certain physiological changes take place in each stage. These should be studied, and lovers should experiment to the point of learning what to expect in each of these phases.

Various Positions

Since the earliest days of writing, various lovemaking positions have been recorded. One author claims there are ninety-nine different positions. The trouble with about ninety-five of them is that only a gymnast could enjoy them. Actually there are only four positions used frequently enough to consider here. Dr. Miles shares his research findings on the first three.

1. The husband above

Our research indicates that 91 percent of couples use the man above position all of the time or most all of the time. Fifty-four percent of couples experiment frequently with other positions, but usually finish with the man above position. Only 4 percent use some position other than the man above position more than half of the time, and only 5 percent use some other position all of the time.

It is important to the husband to have his feet firmly against the foot of the bed or some solid object to aid him in giving full expression to his sexual orgasm. In case of a bed that has no footboard, the couple may reverse their position, placing his feet against the headboard.

2. The wife above

The wife above position allows the husband to relax and control himself, and permits the wife to initiate the movement necessary to give her the most stimulation by forcing the clitoris to move over the penis. The disadvantages are that this position is often not comfortable for the wife, the husband may have difficulty in controlling his arousal, and neither are in proper position to give fullest expression during orgasms. For some couples the advantages outweigh the disadvantages. This position is often advantageous for a large husband and a small wife.

3. Both on their sides

Another useful position is for both husband and wife to lie on their sides facing the same direction with the husband back of the wife. The penis is moved into the vaginal passage from the rear. The disadvantages are that the penis cannot contact the clitoris and the couple cannot kiss during the experience. The advantages are that the position is very comfortable, the husband can easily use his fingers to stimulate his wife's clitoris, and he can control his own arousal. There are other slight variations of this approach. Many couples use this position for the arousal period and shift quickly to the man above position for orgasms.[9]

4. Husband seated

Depending on their comparative heights, a couple may sometimes enjoy the position of the husband seated on a low couch or backless chair. The wife can lower herself onto his penis at her discretion. This position is good for those wives who find that the entrance of the male organ is painful. By controlling the entrance, a wife can minimize the pain. Such sensations will be short-lived, and couples should not give up or use pain as an excuse to avoid lovemaking permanently. If pain is not eliminated by application of generous amounts of lubricant, see your physician.

Most couples experiment with these and other positions, but return to the man above. It seems to be the most satisfying to the largest number of lovers.

Summary

The art of mutually enjoyable lovemaking is not difficult to learn, but neither is it automatic. No one is a good lover by nature, and thus the more selfish the individual, the more difficulty he will have learning this art. If two people love each other with an unselfish love and are willing to control themselves while seeking to learn how to render emotional and physical satisfaction to their partner, they will learn. It does, however, demand time and practice. Anyone who takes time to read this book has indicated he or she is concerned enough to try. Dr. Ed Wheat has sagely said, "Every physical union should be a contest to see which partner can outplease the other."

With this concept in mind, I told a story in the chapter on "Physical Adjustment" in my book *How to Be Happy Though Married.* It was given to me by a minister friend who had counseled a frustrated couple in the art of clitoral stimulation so that in a very brief period of time they resolved their problem.

Four months after that book was published, I was speaking at a banquet in a very small city in northern California. A dentist told me privately that he had read the book and had been reminded of his own case. When he related his story, I found it an exciting corollary to the earlier tale.

The young dentist and his wife of three years were deeply in love, but his wife had never reached orgasm during their marriage. He found this almost as frustrating as she did. As a dentist, he had studied anatomy and felt that he knew more than the average person about the functions of the human body. This knowledge, however, did not seem to resolve their difficulty, and their sexual frustration soon produced marital conflict. Since they were not Christians at the time, they decided to start going to church as a last resort to save their marriage. They fortunately selected a gospel-preaching church, and in about three months they both had accepted Christ as their personal Lord and Savior. But, of course, this still did not resolve their problem of orgasmic malfunction.

One Sunday morning their pastor was preaching on the text of Proverbs 3:6, "In all your ways acknowledge him, and he will make your paths straight." They heard him say, "You do not have a problem in your life that you cannot take to the Lord in prayer." The dentist looked at his wife and realized that they had not prayed about it. Afterward they discussed it and decided to do so.

On Friday of that week they were invited to a social gathering. Being the first to arrive, they were ushered into the family room to await the arrival of the other guests. It was a large room with a couple of conversation areas, so they chose a couch on the far side of the room. They were no sooner seated than another couple came in and sat on the first couch behind them, a large floral arrangement preventing them from being seen by the new arrivals. Thinking they were alone, this sanguine husband put his arm around his wife and exclaimed, "Hasn't our relationship been beautiful since we discovered clitoral stimulation?" The dentist silently glanced at his wife and thought, "We have never tried that." That night they did, and it was the beginning of a new experience for them both.

With obvious emotion the dentist told me, "That simple technique was like a key that opened the door to a beautiful relationship which we have enjoyed for the past three years."

This story shows evidence of God's abundant grace. In a small town without counselors, and under the ministry of a young, single seminary student, this young couple told their heavenly Father of their need and sought His help. He guided them to the right place at the right time to hear the information He wanted them to know.

No doubt the wife of the man who unknowingly gave their secret away would be horrified to know that her husband had been overheard that night, but I have a hunch that living with a super talker like him she was used to being embarrassed. Besides, if she knew how much joy they had introduced into the lives of the dentist and his wife, she might think it well worth the exposure.

No one has a problem that cannot be taken to the heavenly Father. No one need settle for a lifetime of sexual frustration. When God's children pray for His guidance and His will for their lives, He is always faithful in revealing it to them. This relationship with God will bless the lives and strengthen the faith of those who trust in Him for help.

The Key to Orgasmic Love

One of the unexpected results of publishing *The Act of Marriage* was that my counseling room became crowded with what was called in southern California at that time, "sex-dysfunctional counseling." Two of the most dysfunctional people I ever counseled happened to be a forty-eight-year-old doctor and his wife, a thirty-six-year-old nurse. As they disclosed one of the most miserable sex lives I had heard of, my first thought was, *What can I tell these two medical experts about human anatomy that they don't already know better than I do?* But as I listened, I realized sexual ignorance was not their problem; they were the two most selfish people I had ever encountered! Selfishness was destroying what could have been a beautiful expression of love.

Compare that with the two eighteen-year-olds who came in just six weeks after their wedding. Jim was a sailor who had married his childhood sweetheart and moved her from their Minnesota farm home to San Diego, where he had just been stationed. Their problem? Jim blurted it out painfully, "Pastor, we have been married six whole weeks and Sarah hasn't had an orgasm yet."

Needless to say, Sarah blushed all the way up to her blond hair. But she mustered, "I don't mind; I told Jim I just love being close to him and having him tell me he loves me."

Jim responded, "That's not good enough. I want her to enjoy our lovemaking as much as I do." What do you hear in that conversation? I hear two unselfish lovers who wanted to bring pleasure into their partner's life so much they were willing to be embarrassed in order to do so. Very honestly, that is not a difficult problem to solve when love is the motivation. Many of the suggestions I gave them are found in the next three chapters. One day a short time later, as Sarah was going out of church, she whispered, "We don't need your help anymore." Unselfish love had done it again! It works every time.

Notes

1. William H. Masters and Virginia E. Johnson, *Human Sexual Response* (Boston: Little, Brown and Co., 1966), 131.

2. Herbert J. Miles, *Sexual Happiness in Marriage* (Grand Rapids: Zondervan, 1967), 96.

3. Ibid., 97.

4. Ibid., 79.

5. Ibid., 78.

6. From *The Key to Feminine Response in Marriage* by Ronald M. Deutsch. Copyright © 1968 by Ronald M. Deutsch. Reprinted by permission of Random House, Inc., New York.

7. Ibid.

8. Ibid.

9. Ibid.

Seven

For Men Only

During the first decade of marriage most men are more aggressive sexually than their wives. This is not always true, of course, depending on their temperaments and the monthly cycle of the wife, but it does provide a useful generalization. We might more accurately observe that sex is instinctively the most universal drive in men during their first decade of marriage, whereas for women it is a potential appetite that can be cultivated.

The wise and loving husband will therefore learn as much as he can about this subject in order to bestow on his bride the greatest lovemaking experiences possible for both her benefit and his own. The more he strives for her enjoyment, the more he will help to create in her a favorable and exciting attitude toward the relationship. And the more she enjoys it, the more she will welcome and take delight in it.

The following suggestions will guide husbands in helping to create in their brides a wholesome appetite for lovemaking:

1. *Learn as much as you can.* The average man knows more about overhauling the carburetor on his car or motorcycle than he knows about the intricate young woman who will spend the rest of her life with him, providing the most thrilling and satisfying experience he will ever have. We have already alluded to Dr. Ed Wheat's observation that almost all of a man's natural instincts that bring him sexual satisfaction are not what bring his wife satisfaction. Since skilled lovemaking is not instinctive, a wise husband will learn as much as he can from a reliable Christian source. By studying carefully our chapter on sex education and the art of lovemaking, he can gain much of the basic information that every husband should know. In addition, we recommend that every couple send for Dr. Wheat's three-hour cassettes and listen to them together.[1] Since discovering these fine taped lectures, I have required prospective bridegrooms to listen to them alone just before the wedding and urged the couple to take the tapes with them on their honeymoon to listen to them together. The material is highly informative and inclusive; more than one hearing is necessary to absorb all the information presented. For the couple who has been married longer, listening together to these tapes will open lines of communication that will enable them to discuss subjects that previously may have seemed too difficult or personal for discussion.

2. *Practice self-control.* The apostle Paul said, "Each of you should look not only to your own interests, but also to the interests of others" (Phil. 2:4). The principle of unselfishly acting as a blessing to one's partner certainly

applies to lovemaking. As a man, your sexual needs can often be satisfied within a matter of seconds; your wife's situation is just the reverse. She begins more slowly, then gradually builds to her sexual climax. Most men who accuse their wives of being averse to sex because they cannot reach an orgasm are often themselves the problem. About the time she is really getting excited, her husband ejaculates and leaves her with a limp penis, thus denying her an opportunity for a satisfying climax in intercourse.

By what means can we solve this problem? The husband must learn to control ejaculation, and this demands strong self-discipline and practice. Some have suggested that men during intercourse may profitably contemplate nonstimulating things—sports, business, or, as one husband said, "I think about paying the monthly bills." Be careful not to overdo it, but concentrate on something that will delay your ejaculation and give your wife sufficient time for her emotional buildup. Remember, she usually requires ten to fifteen minutes of manipulation, either with your hand or through intercourse, before she can climax. Add to that a stimulating period of foreplay, and you will find plenty of time to practice self-control. Certain techniques that enable a man to postpone his ejaculation will be dealt with in detail in chapter 11.

3. *Concentrate on your wife's satisfaction.* Since a woman's orgasm is much more complex than a man's, it takes her longer to learn this art. A wise husband will make his wife's satisfaction a major priority early in their marriage so they can both benefit from her accomplishment.

Modern research has revealed some interesting feminine responses that a husband should understand. For instance, the intriguing creature known as his wife does not regard foreplay as "a warm-up before the game" as men often do; rather, to her it is an integral part of the big game. No husband should rush this activity just because his instincts suggest it. Instead, he should be aware of the four phases his wife goes through in the lovemaking process. Then he can devote his attention to bringing her through each stage.

Dr. Gary Smalley in his family seminars on TV makes a big point of the power of tender touch. He claims that a woman needs at least twelve touches a day to be assured of her husband's love. Such touches should not be saved until just before bedtime and administered one right after another, while counting out twelve instant love pats. His suggestion is that these love touches start in the morning and go on whenever they pass each other or are together. Such touches silently communicate approval, closeness, and love. I would add that you make sure they are not all sexual touches, particularly if there are other people in the house. A woman needs to be assured that her husband loves her, not just her body. The husband who makes it clear that he loves the woman who resides in her body more than just her body seldom lacks for the responsive love that only her body can provide. And always keep in mind, married sex comes without guilt and the greatest sex in the world is married love!

4. *Remember what arouses a woman.* The sight of his wife getting ready for bed is sufficient stimulation for most men to be ready for the act of marriage. By contrast, the wife at this point is probably only ready for bed! Why is this so? Because men are stimulated by sight, whereas women respond more to other things— soft, loving words and tender touch.

Although not registering on a decibel tester, the auditory mechanism of a woman seems uniquely responsive to the male voice. For instance, teenage girls are more actively stimulated to emit screams and groans at rock concerts than are their male escorts. Rarely does one hear a man say, "Her voice excites me," whereas it is common to hear a woman exclaim, "His voice turns me on!" That auditory mechanism can be likened to the thermostat on the wall of your home. Entering the house at night, you can turn her thermostat up by speaking reassuring, loving, approving, or endearing words. You can likewise turn her thermostat down through disapproval, condemnation, or insults. In such cases it is safe to conclude that the louder your voice, the more rapidly you turn her down. It is a wise husband who from the time he gets home from work until he goes to bed uses his voice and his wife's auditory receiver to turn her on consistently.

Many a wife can identify with Mary: "My husband criticizes me from the time he walks in the house at night until we go to bed, and then he cannot understand why I'm not interested in lovemaking. I'm just not made that way!" If only more husbands were alert to this strong influence on their partner's emotions!

5. *Control your anger.* Anger makes matters worse! Male anger has reached a fevered pitch today and is apparent everywhere from hostile drivers to explosive outbursts at sporting events and other activities that should give us enjoyment. Anger seems to be the response of preference when men face frustration. Admittedly, the frustration level at work, school, church, and throughout our culture in general has reached an all-time high. Unfortunately, too many men bring such anger home and take it out on their wives. Anger is not a sexual

motivator! And the first way that anger is usually demonstrated is in words. Yelling or caustic and unkind speech is almost as demotivating to a couple's love life as physical abuse. We are convinced that "Spirit-filled homes are angry-free" homes most of the time. A godly husband who wants to communicate true love to his wife must use both tender touch and kind gracious speech. And what does a real man do when he loses control? He apologizes. That is God's way of removing a potential root of bitterness that otherwise would fester in the heart of a wife.

The Bible is not silent on this subject, but commands, "Husbands, love your wives and do not be harsh [or bitter] with them" (Col. 3:19). Harbored bitterness produces angry actions and outbursts that cut to the heart. Every couple I have ever counseled who claimed they had lost their love for each other started the damage with their mouths. Our gift of speech is a gift of God that was provided for edification and gracious communication. It is a wise man who leaves his anger, particularly angry speech, outside the home. It is an even wiser man who uses the resources of the Holy Spirit to cure his anger altogether.

6. *Do not use crude words.* A woman's verbal receiver responds not only to the tone of voice but also to the message of the words. One couple requested help regarding the wife's "frigidity problem." After seven years of marriage, they had three children and claimed mutual love and respect. Upon questioning, we discovered that he spoke lovingly to his wife, wooed her tenderly, and gained a warm response up to a point. Then suddenly she would turn "cold as ice." Eventually we discerned that his language was the culprit. In the heat

of lovemaking excitement, he would introduce crude terms and crass expressions he had picked up in the army, forgetting that women tend to be more delicate in their word selections and often cannot understand why men use such uncouth speech to describe beautiful things. To solve that problem of her turning "cold," he had only to learn better terminology. Such things are important to women.

7. *Protect her privacy.* Men are far more inclined than women to be sex braggarts. Many a thoughtless man has spoiled a vital relationship by indiscreetly revealing his wife's intimate secrets to his buddies. If such a thing gets back to his wife, she feels betrayed. Such impropriety is not worth the risk. The beauty and sanctity of the intimate relationship you share is strictly confidential. Keep it that way.

8. *Beware of offensive odors.* The power of smell is one of our primary senses. Unfortunately some people experience more difficulty in this area than others, but today there is little excuse for bad breath, body odor, or any other offensive smells. A thoughtful lover will prepare for lovemaking by taking frequent baths, using effective deodorant, and practicing good oral hygiene.

On the subject of odors we share an observation made in the counseling room about extremely sensitive men. A melancholic man is a perfectionist, a very sensitive idealist. Consequently he may become "turned off" by the odors emitted by his wife's natural vaginal fluids. Women have a problem unshared by men, for the strong odor of a man's seminal fluid is usually not detected because it remains inside him until he ejaculates it into his wife's vagina, where it is not easily detected until after the resolution phase. But for the wife to permit penile entrance, she must secrete a vaginal lubricant that usually gives off an odor. A husband should simply learn to disregard that odor.

One such melancholic husband strongly complained that such an odor "turns me off so much that I cannot maintain my erection." Taking note of his limited sex education, I took the time to explain the function of his wife's vagina during sexual arousal. After convincing him this was a normal procedure over which his wife has no control, I concluded, "You should recognize that odor as the smell of love. Your wife's response to your love causes the lubricant to flow in anticipation of coitus with you; therefore you are the one causing the odor." With a sheepish grin he conceded, "I never thought of it that way." He later indicated that the "smell of love" concept had transformed their love life.

9. *Don't rush lovemaking.* Occasionally, when an experienced wife's monthly cycle causes her to be unusually passionate at a time when coitus is convenient, you both may attain exciting orgasms in a matter of two minutes or less. When it happens, enjoy it—but don't expect it to be the norm. Most couples find that time in loveplay is a major key to feminine response. Therefore the husband who would be a good lover will not advance too quickly, but will learn to enjoy loveplay. He will not only wait until his wife is well-lubricated, but reserve his entrance into her vagina until her inner lips are engorged with blood and swollen at least twice their normal size.

The time spent in lovemaking varies with the culture. Researchers have indicated that the average experience runs from two minutes in some cultures to thirty minutes in others. Their comparisons suggest that the more a culture is masculine-oriented and views sex as existing purely for male satisfaction, the shorter the time spent in the experience. In such a case, wives view it as a wife's "duty" or as an unpleasant function of life. In cultures where women are cherished and their satisfaction is sought, lovemaking is a time-consuming art.

A wise husband will keep in mind that his wife usually requires ten to fifteen minutes more time to reach her satisfaction than he does, but he will reckon it time well spent. Once he understands that a woman's nature ignites slowly and that her sexual tension increases gradually, he will cooperate with her needs.

10. *Communicate freely.* Most Christian women go into marriage relatively uninformed about sex and often retain the naive idea that their husbands know it all and will teach them. Rarely has she anticipated the fact that discussion of their intimate relations is difficult for most men. In fact, it is frequently the most difficult subject with which a couple has to cope. Consequently those who are most in need of the free-flowing expression of ideas on the subject practice it the least.

I have been appalled to learn that even well-educated people find it difficult to discuss their love lives frankly. But this explains why couples get embarrassed when their children ask questions about sex—they have never been able to communicate with one another on the subject. An engineer married to a schoolteacher for ten years reported, "After all this time my wife still doesn't know what turns me on." When I asked, "Have you ever told her?" he replied, "No, I find it embarrassing to talk about sex. Besides, I think she should know." He was surprised when I responded, "How should she?

You're different. You feel and react differently than a woman, and you possess an entirely different reproductive apparatus. Who did you think was going to tell her?" Most young brides expect their husbands to inform them of male needs. Unfortunately this does not usually happen. We have found that open communication between a husband and wife remains the best possible sex education. After all, a young bride does not need to know how men function; she must simply learn to recognize the sexual responses of one. Who best can teach her about his needs but the object of her love—her husband?

11. *Love your wife as a person.* No human being likes to be considered an object, for in the quest for identity, everyone wants to be accepted as a person. A young man wins the affection of a young woman because he loves her as a person, showering his attention and affections upon her. After the wedding he too often becomes involved in business and work while his wife is busy raising their children. The two gradually become preoccupied with activities that do not include each other. Consequently the wife soon feels that the only thing they share is their bedroom life. That is always unacceptable to a woman. This is what gives rise to the complaint often heard in the counseling room, "The only time my husband is interested in me is when he wants sex"; or "I am no longer a person to my husband; I am just a sex object"; or "When my husband and I have relations, I don't feel it is a natural expression of love. Instead, I feel used."

It is interesting that when confronted with the wife's discontent, most husbands admit the validity of her complaint. But they are mystified at how it occurred so gradually, and they are not always sure what to do to correct it.

There are many things a man can do to express his love for his wife as a person. As he does, he will find them mutually therapeutic. Such expressions not only reassure his wife of his love, but also reaffirm it in his own heart. The little thoughtful things that he does or does not do confirm to his wife's heart that he loves her as a person.

For example, when a man comes home at night, he should indicate a personal interest in her and what she has been doing during the day, rather than become obsessed with the sports page, what is cooking for dinner, or what is on TV. In the evening, giving a hand with the children, relieving her of some of the responsibilities she has borne all day, is a further expression of his love. His spending time with the children rather than being enslaved by the boob tube does as much for the wife as it does for the children.

Moreover, a weekly night out for dinner away from the children is vitally important to the wife, even though the husband's yearnings may be for a quiet evening at home. Then occasionally there are those little birthday and holiday remembrances and, most of all, verbalized expressions of love and approval all through the evening.

A man who treats his wife as someone very special will usually find her eagerly responding to his expressions of love. When his words and actions together convince her that he dearly loves her, their intimate lovemaking is the natural, culminating expression of that love.

God had a wise plan in establishing one man for one woman. It is impossible for a man to love a woman as a person when there is another woman involved. A close friend expressed that beautifully to me at lunch one day. We were discussing my Sunday sermon on King David. I asserted that I could not understand why a fifty-year-old man with twenty wives would stoop to committing adultery with Bathsheba. Jim surprised me by saying, "I can understand that. David had so many wives he never knew what it was to have one true love."

God designed the beauty of marriage to be a lifetime of sharing experiences with one true love. As long as a man convinces his wife that their lovemaking is the expression of the true love he has for her, he will find her a willing and cooperative partner.

Notes

1. Ed Wheat, M.D., "Sex Problems and Sex Technique in Marriage," available from Bible Believers Cassettes, 130 N. Spring, Springdale, AR 72764.

Eight

For Women Only

One outstanding observation gleaned from my years in the counseling room is that women enjoy a greater capacity for love than do men, a capacity that includes both giving and receiving. For this reason it seems women usually try harder than men to be good and faithful lovers. One thing has been obvious—far more women than men are willing to settle for a second-rate love life. Fortunately neither must endure such a condition any longer.

It is vitally important to a married woman's self-acceptance that her husband be satisfied with her as a love partner. One loving wife with a self-acceptance rating of zero lamented, "My husband thinks I'm an ideal cook, homemaker, and mother for his children, but he left me because I was a failure in the bedroom." Most men will accept mediocrity in other areas if the bedroom activity gives satisfaction. We have regularly noticed that nearly every wife genuinely wants to succeed in this important area of marriage, but too many just don't know how to proceed. Therefore some suggestions directed specifically to wives will be helpful.

1. *Maintain a positive mental attitude.* When en route to Hawaii with my wife for a few days' vacation before a seminar, I was reading Marabel Morgan's book *The Total Woman.* Beverly was startled when I suddenly started to laugh, but her response was identical when I showed her the cause. Mrs. Morgan indicated that the brain is the control center in women for making love. I had long been aware of that fact, but was astounded to find a woman who would admit it.

Proverbs 23:7 (mg.) reminds us, "For as he thinks within himself, so he is." Students of the mind are discovering that people never rise above their expectations. When they anticipate failure, they will never succeed. If, however, they expect success, they will achieve it. For the woman concerned about lovemaking success, talent, I.Q., and age have little to do with it; her mental attitude is the determining factor. We all have observed people who outperform their natural capabilities. It is our conviction that all Christians, empowered by the Holy Spirit, should outperform their own natural abilities in whatever situation they find themselves.

As a counselor I have been surprised by the number of beautiful women, the embodiment of sexual appeal, who confess that they are completely inept in the bedroom. On the other hand, some "plain Janes," flat-chested or overweight, admit to an exciting love life with their husbands. This proves that it isn't primarily the size, shape, or appearance of a woman that makes her a good lover; it suggests that her mental attitude is of utmost importance.

Three areas in a woman's sexual thinking pattern are very important to her: (a) what she thinks about lovemaking; (b) what she thinks about herself; and (c) what she thinks about her husband. Her attitude toward these will determine her success or failure.

(a) *What she thinks about lovemaking.* Although we cannot endorse the sexual revolution, it may be somewhat responsible for exposing the false concept that married love is "dirty," "evil," or "for masculine enjoyment only." Such impressions certainly did not emanate from the Old or New Testament or from the early church. They sprang from the "Dark Ages" when Roman theologians tried to merge ascetic philosophy with Christian thought. The pagan philosophy that assumed that anything enjoyable must be evil took precedence over the biblical concept that "marriage should be honored by all, and the marriage bed kept pure" (Heb. 13:4). It is difficult to describe some of the unbelievable and ridiculous distortions to which the sacred relationship of married love has been subjected. One author wrote,

> Peter Lombard and Gratien warned Christians that the Holy Spirit left the room when a married couple engaged in sexual intercourse— even if it were for the purpose of conceiving a child! Other church leaders insisted that God required sexual abstinence during all holy days and seasons. And in addition, couples were advised not to have sex relations on Thursdays in honor of Christ's arrest, on Fridays in memory of His crucifixion, on Saturdays in honor of the Virgin Mary, on Sundays in remembrance of Christ's resurrection, and on Mondays out of respect for

the departed souls (leaving only Tuesday and Wednesday)! The Church sought to regulate every facet of life, leaving no room for the individual's right to determine God's will, nor for the rights of a married couple to decide for themselves how the most intimate aspects of married life should be conducted.[1]

The Reformation fortunately called Christians back to studying the Word of God rather than blindly accepting dogma. In gaining new insights into God, salvation, sin, and theology, Christians discovered that God is the author of sex, that both men and women have sexual needs that a partner is obliged to fulfill (1 Cor. 7:1–5), and that their fulfillment is honorable and undefiled. Obedient Christians over the centuries have discovered in the privacy of their bedrooms that sexual relations provide the most exciting experiences in their lives. Any young woman who enters marriage without knowing that sexual union is a blessing from her heavenly Father, to be enjoyed without reserve, does not fully understand the Bible.

Confused church leaders of the past are not the only ones who seemed to delight in warping the mental attitudes of young virgins just prior to marriage. Some communities have been disturbed by little old ladies who were self-appointed evangelists of aversion to sex and took it upon themselves to visit brides-to-be before their weddings to inform them of the "facts of life." Their version was something like this: "S—is the worst part of marriage. It is distasteful and disgusting but something every wife must endure." By the time the "evangelist" was through, no young virgin could possibly anticipate the joys of married love. Such sexual misfits are contagious.

Having never welcomed the experience, they feel duty-bound to keep everyone else from enjoying it.

One wife who was sexually unresponsive told the following story in the counseling room. About two weeks before her marriage, her Aunt Matilda caught her and psychologically marred her for the first five years of marriage. Apparently her aunt, whose marriage was arranged by her parents in the old country, found herself petrified of sex on her wedding night. When her embarrassed and clumsy farmer husband, who was twenty years older, brought her to their wedding bed, he "stripped me naked and raped me in my own bed. I fought and screamed to no avail. My virginity was gone and I cried for three days. I have hated sex faithfully for thirty-five years." Her conclusion to her niece was, "As far as I'm concerned, marriage is just legalized rape."

As much as one might feel compassion for poor Aunt Matilda and her equally unhappy spouse, we can hardly envision more unhealthy concepts to pump into the impressionable young mind of a bride-to-be. It is little wonder that it took her niece several years and several counseling experiences to overcome such disastrous ideas.

How much better it would be for the young bride if her mother, whose love relationship for her husband had been accepted by their children through the years, would explain to her that married love is beautiful, exciting, meaningful, and mutually enjoyable. Such young virgins are mentally fortified against the false notions of Aunt Matilda and rarely become women who disdain sex.

The following illustration clarifies that a woman's mental attitude is the key to the use of her sexual apparatus. After listening for an hour as a couple who had come for counseling discussed their miserable sex life, I excused the husband for a few minutes in order to ask the woman why they made love only two or three times a month. The wife reported, "I'm not as robust as most women; I think my female organs are too small, and I can't function like other women." (Modern research indicates that all female organs, like those of their male counterparts, are approximately the same size regardless of the person's size.) When she admitted to suffering from arthritis, I shared with her some information that I had recently read reporting that tension accentuated pain in arthritis patients. Inasmuch as marital relations are a God-given means of relaxing emotional tensions, I counseled her to try more frequent lovemaking to help ease her arthritic pains. One week later I received a frantic phone call from her husband. "I don't know what you told my wife after I left the room, but she has made love to me seven times in the last seven days—and I'm not sure I can keep up with this pace!"

What turned the wife on? I suggested no medication, vitamins, or mechanical devices—merely a change in her mental attitude, the most powerful tool in combating sexual dysfunction.

(b) *What she thinks about herself.* Self-rejection is one of the most common maladies of our day. Men fret about a penis being too small or too soft; women worry about having miniature-sized breasts or being undersexed. Actually, the percentage of sexually normal people is enormous. In fact, tests have proved that "undersized" people (whatever that is supposed to mean) are just as responsive or sensitive sexually as anyone else—and sometimes more so.

Anxiety over one's ability to function sexually is the primary cause of sexual malfunction. Researchers report that men have functioned normally after various parts of their reproductive systems were removed, such as testicles or prostate glands. Interestingly enough, women who have had the clitoris removed for some reason reported no adverse effect on their sexual capability, and many women indicate increased marital enjoyment after having had a hysterectomy. From all the evidence we must conclude that the organs themselves are not of primary importance, but what we think about them—and ourselves. If we regard ourselves as sexually expressive and responsive love partners, we are—or at least have that capability.

(c) *What she thinks about her husband.* "I can't stand to have my husband touch me!" Thus began the mother of five who had become infatuated with another man. She confessed, "Ten minutes to five is the most miserable time of my day because as I stand at the sink, getting dinner ready, I know that Tom will be home in ten minutes and will kiss me when he comes in."

After we seriously dealt with her mental love affair with a divorced man as a sin, Julie got down on her knees and confessed her sins through her tears. Two weeks later my phone rang at 4:55 P.M., and Julie reported excitedly, "God has changed my heart! I'm all dressed up, excited that Tom is due home in a few minutes. I called because I wanted you to know that this has now become the most exciting time of my day."

Love is not a whimsical vapor that comes and goes without rhyme or reason. It is a vital emotion that grows or dies in direct proportion to one's thinking pattern. If a person gripes and mentally criticizes his or her partner in his mind, before long love for the partner will die. If however, that negative mental habit is replaced by thanksgiving for the positive characteristics in the partner's life, love will blossom as surely as night follows day.

"Since we belong to the day, let us be self-controlled, putting on faith and love as a breastplate, and the hope of salvation as a helmet" (1 Thess. 5:8). Love is the result of thinking wholesome thoughts about one's partner. "Finally, brothers, whatever is true, whatever is noble, whatever is right, whatever is pure, whatever is lovely, whatever is admirable—if anything is excellent or praiseworthy—think about such things" (Phil. 4:8). Many times we have seen love return to a marriage when one or both were willing to obey the principle "Give thanks in all circumstances, for this is God's will for you in Christ Jesus" (1 Thess. 5:18).

One day a couple came to my office as a last resort. They told me, "We have an appointment with our attorney on Thursday to get a divorce." It was then Tuesday. "Is there anything you can do to bring love back into our marriage before it is too late? We have three children."

"No, there is nothing I can do," I responded, "but I know Someone who can." They quickly admitted to being Christians, but added that they "hadn't worked at it lately." I explained, "God commands married couples to love one another, and He never demands that we do anything for which He will not provide the strength." They remained dubious.

Sensing their spirit of hopelessness, I offered a quiet word of prayer for instruction and found myself asking, "How would you like to fall madly in love with each other again in three weeks' time?" They brightened at the thought, but doubted it was possible. I began to explain to them that criticism, nit-picking, faultfinding, and griping in our minds is destructive of love (and verbalizing those feelings is even worse). I further stressed that God condemns such thinking, commanding us instead to think with love and thanksgiving about everything. Taking two three-by-five cards from my desk, I turned to the husband and asked him to list ten things about his wife that he liked. The first items took a while, but soon the others flowed out. When the wife's turn came to list his good points, it was easier, for she had been planning her list as he proceeded with his.

When their lists were complete, they agreed to review them every morning and night and thank God for each of these blessings. Within three weeks they called to break their next appointment, saying, "We don't need any more counseling; our love has returned stronger than before."

If your love has become stagnant, your mind is the culprit. Try mental praise; it will change your love life.

2. *Relax! Relax! Relax!* It should come as no surprise that a virgin will be rather tense in anticipation of her first intercourse. Why shouldn't she be? Every new experience produces nervous excitement—it's perfectly normal. But like anything else in life, repetition leads to relaxation. It is vitally important that a wife learn to relax in the act of marriage, for all bodily functions operate better under such conditions.

This need for relaxation may be illustrated in a woman's production of vaginal lubrication. Almost all women have the glands necessary to produce this needed fluid that makes possible the entrance of the penis without pain. But when she is tense or nervous, the glands will not function adequately, and she will experience some friction that may be painful. Actually the very fear of that pain can restrict the normal flow of fluids the next time.

Most counselors recommend using a lubricating vaginal jelly during the first few weeks of marriage, which will eliminate the probability of pain and help attain more relaxation. The less tension in the wife, the easier her reproductive organs cooperate with her in the accomplishment of an orgasm.

A wife's relaxation is important to her loving husband, because if he senses that she is tense or afraid, he may interpret that to signify her fear of him. Her relaxation inspires his own.

3. *Chuck your inhibitions.* Although modesty is an admirable virtue in a woman, it is out of place in the bedroom with her husband. The Bible teaches that Adam and Even in their unfallen state were "naked, and they felt no shame" (Gen. 2:25). Frankly speaking, that means that even in their nakedness they were uninhibited. It may take time for a chaste woman to shake off the inhibitions of her premarriage days and learn to be open with her husband—but it is absolutely essential.

An attractive couple requested guidance to overcome what they called "sexual frustration." The wife of twelve years was too embarrassed to let her husband watch her disrobe at night. "My mother taught me that good women never do that kind of thing," she explained.

I responded, "Just because your mother made the lifetime mistake of failing to make her husband and your father an exception to her modest standards, there is no reason for you to perpetuate that error." I suggested that she let her husband help her undress, and I encouraged her to relax and enjoy it. It took a while, for she even felt guilty when she found it exciting; but gradually she overcame her acute reticence.

4. *Remember that men are stimulated by sight.* Our Lord said, "Anyone who looks at a woman lustfully has already committed adultery with her in his heart" (Matt. 5:28). Has it ever occurred to you that He made no such directive concerning a woman lusting after a man? The reason is clear. Men are quickly stimulated visually, and the most beautiful object in a man's world is a woman.

Many women counselors urge wives to make the daily homecoming of their husbands the most significant time of the day. By bathing, fixing their hair, and putting on fresh attire, they are prepared to give their husbands an enthusiastic welcome home each night. A contented husband is one who is assured that the loveliest sight of the day greets him when he opens the door at night.

Some women resent making their husband's homecoming the object of such attention. Others greet Prince Charming in their work clothes and curlers in an attempt to impress him with the grievous nature of their daily chores with "his kids." The sight of a bedraggled wife may engender sympathy (though it's doubtful), but it will rarely inspire love. A woman has more assets than she thinks, so she might as well take advantage of them. "Clean up, paint up, fix up" is a good motto for every loving wife to remember just before the time of hubby's arrival. We have observed that the women who go that extra mile seem to avoid the problem of "How can I get my husband to be content to come home at night and spend the evening with the family?" If he is provided with a good reason to come home, he usually will.

5. *Never nag, criticize, or ridicule.* Since we have already noted that most young men are insecure and desperately need the loving approval of their wives, we will not belabor the point here. Nevertheless, it is

important to remember that nothing turns a man off faster than motherly nagging and criticism or ridicule of his manhood. No matter how upset a wife may become, she should never stoop to such conduct, or she may jeopardize a beautiful relationship.

A brilliant doctor with a beautiful, cultured wife had an affair with a woman who had almost no education and was not nearly so attractive as his wife. In fact, he admitted that she was not as sexually enjoyable as his wife. When asked to explain his behavior, he replied, "She makes me feel comfortable." Upon reflection, his wife realized that she had gradually become very critical of his actions and nagged him about the long hours he spent at the office. Not being gifted with ready speech, he had responded by staying away in pursuit of a haven of peace. The other woman was the way he found the peace and quiet he had longed for.

6. *Remember that you are a responder.* God has placed within the feminine heart the amazing ability to respond to her husband. Most women admit to having exciting experiences they would never otherwise have attempted except in response to something initiated by their husbands. This is particularly true of their love lives.

Except for those occasions when a wife is particularly amorous and initiates lovemaking, the husband makes the first approach most of the time. Since men are quickly stimulated visually, on many occasions a husband will approach his wife with amorous intentions when lovemaking is farthest from her mind. The nature of her response often determines the outcome. If she reacts with a sign of indifference (perhaps a groan or yawn), it will probably end right there. On the other hand, if she cuddles close to him for a few minutes and accepts his advances, however passively at first, she will gradually find her mood beginning to match his as her own motor of amorousness ignites.

Many a wife has cheated herself and her husband out of countless lovemaking experiences because she did not understand the unique responding ability of a woman.

7. *Observe daily feminine hygiene.* When Beverly was in high school, her girls' physical education instructor told the class that men have a stronger sense of smell than women. That made such an impression on her as a teenager that she has always been exceedingly careful in this matter.

Whether that coach was right I do not know, but every woman must be careful of body odors for two reasons: first, in some women the vaginal fluids, especially those that have dried on the outside, can emit a strong odor unless removed by regular bathing; and second, she may become immune to her own body smells. In this day of various special soaps, lotions, and deodorants, body odors should never be a problem.

8. *Communicate freely.* One of a woman's biggest sexual misconceptions is that her husband knows all about sex. That is rarely, if ever, true. Men may be interested in the subject from the day after they graduate from kindergarten, but they may also be too embarrassed to go to the right sources for the proper information. To complicate the problem, men can be notorious liars whenever they discuss the subject of sex.

As an eighteen-year-old in the air force, I listened with fascination to the "big boys" tell of their sexual exploits. When those old stories come back to mind now, I have to smile. Most of them were either lies or exaggerations, for many of them were impossible.

Unless a man has read the right books or sought knowledge in the right places, much of what he thinks about women is likely wrong when he enters marriage. The wife should not feel discouraged about this; she should look on it as an exciting opportunity to inform him about the one woman in the world whom he should know intimately. She must learn to communicate freely. Besides telling him how she feels, she should guide his hand to show him what gives her pleasure. Unless she tells him what excites her, he may never know. A wife will probably have to teach only one man in her lifetime about her intimate self. She should do it thoroughly and make it an exciting experience, rewarding to both her and her husband.

9. *When all else fails, pray.* That may sound strange for a minister to say, but if you understand my meaning, I think you'll consider it a valid suggestion. I am convinced that God never intended any Christian couple to spend a lifetime in the sexual wilderness of orgasmic malfunction. He has placed within every woman the sexual capabilities He meant for her to enjoy. His only real prohibition relates to their use outside of marriage. When kept within the confines of that sacred institution, these capabilities should provide pleasure for both partners. If it isn't a pleasurable experience, He has something better in store for you, so pray about it and expect Him to direct you to an adequate solution. "Until now you have not asked for anything in my name. Ask and you will receive, and your joy will be complete" (John 16:24).

Notes

1. Letha Scanzoni, *Sex and the Single Eye* (Grand Rapids: Zondervan, 1968), 31.

N i n e

The Unfulfilled
Woman

Karen, a lovely twenty-nine-year-old mother of three, came for counseling. She was obviously distressed: "Pastor, I really love my husband, but lately I have noticed that my resentment toward him is growing something fierce. If something doesn't happen pretty soon, I'm going to end up hating him!" Although it was hard for her to express it, she finally admitted that the problem concerned their love life. "He is the only one who gets satisfaction out of it! I have always considered myself an affectionate woman and have rarely refused to make love to him; but just about the time I really get excited, he comes inside me and it's all over. He flops over on his side of the bed and falls sound asleep—and that's when I get mad! It takes me over an hour to unwind enough to go to sleep. He says I must be frigid."

Karen was anything but "frigid." Like many other unfulfilled wives, she knew very little about sex, and

148

much of her information was wrong. Unfortunately her husband, Jeff, knew less than she did. Without the benefit of premarital counseling, and limiting their sex education to birth control, these two Christian young people had entered marriage with the naive idea that their love was so powerful that "everything will just work out naturally." That may be true of pregnancy, but it certainly isn't true of female orgasm. With a little guidance and encouragement, she was functioning like a new woman within two months.

During my years as a pastor, I have conducted premarital counseling sessions with every couple before the marriage ceremony. After performing nearly 450 weddings preceded by such counseling sessions, I am convinced that even in this sexually enlightened era, many young people get married with much the same sexual ignorance Karen and Jeff had. As I engage each prospective couple in a one-hour discussion on lovemaking, I am astounded to note how few have heard the most basic principles relative to husband-and-wife relationships. Many women get married with the assurance that the prospective husband knows all these principles, but rarely is that true. As we have already seen, most young men are steeped in sexual information, but much of it is wrong. In fact, their ignorance contributes largely to the frustration of their wives and is a cause of much marital disharmony. But if ignorance creates the major problem, it can be dissolved by proper information as long as both partners are willing to face the problem.

The strangest paradox in the realm of sexuality is the widespread idea that a woman's orgasmic capability is less than a man's, whereas in reality it may be even greater. Equally difficult to understand is why such a pleasurable and exciting experience has been hidden from so many women while their male counterparts almost universally have tasted the delight of ejaculation. No research or tradition suggests that the male orgasmic capability has ever been questioned in any culture. Yet the tragic tale of female sexual frustration winds its way through almost every tribe and people, leaving literally billions of married women sexually unfulfilled. Fortunately there is no longer any reason to perpetrate this hoax on potentially one-half the world's population.

Many fanciful ideas attempt to explain why this dilemma has arisen, when it is entirely unnecessary. It is true that a woman's orgasm is not essential for propagation, whereas a man's ejaculation is required to perpetuate the race, but both need the psychological satisfaction that orgasm gives to marital relations. Many have blamed religion; others criticize culture. Actually no one really knows why such a one-sided fraud should be so universally accepted for centuries. Even Masters and Johnson have admitted, "Neither totem, taboo, nor religious assignment seems to account completely for the force with which female orgasmic experience often is negated as a naturally occurring psychophysiologic response."[1]

Thanks to the dissemination of scientific information based on detailed sexual research, most women are no longer willing to settle for a second-rate response when they can proceed to an ecstatic experience. We are forced to admit that some of the research methods would shock the modesty of many people, and Christians in particular would look askance at the moral decadence of hiring prostitutes or using electric manipulators equipped with electronic recording devices; but regardless of the methods, facts are facts. We accept the law of gravity not because it was discovered by a Christian, but because it is true. Today we know more about female sexual capability, function, and response than ever before. Some will use this data to flout God's principles for observing the sacredness of the marriage act—at their own peril, of course—but a wise Christian couple will utilize these facts to understand better their own bodies' function and consequently enrich their mutual enjoyment.

This chapter deals frankly with several intimate aspects of female sexuality that some may consider controversial. It is our hope that this information will prove helpful to those who either are sexually frustrated or regularly settle for a second-rate experience. If you are offended by intimate honesty, you may wish to skip these pages. However, putting one's head in the sand has never helped anyone—not even the ostrich.

The Great Sex Swindle

Until around the turn of the century, millions of women each year were cheated out of the exciting sexual climax that most men enjoy regularly. If they weren't cheated entirely, they settled for far less than they were created to enjoy. Rather than "revolt against the male establishment," they suffered in silence. Each decade since then has produced research that increases our knowledge of this very intimate subject. When properly used, these facts contribute to the liberation of millions of married women. Unfortunately it has been a slow process.

Ronald M. Deutsch, in his excellent book *The Key to Feminine Response in Marriage*, cites several researchers in the field of female sexual satisfaction. Of the Kinsey report he writes,

By drawing some general averages, it appears that by the end of the first year of marriage, perhaps a little more than a third of women have rather dependable orgasm. By the tenth year of marriage, this percentage increases to no more than perhaps 40 percent.

In more recent studies, Dr. Paul Wallin and Dr. Alexander Clark concluded that probably no more than 15 percent of American women depend upon a fully satisfying sex life. And they find that a large minority of women still never have orgasm.

Apparently, most American women suffer from some degree of sexual failure. In 1950, Kroger and Freed estimated, in the *American Journal of Obstetrics and Gynecology:* "Gynecologists and psychiatrists especially are aware that perhaps 75 percent of all women derive little or no pleasure from the sexual act. . . ."

Wallin and Clark . . . gave questionnaires to four hundred and seventeen women, most of whom had been married between seventeen and nineteen years. Nearly all had children and seemingly normal lives. Wallin and Clark wanted to know if these women, though they might not have dependable orgasm, nevertheless experienced other normal responses to lovemaking.

Of those women who said they *never* had orgasm, or did so only rarely, fully *half* reported enjoying sex relations either "much" or "very much."

Of the women who said they had "some" orgasms, fully two-thirds reported "much" or "very much" enjoyment.[2]

Years of counseling predominantly Christian couples have convinced me that Christian men and women experience a higher degree of orgasmic enjoyment than non-Christians. This was confirmed by Dr. Herbert J. Miles, a counselor for over twenty years who made a detailed survey of 151 Christian couples. It being a highly controlled study, since the subjects (1) were young married couples, (2) had spent one to four years in a Christian college, and (3) had been given thorough premarital counseling by Dr. Miles, the report that 96.1 percent of the wives experienced a "definite orgasm"[3] does show a remarkable improvement over the secular norm.

Our own survey, taken by more than seventeen hundred couples who had attended our Family Life Seminars and registered a willingness to take the test, produced results almost as favorable. It should be kept in mind, however, that our survey was of a much wider age spread, covered various stages of Christian maturity, and concerned people who had undergone little or no premarital counseling. Even so, 89 percent of the women registered orgasmic experiences.

It is safe to say that, except for Christians, the majority of women do not regularly enjoy orgasm in the act of marriage. In fact, many don't even know what it is.

Consequently, every woman can expect to experience the ecstasy of that event, not just once or occasionally but almost all of the time. The first orgasm is the most significant, for it prepares a woman for success. Once it is achieved, she anticipates another and eventually her mental attitude is changed from negative to positive, which is half the battle.

What Is an Orgasm?

Most of the current sex manuals have been written by men. Consequently they are less than accurate when it comes to describing the female orgasm. Dr. Marie Robinson is a psychiatrist, medical doctor, and married woman whose counseling practice is predominantly with women. She has described the female orgasm as follows:

> Orgasm is the physiological response which brings sexual intercourse to its natural and beautiful termination.... In the moment just preceding orgasm, muscular tension suddenly rises to the point where, if the sexual instinct were not in operation, it would become physically unendurable. The pelvic motions of the man and the movement of the penis back and forth within the vagina increase in speed and in intensity of thrust. The woman's pelvic movements also increase, and her whole body attempts with every move to heighten the exquisite sensations she is experiencing within her vagina. According to many women with whom I have discussed this experience, the greatest pleasure is caused by the sensation of fullness within the vagina and the pressure and friction upon its posterior surface.
>
> At the moment of greatest muscular tension all sensations seem to take one further rise upward. The woman tenses beyond the point where, it seems, it would be possible to maintain such tension for a moment longer. And indeed it is not possible, and now her whole body suddenly plunges into a series of muscular spasms. These spasms take place within the vagina itself, shaking the body with waves of pleasure. They are felt simultaneously throughout the body: in the torso, face, arms, and legs—down to the very soles of the feet.
>
> These spasms, which shake the entire body and converge upon the vagina, represent and define true orgasm. At this moment the

woman's head is thrown back and her pelvis tips upward in an attempt to obtain as much penetration from the penis as is possible. The spasms continue for several seconds in most women, though the time varies with every individual, and in some women they may continue though with decreasing intensity, for a minute or even more.

Many women can repeat this performance two or three times before their partner has his orgasm. The pathway, neurologically and psychologically, has been set for orgasm and, if her partner continues she can respond. I have had women report that the last orgasm is sometimes more intense and satisfying than the first.

If a woman is satisfied by her orgasmic experience she will discharge the neurological and muscular tension developed in the sexual buildup. When satisfaction has been achieved, her strenuous movements cease and within a short period blood pressure, pulse, glandular secretion, muscular tension, and all the other gross physical changes which characterize sexual excitement return to normal, or even to subnormal, limits.

There have been detailed studies made of the physical reactions of both men and women during intercourse. I think it is important to realize that in almost every detail, including orgasm, these reactions and the subjective experience of pleasure parallel each other in the sexes. The major differences are that the woman is slightly slower to respond at the outset than the man, and the orgasm of the man is characterized by the ejaculation of sperm into the vagina.

Full sexual satisfaction is followed by a state of utter calm. The body feels absolutely quiescent. Psychologically the person feels completely satisfied, at peace with the world and all things in it. The woman in particular feels extremely loving toward the partner who has given her so much joy, such a transport of ecstasy. Often she wishes to hold him close for a while, to linger tenderly in the now subdued glow of their passion.

As you can see from this description, orgasm is a tremendous experience. There is no physiological or psychological experience that parallels its sweeping intensity or its excruciating pleasure. It is unique.[4]

Note Dr. Robinson's expression "excruciating pleasure"—an apt description to say the least. And coming from a married woman doctor, we have every right to believe she knows what she is talking about. We already pointed out in previous chapters that the most exciting experience for both a man and a woman is simultaneous or nearly simultaneous orgasms, for which they need each other. When properly consummated, we could say simultaneous orgasms provide a loving couple excruciating pleasure. We are so convinced that such is possible for all couples that we encourage them to lovingly work toward that ideal. Open communication of how they really feel is very important, particularly what they do find most pleasurable and what is a turnoff.

Lack of Desire for Sex Versus Orgasmic Impairment

Many women have erroneously come to Diane's conclusion that she was "frigid"—that is, she lacked the desire for sex. However, that just was not true. Diane had never learned the art of orgasmic expression. She and her husband probably had been married fifteen years when she told me, "Although I enjoy loving, I really don't get much out of it except for the closeness I enjoy with my husband."

Much current literature unfortunately brands any woman who has difficulty reaching orgasm as being averse to sex, but that is a fraud. Dr. Robinson has provided a good definition of what was popularly known as frigidity.

> Sexual frigidity is the inability to enjoy physical love to the limits of its potentiality. The frigid woman is, to a greater or lesser degree, blocked in her sensual capacities. Generally she cannot experience orgasm. If she has one at all, it is weak and unsatisfying. Many frigid women, however, not only do not have any orgasm, but may also lack the capacity to feel even the beginnings of sexual excitement. To some the sexual act is painful.[5]

We may thus briefly define frigidity as a lack of desire to initiate or enjoy the sex act.

Dr. David Reuben, author of three best-selling books on sexuality, is reluctant to label it *frigidity*, so he has conceived the term *orgasmic impairment*.

> Many of the women who have been solemnly diagnosed as frigid are simply understimulated sexually. Under the old rules, once a man delivered an erect penis into the vagina, the responsibility for reaching her orgasm shifted to the woman. It just isn't that way. No woman deserves to be labeled sexually frigid unless her sexual partner provides her with at least enough mechanical stimulation to trigger the orgasmic reflex.
>
> For the average couple, [the needed stimulation] is about eight minutes of actual intercourse or seventy-five to eighty pelvic thrusts.

This assumes, of course, a reasonable amount of foreplay—enough to start vaginal lubrication—and an emotional atmosphere of mutual affection. Under these circumstances the average woman should be able to reach orgasm a good part of the time.

What if she can't? Then she may be suffering from some degree of orgasmic impairment (a more descriptive term than *frigidity*) based on an underlying emotional conflict. But if her partner furnishes her with a rapid entry, a few halfhearted thrusts, a quick spurt of sperm, and a mumbled apology, it is more likely his problem than hers. Tragically, the man who cannot delay his orgasm and thus prolong his erection long enough to satisfy his partner expends a tremendous amount of time and energy trying to convince her that *she* is to blame. Even if she is convinced, that doesn't really solve his dilemma—he still has the problem of premature ejaculation. It would seem much more sensible for him to undertake the cure of his own disease rather than invent a new one—delayed female orgasm—to prove he's normal.[6]

Reuben concludes, "To the millions of women in America who don't have regular orgasms, orgasmic impairment is a personal disaster."[7]

There was a day when a "frigid" woman was doomed to spend the rest of her life in the despair of sexual frustration or, what is worse, in emotional self-defense. She became cold and indifferent to expressions of affection from her husband, for whether she admitted it or not, being a sexually unfulfilled wife was emotionally traumatic. Thankfully, that day is over. Modern research has made it abundantly clear that all married women are capable of orgasmic ecstasy. No Christian woman should settle for less.

Clitoral Versus Vaginal Orgasms

One of the most confusing aspects of our research in this field concerns the varied opinions among medical doctors as to whether a woman experiences an orgasm by clitoral stimulation only or through vaginal stimulation. Very strong feelings have been expressed by those who believe that a woman can have orgasm only by manipulation of the clitoris. Some researchers have discovered that the tissue of the walls of the vagina contains very few nerve endings and thus is not capable of great feeling; hence they conclude that the clitoris is the only source of female sex stimulation.

Ronald Deutsch describes the vagina this way:

> The walls of the vagina are covered with a delicate mucous membrane. They have many folds or *rugae*. The walls are supported by muscle fibers, which surround the passage and run its length. And it is in these vaginal walls that researchers have hunted in vain for one perplexing factor—physiologists could find virtually no nerve endings in the vagina. This organ, though the woman's sexual center, appeared to be almost incapable of perceiving sensation.
>
> As recently as 1962, Baruck and Miller described in *Sex and Marriage: New Understandings* the general scientific view that the walls of the vagina were "not endowed with sensitive nerve touchspots.... The vagina is made of the same kind of tissue the intestines are made of." They concluded that the vagina could not be the pathway to orgasm.[8]

Deutsch describes the clitoris as the female parallel of the male penis.

> The clitoris has been a source of confusion in understanding how women function sexually. The most keenly sexual part of a woman's body, it was long taken as the seat of all sexual satisfaction. And because stimulation of the clitoris alone will produce an orgasm in nearly all women, it has been assumed that, whatever else happened in the act, it was direct clitoral stimulation alone which produced the climax.
>
> Most doctors thought the reason why a few women were regularly satisfied in love was a fortunate placement of the clitoris, so that it came in contact with the penis during intercourse. Size, too, was thought significant, for much the same reason. The result was that doctors actually performed surgery to expose the clitoris more, or to bring it closer to the vagina. Much of this confusion is not resolved.[9]

Dr. Miles's studies are in agreement.

> Since the clitoris is the arousal trigger of the wife, and since the penis does not contact the clitoris in normal intercourse, marriage counselors recommend what is called "direct" stimulation. That is, the husband, in the process of love-play before intercourse starts, will gently stimulate his wife's clitoris with his fingers for ten or fifteen minutes, or whatever time it takes, until he is certain she is fully aroused sexually and ready for intercourse. There is nothing wrong in this procedure. Remember the piano-violin duet. A couple must do the right thing at the right time in the right attitude for full arousal and complete love harmony. It is normal in the

love-play and arousal period for a couple to touch and handle each other's sexual organs. This is a pleasant and meaningful part of love expression. It was planned this way by the Creator.

... The important point to remember here is that the *clitoris is the external arousal trigger*; that there must be uninterrupted stimulation of the clitoris and the area close to the clitoris for a wife to have an orgasm. The *method* of stimulation of the clitoris is not so important. Any one of several different methods may be satisfactory. The fact that the clitoris *has to be stimulated* is the *important thing* to remember. If a couple can give the wife sufficient stimulation simply through the process of intercourse alone to experience orgasms regularly, fine, wonderful! We have simply said that direct stimulation in the arousal period is one of the surest ways for a young bride to reach an orgasm in the early part of marriage. Our research shows that 40 percent of wives, after they have gotten used to sex life in marriage, are able to become aroused and experience orgasm through intercourse only, and no manual stimulation of the clitoris is necessary. It took several weeks for most of these couples to learn how to succeed in this manner. All couples would do well to work toward this goal. However, we need to be reminded that 60 percent of all women need direct stimulation of the clitoris in the arousal process before they can reach orgasms in intercourse. Couples should not hesitate to use this method when there is need for it.[10]

Dr. Marie Robinson, in her book *The Power of Sexual Surrender*, is scathing in her indictment of women who experience only clitoral orgasm. She equates clitoral orgasm with sexual infancy, vaginal orgasm with sexual maturity. Many normal women doubtless have been unnecessarily frustrated by thinking they were missing something by having only a clitoral orgasm. Frankly, I have found many women who would be delighted if they could accomplish even that.

Dr. Robinson states her case thus:

> I have already described the so-called clitoridal woman to you, but now I must tell you more about the implications of her problem. You will remember that in the female genitalia both the clitoris and the vagina are capable of experiencing orgasm. This fact is of decisive importance to the problem of frigidity in women.
>
> Why? It means, in effect, *that women have two distinct sexual organs, both capable of bringing her release from sexual tension.* In the unconscious sense many women can "choose" one type of sexual satisfaction in preference to another. This ability to choose often spells disaster, for one of these methods of gratification represents immaturity and is allied to neurosis.[11]

Fortunately for womanhood, modern research has disproved this notion. Masters and Johnson have uncovered more data in this field than anyone to date.

You might wonder about the origin of all the misunderstanding concerning such basic and essential truth. Although we cannot give him all the blame, Sigmund Freud is more responsible than any other person. Dr. David Reuben in his inimitable way has explained the situation admirably:

> For the most part women have come to rely on men for information on how their bodies work; the results have been good and bad.

Sigmund Freud was one of the major (though certainly not the first) researchers who pointed out that the brain was inseparably linked to the genitalia. That helped bring a lot of sexual problems into clearer focus. *Regrettably, Dr. Freud was not aware that the clitoris was inseparably linked to the vagina.* He can be considered the father of modern psychiatry for his first discovery; he must be considered the father of the next myth of female sexuality for his related omission. He forced at least two generations of women to pay the penalty for believing: *There is a difference between vaginal and clitoral orgasm and vaginal orgasm is somehow superior* [emphasis ours].

Didn't Freud know any better? As a scientist he *should* have known better. His early studies in psychoanalysis led him to the awareness that little girls masturbated. Academically this was a dramatic discovery but realistically it was something that other little girls and mothers of little girls had known for centuries. He also observed that most female masturbation in this age group (and though he didn't realize it, in *every* age group) centered around the clitoris. As the girls matured and grew into young women they began to replace masturbation with sexual intercourse and showed *apparently* less interest in the clitoris and more interest in the vagina. Freud then leaped to the conclusion that there were two types of orgasm. The clitoral variety was childish and only suitable for the Viennese equivalent of teeny-boppers. Any mature woman immediately relinquished all clitoral sensation and felt everything she was going to feel exclusively in the vagina. It was a magnificent theory, at once profound and dazzling. There was only one problem—it was completely wrong.

If it was wrong, why didn't someone set the record straight? Unfortunately the only people who knew for sure that Freud was in left field were women—and no one listened to them. Psychiatry in those days was exclusively a man's domain (and things haven't changed that much since then) and all important decisions relating to how women were supposed to feel were made by men. But there was another more compelling reason for the myth of vaginal-clitoral orgasm—it was flattering to men. Many psychiatrists lost their objectivity when they put on their pajamas and every theory that made them more comfortable in bed was greeted with eager delight. The traffic from New York to Vienna took on rush hour proportions and every American analyst who could afford passage made the pilgrimage. They returned with the new and exciting revelation that American women were copulating all wrong and if things didn't work out, it wasn't the man's fault. According to the psychoanalytic smoke signals at the time, all a man had to do was get an erection and ejaculate—if a woman wasn't satisfied it was her own fault.[12]

Dr. Reuben—a practicing psychiatrist whose medical qualifications are superb but whose moral principles and judgments are usually shocking to Christians—goes on to describe a patient named Nina who regularly experienced orgasm but became "frigid" after reading a magazine article suggesting that a woman who didn't experience a vaginal orgasm was "missing it all." The more Nina tried, the more frustrated she became, and eventually she even lost her capability for clitoral orgasm.

After three years of treatment with two different psychiatrists without relief, Nina came to Dr. Reuben. He explains how he advised her:

Instead of telling Nina why she shouldn't have orgasms, it made more sense to tell her how to go about having them again. And the first step was to explain the mechanics of orgasm in the female. It goes something like this:

The clitoris is directly connected to the spinal cord and brain by the same plexus of thousands of nerve fibers that supplies the vagina. Stimulation of either organ immediately affects the other. In addition, the extremely sensitive roots of the clitoris extend deep into the walls of the vagina itself. As the penis rubs against the vaginal wall it applies exactly the same pressure to the internal part of the clitoris and to the vaginal lining. The third factor is probably the most important. The labia minora, those two thin curtain-like membranes that extend over the vaginal opening, are attached above to the body of the clitoris. Even though the shaft of the penis may never actually come into contact with the top of the clitoris, as the penis slides in and out of the vagina it successively pulls and releases the lower ends of the labia. This causes constant and rhythmic friction against the head and shaft of the clitoris and if everything else is right, orgasm is rapid and inevitable. *Every orgasm that occurs in a woman is basically clitoral.* Orgasms occurring by sexual intercourse may be clitoral *and* vaginal— which only means that the penis is stimulating the vagina and clitoris simultaneously. But for Nina—and every other woman—that part was academic. The only real question was whether or not she was able to enjoy sexual intercourse.

The answer wasn't long in coming. Once she clearly understood that all orgasms were identical and were basically dependent on stimulation of the clitoris, things began to improve.[13]

Naturally some women will ask, "But isn't a vaginal orgasm better in some ways than just a clitoral orgasm?" To that question Dr. Reuben responds,

> Nope. From a sexual point of view, there is an Orgasmic Bill of Rights—all orgasms are created equal. Every orgasm, whether produced by intercourse or foreplay ... depends on the same sensory triple play—clitoris to spinal cord to brain, instantaneously followed by a reverse explosion—brain to spinal cord to clitoris. Every other part of the body—vagina, heart, lungs, skin—also participates, but the center of attention, as always, is the clitoris.[14]

Much of this controversy was caused by the fact that many women can experience orgasm when their husband tenderly manipulates their clitoris, but they cannot come to a climax in intercourse. This usually leaves both husband and wife with a sense of frustrating inadequacy. Freud and his followers have tried to blame everything on some "deep-rooted emotional problem." This usually required a battery of psychological tests and a long series of counseling encounters, all of which are enormously expensive and not always productive. Dr. Reuben has pointed out that until recent years most psychiatrists have been men; consequently most women have been tricked into believing that some psychosis or neurosis was the primary cause of the problem, when in reality it probably wasn't that at all.

Ronald M. Deutsch explains the paradox:

> Recent research has asked some important questions about this long-accepted concept. Is this the only way in which women fail sexually? If not, what proportion of women who fail are emotionally normal? And what are the other causes of the failure?
>
> It has now been widely reported that many women who are quite normal psychologically nevertheless fail to reach full sexual completion. A typical report is made by Dr. Peter A. Martin, clinical professor of psychiatry at Wayne State University in Detroit: "When I started in psychiatry, I was taught that orgasm in the female is related to the psychosexual level of development. Thus, a mature, emotionally healthy woman who had achieved a genital level of development should have a vaginal orgasm ... [but] I have seen the emotionally sickest of female patients report ... several consecutive orgasms. Also, I have seen women who were the epitome of emotional maturity in all other areas incapable of vaginal orgasm."
>
> Reading back into the psychiatric literature, one finds that long ago some of the chief exponents of psychoanalysis had second thoughts as they treated unresponding women. One was the famed Dr. Wilhelm Stekel, an associate of Freud and Adler, who wrote volumes on sexual problems. By 1926 Stekel felt "frigidity" has to be viewed in three different forms. The first was "the absolutely frigid woman," who experienced no orgasm and felt no response to any level of physical affection. The second was "the relatively

frigid woman," who felt a little more in both ways. And third was "the passionate-frigid woman, who in spite of great longing and keen forepleasure is unable to achieve orgasm." Of this last type, Stekel wrote, "This is the form most often seen by us as specialists."

For "the passionate-frigid woman," clearly a better concept was needed. She wanted the physical relationship. She was moved by it. Only at the last was she thwarted. Was she also a neurotic?...

One factor which certainly led to some early questions about an unqualified view of "frigidity" as a neurotic symptom was the overwhelming number of women who seemed to suffer from it. This was one reason why Stekel, for example, began to look for sociologic and physical causes. He wrote long and ardently about social injustices to women which made them resent the feminine role and the masculine assumption of authority. And he began to study the work of Rohleder, a sexologist of the time, who advocated, among other things, premarital examinations of men and women to assess their physical compatibility....

Perhaps the first important study of how commonly women reach orgasm was made at the turn of the century, by the noted gynecologist Dr. Robert L. Dickinson. Dr. Dickinson asked four hundred and forty-two of his patients if they experienced orgasm. One woman in four answered, "Never." Only two of each hundred answered, "Usually."

Between these two extremes, the answers were suggestive, but rather vague. Forty percent said they had the experience "rarely." And another 40 percent answered, "Yes," without stating the frequency. Of this last group, however, Dr. Dickinson believed that about one-third were not really achieving true orgasm in intercourse.

Three studies were made in Europe during the next few years. Otto Adler found that 30 to 40 percent of women had no orgasm and probably felt little sexual response or desire during actual sexual union. Guttceit said that 40 percent of women "felt nothing" during intercourse, "participating in the act without any pleasurable sensation during the friction of the sexual parts and without the suspicion of a climax on their part." And Debrunner reported, "Over 50 percent of our women in eastern Switzerland know nothing of the sexual libido," without specifying precisely what he meant.

Still later, in the United States, Dr. Carney Landis studied forty-four women. He found that only seventeen of them reported "satisfaction," though he did not specify what kind or how frequently.

Though these studies took place at different times, and in only a general way measured the same things, one may draw from them some rough conclusions about sexual response in the first few decades of the century. First, only a rather small minority of women appear to have reached orgasm dependably. Secondly, a much larger minority, a group ranging from one-fourth up to one-half of the women sampled, never reached orgasm at all.[15]

On the basis of these and many other statistics, it is safe to assume that the majority of married women do not experience orgasm regularly. *If*, as many psychiatrists try to suggest, such women are "neurotic," "psychotic," "sexually infantile," or in some way "abnormal," it would mean that most women are abnormal! Frankly, that is just too big a psychological pill to swallow. It would be better to look for other causes.

The Causes and Cure of Orgasmic Incapability

At best an orgasm is a complicated maneuver that culminates many activities. Consequently a malfunction of any one or a combination of several of these functions could keep a woman from experiencing all that God intended for her. For that reason we will examine the most common contributing causes of orgasmic incapability and offer some workable remedies.

1. *Ignorance*. The average woman knows far more about the operation of her sewing machine than she does her own reproductive organs. That's not hard to understand when we realize that her sewing machine came equipped with an operation manual; if she gets into trouble, she merely has to call the serviceman to rectify the malfunction.

Unfortunately most women and their equally uninformed husbands have never read a good sex manual, and when they run into trouble, they are often too proud to go for help. Even when they do seek counsel, the materials they read or the counselor they find is woefully inadequate. One writer asks,

> Where do women learn about their own sexuality? From those who are least able to teach them. Ninety-nine percent of "experts" in the sexual problems of women never had a menstrual period, a hot flash, or a baby—and never will. In fact they will never have any female sexual experiences at all—because they are men.

What makes these men qualified to explain female sexual responses to women? Nothing. Scholarly books on women and their sexual behavior began to be written about five hundred years ago, during the Dark Ages. At that time women occupied a social position somewhat higher than cattle and somewhat lower than male lunatics. Just as no self-respecting scientist would think of asking a cow how she felt, no medieval scholar would stoop to interviewing a woman. The next generation of sexologists prepared for their projects by reading the books written by their forerunners. They piously pored over the questionable revelations they encountered there and mumbled something like, "Hmmm, that's just what I suspected. I knew it. I knew it all along." Fortified with the ignorance of the Dark Ages, they sallied forth to further muddy the sexual waters. No one ever took the time to ask the ladies what they were feeling (or not feeling) in the sexual department. They didn't have to—after all, they had the word of a whole generation of experts—all of whom would be more likely to interview a cow than a woman.

Did these experts do any harm? Only to women. Most of the early "facts" about female sexual behavior consisted entirely of male wishful thinking. Little things about women not really being capable of enjoying sex and men being sexually superior to women began to appear in medical textbooks with monotonous regularity. As the same misconceptions and misunderstandings were repeated over and over again, they began to take on the veneer of facts. As one expert repeated some scientific gossip to another, the errors took on an aura of authenticity. Gradually the platitudes found their way into magazines and newspapers and became part of American sexual folklore. By relentless repetition they finally achieved wide acceptance as facts.[16]

Deutsch expands on this theme:

> The fact is that women who are sexually unfulfilled to some degree appear to make up a majority of American womankind. The old idea that she is thus, by definition, psychoneurotic is fading. For it has now been widely demonstrated that the key to relieving such a woman is usually a true understanding of her body and her sexual role.
>
> This is not to say that emotion cannot block sexual response. It can. And I have no intention ... to convey a mechanistic view of love, which I abhor, or to challenge the emotional or spiritual bases of love, in which I believe.
>
> Yet the act of love remains a physical act. As we shall see, most authorities agree that in most respects this act is not instinctive, but is learned. And we shall see that for most men and women, the understanding of the act persists as a melange of myth, confusion and superstition. As a result, in a day of supposedly great sexual sophistication, only the unusual couple achieves anything like the fully satisfying expression possible for almost any good marriage.
>
> Though science has learned much about the physical side of sex in the last two decades, little of this knowledge has been communicated. As sex researcher Dr. William Masters wrote recently in the *Journal of the American Medical Association*, in answer to the question of a doctor who asked help in treating an unresponsive wife:

"With any marital unit, one can anticipate that the couple has a vast amount of mis-
information, misconception, and quite simply,
inadequate knowledge of sexual physiology."

This may seem curious in a time when we
are so open about sex, when the subject is so
frankly overworked and coldly exploited by com-
merce of every kind. Oddly, it seems to be only
the useful and accurate information which is
excluded from the torrent of sexual dialogue.[17]

Until the last few years, the Christian wife has
faced an even greater problem. Because of the humanistic philosophy and lack of moral values reflected in
most of the literature on sex information available
today, most Christians are apt to discard it all. This is
most unfortunate, for I have found that those who tend
to reject it are the ones who need it most. In addition,
"doing what comes naturally" is likewise inadequate.

Within the past few years some Christian publishers have had enough courage to print books dealing
frankly with this subject. Thirty years ago I could not
recommend a single book in the field, and thus I devoted
forty-five pages to physical adjustment in marriage in my
book, *How to Be Happy Though Married*. Later I discovered that the publisher came within an eyelash of not
producing that book for fear it would be offensive to the
Christian public. However, the firm did publish it, and
now the climate has changed to such a degree that no
Christian wife or husband should be ignorant of the intimacies of lovemaking, nor should they limit themselves
to the information they discover only by themselves.
Both should study some of the excellent books by Christians now on the market. Of course, Dr. Ed Wheat's

tapes mentioned in chapter 7 should not be overlooked. These resources will do much to dispel ignorance and will enable both partners to achieve open communication about physical pleasure.

No Longer an Excuse

A few decades ago, sexual ignorance was a reasonably acceptable excuse for orgasmic incapability, but that day is past. Regrettably some husbands are carryovers from the Dark Ages, like the one who told his frustrated wife, "Nice girls aren't supposed to climax." Today's wife knows better, for modern research has proved that women, unlike men, can experience several climaxes in a single lovemaking experience. That is hard for a man to understand, because after ejaculation, he is finished with lovemaking for from one to twenty-four hours (depending on age, tension, and energy). Well-documented tests have proved that a woman, if continually stimulated after orgasm, is capable of four, five, or even more climaxes, and some women report a continued increase in intensity. In fact, some women do not feel sexually fulfilled by experiencing only one orgasm.

If more husbands knew that fact, they would be more inclined to bring their wives to orgasm manually once or twice before entrance (and some wives may desire manual stimulation after his ejaculation). An uninformed man may be afraid that if he tenderly massages his wife to climax before entrance, she will not have anything left for him. In reality, quite the opposite is true! He would find his wife much more sexually exciting and cooperative.

Every couple I marry must promise me that before separating for a single night under duress, they will come to see me for counseling. That is probably one reason for such a low divorce ratio (17 known divorces out of 450 weddings). Among those who have returned for help, the most common cause of difficulty is the lack of orgasmic capability in the wife. One such couple came in six weeks after their wedding. After talking with them for an hour, I lent them about five pounds of books I keep in my study for such occasions. Three weeks later the wife stopped at my office after a church service carrying the books in a brown paper bag. Grinning, she thanked me and said, "We don't need these books anymore!"

Reading this book, it is hoped, will provide for you the necessary information to produce a normal, healthy love life that includes orgasmic ecstasy for both husband and wife.

An All-Time First

2. *Resentment and revenge.* At the conclusion of a seminar, a twenty-six-year-old mother of three children asked, "Would you explain why I am unable to respond to my husband after six years of marriage?" She not only had never reached orgasm, but also quickly acknowledged, "I hate sex!" What amazed me most was the fact that she described her husband as "kind and considerate, even after no sex relations in two years!" That violated my long-standing conviction that a woman will always respond to a man who is kind, considerate, and thoughtful of her. I was curious because she was an all-time-first exception to me.

By my watch, I could see I had less than thirty minutes to catch the last plane out of their little city and return to San Diego for services the next day. So I got right to the point by saying, "Describe the relationship between you and your father." Her lovely features immediately changed as she angrily berated him as a miserable excuse for a human being. "He is the biggest hypocrite I have ever seen. He is an official in this church, yet he has molested both of my younger sisters and has tried to be fresh with me."

Although suspicious by her reaction that she wasn't telling me everything about her father's relation with her, to save time I asked, "Do you *really* want to freely love your husband?"

"Certainly," was her reply.

"Then you had better forgive your father. Get on your knees and confess your sins of resentment and bitterness, for you cannot indulge in bitterness toward one person without it spilling over and spoiling your relationship with those you love."

"But he doesn't deserve that forgiveness," she replied emphatically.

"No, but your husband does!" I tried to assure her. "You are not responsible for your father's behavior, but you are responsible for your reaction to it. God holds you accountable to forgive others their trespasses and sins, and what He commands us to do, He will always enable us to do."

She started to cry, and in a matter of moments she dropped to her knees, confessing her sin.

I got to the airport just in time. As the plane took off, I prayed that God would help this young couple, but soon I forgot about them. One year later at a second Family Life Seminar in the same city, a young couple came to me after the first session. "Do you remember me?" asked the wife. She had to prompt my memory by recounting our discussion of her father at the previous seminar. She then added with a beautiful smile, "God has forgiven me, and this has been the greatest year of our marriage! I want you to meet my husband."

As he shook my hand, I feared that this big, silent-type man would crush it as he exclaimed emotionally, "Thanks, preacher. My wife's a different woman!"

Hostility Devastates

Revenge, bitterness, resentment, and other forms of hostility are not only devastating to one's spiritual life, but sexually demotivating. That is true whether the object of one's wrath is many miles from one's bedroom or lying in the same bed.

A minister's wife of twenty-two years came in to explain that she was "having an affair" (the Bible labels it *adultery*) with the choir director. What would cause a mother of three, a virgin when married and never unfaithful before, to violate her Christian principles with a three-times-divorced "Don Juan" who has pursued affairs with two choir members? The same thing that had impaired her orgasmic capability during the past two years—deep-rooted hatred of her husband, who had always been a stern disciplinarian. She complained, "His awful beatings of our children made me ill. Two years ago our nineteen-year-old son left home to join a commune because he couldn't do anything to please his father."

When she finally stopped looking at her husband's sins, she could face her own scarlet sin. Then she repented and asked God to restore her love for her husband, which He did. The husband also repented, and today they enjoy an excellent relationship and love life because God removed the root of bitterness that had built up a wall between them.

The Bible says, "Get rid of all bitterness, rage and anger, brawling and slander, along with every form of malice. Be kind and compassionate to one another, forgiving each other, just as in Christ God forgave you" (Eph. 4:31–32).

Guilt Consciousness

3. *Guilt.* Modern psychology notwithstanding, every human being begins life with an intuitive guilt consciousness. The Bible explains that all people possess a conscience, "now accusing, now even defending them" (Rom. 2:15). Today's free-love advocates try to explain away the conscience or educate it into oblivion during the teens and twenties, but I find that after marriage and the birth of children, the once-dead conscience often comes to life and haunts the individual. Particularly is that true of women. A twinge of guilt over sexual misconduct performed once or many times can later serve as a mental block to sexual enjoyment.

Guilt is a common cause of orgasmic malfunction, as verified by the fact that every book we have read on this subject refers to it. Whether related to an attempted rape for which the unwilling victim feels guilty, or an ill-advised adulterous liaison experienced prior to marriage, or promiscuity before or after marriage, guilt is a cruel taskmaster that must be confronted spiritually. As a pastoral counselor, I have been privileged to lead many women to the forgiving grace of God, either through accepting Christ as their Savior (as explained in chapter 14) or applying the cleansing principle of 1 John 1:9. Getting things straightened out with God has so relieved their guilty consciences that orgasmic malfunction ceases.

One young couple serves as an illustration. Both Brenda and Mitch lacked a strong spiritual background when they first visited our church, and their marriage was on the verge of collapsing. After they received Christ, I counseled them only once about their marital problems. One year later Mitch said rather hesitantly, "Pastor, I never dreamed when I accepted Christ that He would invade our sex life, but we had never been able to make my wife's bells ring until after we were converted. Now she has a climax most of the time."

Those who have never experienced salvation through faith in Jesus Christ will probably find that difficult to accept, but I have seen it happen so many times that now I almost expect it. The reason is simple. When a person's sins are forgiven, his conscience is freed, thus removing a common cause of orgasmic malfunction.

The Greatest Demotivator

4. *Fear.* Fear is the greatest demotivator and emotional crippler of all time. If indulged in long enough, it can destroy one's health, one's spiritual relationship to God, and, of course, one's love life.

Almost every virtuous bride understandably goes to her wedding bed with a good deal of trepidation. Admittedly, she approaches it with excitement and anticipation too, but probably fear, more than anything else, keeps a woman from experiencing an orgasm on her wedding night.

As we have noted, when a bride experiences pain on first entrance, she may continue to associate pain with lovemaking. Consequently, this restricts the natural flow of her vaginal lubricant and makes lovemaking difficult. The more she fears pain, the more she will experience it. For that reason she should keep a good vaginal lubricating jelly near her bed for ready use until she so learns to relax in lovemaking that her natural lubrication takes over. Especially during the first few months of marriage, the frequency of intercourse demands use of a lubricating jelly almost every time in order to prevent bruising at the opening of the vagina.

Remember that anything we do the first time is usually faced with fear. Do you recall your first driving lesson? Your hands clutched the steering wheel until your knuckles turned white and your palms were moist—that's fear. Now, as an experienced driver, you perform the same maneuvers almost subconsciously; you have learned to relax while driving a car. Clearly, you need to learn the same relaxation in lovemaking.

Concentrate on Joy

Even the fear of another orgasmic malfunction can make it more difficult to experience an orgasm. One very fearful wife came to see us because of orgasmic malfunction. In the midst of lovemaking she would convince herself, "I won't make it this time either." From that moment on, her emotional battery would run down instead of up, and she would be left unfulfilled. After several counseling sessions, I suggested a thought pattern that solved her problem. We had established that she loved her husband, and even though she did not experience a climax in the act of marriage, she enjoyed his closeness and tenderness that lovemaking afforded. So we proposed that she concentrate on this and the joy of giving him pleasure, totally forgetting about herself. We also recommended that she become even more aggressive, embracing him more tightly with her arms and legs and increasing the activity of her hips. Less than three weeks later she called very excitedly to report, "It happened!" Now it happens most of the time. Why? She has eliminated her fearful thinking pattern.

An orgasm, particularly for a woman, is an ultimate expression of love, but fear destroys love. The Bible says, "Perfect love drives out fear" (1 John 4:18). When a woman gives herself lovingly and excitedly to her husband, she will be much less likely to let fear cheat her out of the ultimate feeling.

5. *Passivity*. Many women are much too passive in lovemaking. Their maidenly inhibitions and misconceptions compel them to lie on their backs and allow the vigorous young husbands to satisfy themselves. "Ultimately," they persuade themselves, "it will happen." Pregnancy yes, but orgasm no. Lovemaking is a contact sport that requires two active people. The more active a woman is, the more likely she will learn that positions and movements will bring the maximum stimulus to her clitoris and vagina, building her toward climax. Of the women interviewed who acknowledged enjoying orgasms most of the time, I have yet to discover one who is passive.

Men have a higher rate of orgasm largely because they are more active in lovemaking. Naturally they are going to repeat the activity or movements that bring them the greatest amount of excitement. If wives would do the same, they too would experience a higher ratio of fulfillment.

With reference to experiments by Masters and Johnson, Deutsch says,

> Experts conclude that for virtually all women the initial phases of the orgasmic platform are an almost automatic response to effective

emotional and physical stimulation. If the external stimulation, especially of the clitoris and other parts of the vulva, continues, orgasm is the almost universal result. But to continue the buildup of sexual tension after intercourse begins, authorities agree, is an ability which must be *learned*.

Moreover, this heightened tension during intercourse must be actively sought by the woman, not passively awaited. For most women, no amount of skill or technique on the part of the husband will suffice. The woman must not merely surrender to her husband, she must surrender to her own drive, a drive to seek stimulation emotionally and physically, to seek tension until tension becomes release.

Some women are enabled to attain orgasm simply by adopting this attitude. Many authorities believe this is in large part because the woman, in giving herself over to the pursuit of release, becomes more responsive to her own subtle physical sensations and learns to move her body so as to increase the sensations. For most women, however, a fuller understanding of how stimulation occurs in intercourse appears to be the key.[18]

Consequently the wife must maintain an active role in lovemaking, for both her own and her husband's good. No red-blooded husband will ever complain about a passionate, innovative wife who responds with excitement to his lovemaking. In fact, the only part of the act of marriage a man enjoys more than ejaculation is the satisfying feeling he gains from his wife's amorous and affectionate efforts, confirming that she finds him sexually exciting.

6. *Lovemaking takes time.* A strong corollary exists between the time spent making love and the wife's

orgasmic accomplishment. Men who are "quick lovers" usually have unsatisfied wives. Anything worthwhile takes time, and love is no exception.

Back in the Dark Ages, when the misconception prevailed that a woman's only sexual function was to bear children, intercourse took only from thirty seconds to three minutes. Today it is widely recognized that women have a tremendous capacity for sexual feeling and expression, but it is seldom realized quickly.

Speaking to a group of men, the head of the psychology department of a Christian college said, "There is no such thing as a frigid wife—only clumsy husbands." I do not agree completely with his conclusion, but to a degree his point is well taken. Because men are quickly aroused and quickly satisfied, they tend to think that women should be capable of the same—but that is not true. Most researchers indicate that even under the most favorable conditions and when highly motivated, the average wife requires ten to fifteen minutes or more to reach orgasm. Of course there will be exceptions, but as a general rule, fulfilling lovemaking takes time. A wife should encourage her husband to take the necessary time; even if *he* doesn't need it, *she* does.

Premature Ejaculation

In this connection we should consider premature ejaculation. About 20 percent of today's husbands must cope with the problem of ejaculating too soon. This is most frustrating to a wife, because lovemaking is impossible without an erect penis, and after a man ejaculates, his penis gets too soft to maintain the necessary pressure on the vaginal walls and clitoris to see his wife through to her climax.

One disconsolate bride exclaimed, "On our first night of marriage, he got me all worked up and started to enter my vagina, but as soon as his penis touched me, he ejaculated." He was embarrassed, of course, and his bride was frustrated. They tried again about an hour later, and he did somewhat better, but because of his inexperience he again came before she could reach satisfaction. Finally she admitted, "In the nine months of our marriage, we have made love over one hundred times, but I am still not a fulfilled woman."

Part of his problem was fear. The more he feared premature ejaculation, the more likely it was to occur. A couple must recognize this as a major problem that will not disappear naturally. It must be trained away, and it is well worth the time spent in such a training process. Many a frustrated and unsympathetic wife has turned on her "quick" husband in ridicule or indifference, thus heightening his natural feelings of male inadequacy at the expense of a good relationship. An alert wife will understand that her husband is ashamed of this lack of self-control and will work with him in effecting a solution.

In the next chapter we will go into this problem in detail, even offering several methods for overcoming it, but here we would like to mention just one method, advocated by Masters and Johnson. They suggest that the wife and husband get alone for a protracted time for what they call "squeezing exercises." The wife should caress her husband's genitals until his penis reaches an erection. Then, as she moves her hand up and down the shaft and lightly on the glans (head of the penis), he will quickly start toward ejaculation (the husband must keep the wife informed of his progress). By holding the penis with her thumb on the underside and her two fingers on either side of the ridge which separates the head (glans penis) from the shaft, she squeezes her thumb and fingers together with a very tight squeeze for three or four seconds as soon as her husband gives the signal he is about to ejaculate. She then waits fifteen to thirty seconds as his tension subsides before repeating the light, stimulating movements up and down the shaft. When he signals he is about ready to ejaculate, she again repeats the squeezing process for three or four seconds to prevent his ejaculation. This procedure should be repeated for fifteen to twenty minutes or more. If the husband accidentally ejaculates, the couple should wait forty-five minutes to an hour. Then they may start the exercises again.

When they have learned a degree of control, the wife should get astride her prostrate husband and insert his penis into her vagina *without movement* until he gets used to the new sensation. Sometimes it is necessary to remain motionless for up to two minutes. This will provide the husband with greater control. Then the wife should move up and down very gently, arousing the husband toward climax. At his signal that he is close to ejaculation, she should raise her body and repeat the squeeze technique for three to four seconds. When the feeling has subsided, she should put his penis back into her vagina and repeat the procedure. With much patience, a wife can help her husband learn control that will be a source of great satisfaction to them both. For the husband, it will be the satisfaction of mastering an important aspect of inadequacy; for the wife, it will mean that his controlled delay enables her to reach orgasm.

If at the first consideration this exercise should seem offensive to some wives, they should recognize that premature ejaculation is a heartrending problem to both husband and wife, and it will not improve by itself. A loving wife will realize that it is well worth the investment of a week of vacation or two or three weekends alone in a motel. Three to fifteen such experiences usually suffice to teach the husband ejaculatory control. A couple will earn lovemaking dividends from such an investment for many years to come, besides enriching their intimate relationship.

All learning takes time. A husband and wife will find this learning experience enjoyable and profitable for the time spent.

7. *Fatigue.* All normal body functions are weakened when a person is fatigued. A tired wife is not likely to be an amorous, responsive wife, thus lessening the chances of orgasmic fulfillment. For that reason, lovemaking should be reserved for those times when both husband and wife are rested; and for that same reason, lovemaking should be spontaneous.

A wife should greet her husband at the door with a warm kiss that may predict the future. Through tender words and touch, they can keep themselves in an animated lovemaking mood all evening, which becomes an exciting preliminary to lovemaking if they don't retire too late.

Since opposites tend to attract each other, I have noticed that couples are often opposites in their metabolism (the process by which energy is provided for the body). Early birds, whose good hours are from 6 A.M. to 8 P.M., often marry nocturnalists, whose strongest hours extend from 10 A.M. to midnight. Consequently a nocturnalist husband may find his motor running wide open at 10:30 P.M. only to discover that his wife, who was amorous at 7 P.M., is sound asleep or, worse, is half-asleep and incapable of full response.

Two things can help to equalize this metabolic mismatch. One suggestion is for the early-bird husband to nap as soon as he gets home from work so that he can feel vital at bedtime; the early-bird wife can learn to nap around three or three-thirty when the children are small, and earlier when they are in school. Years ago I learned the secret of a twenty-minute nap lying on the floor with my feet up on the bed to let the blood run back into my head. Many people have asked me, "How can you preach five times on Sunday after losing three hours' sleep coming home from a seminar where you have been speaking for eight hours on Friday night and Saturday?" My answer points to the twenty-minute Sunday afternoon nap with my feet elevated, the equivalent for me of two to three hours' sleep at night lying flat in bed.

Spontaneity Rewards

A second way to equalize your metabolic mismatch is to be spontaneous with your lovemaking. What is wrong with enjoying love when you *feel* like it? Sure, dinner may have to be warmed over if the fancy strikes when the husband first comes home, but I've never heard a husband complain about a cold dinner for the sake of lovemaking. What's wrong with the children being assigned to dinner dishes while mom and dad go to their bedroom and lock the door for thirty minutes to make love? Rarely will you discover love at its most exciting by synchronizing watches and meeting in the bedroom by appointment. Ordinarily you will find that the most enjoyable lovemaking experiences are spontaneous. Analyze the activities that interrupt or delay lovemaking, and you will discover they are usually not nearly so important as the act of marriage.

8. *Illness.* Not only fatigue but also illness stifles lovemaking and leads to orgasmic malfunctions. Although medical science is not my field, I have known cases in which physical problems, hormone imbalance, and even low-grade vaginal infections have kept women from climax. For that reason any woman with a problem of this kind should see her family doctor and probably a gynecologist.

9. *Overweight.* An attractive but grossly disproportioned president of a Christian women's club engaged me in conversation at a luncheon where I was to speak on "How to Get Your Husband to Treat You Like a Queen." After ten years of marriage, she still found sex repulsive. What really interested me about this woman was the fact that she had learned orgasmic fulfillment early in their marriage five years before becoming a Christian. She declared, "Now that I'm on fire for the Lord, I've lost my fire in the bedroom." When I told her that being a Spirit-filled Christian doesn't extinguish a person's natural, God-given desire for sex in marriage, but actually increases it, she was startled.

Upon further questioning I discovered that she had not always been overweight but had gained seventy pounds during her last pregnancy and was unable to lose them. Not surprisingly, she had lost interest in sex and found orgasms impossible for the first time in her married life. When I asked, "Does your being overweight bother your husband?" she replied, "No, it doesn't seem to, but it sure bothers me!" That was her problem. With the increase in weight she experienced a decrease in self-image. For the first time she was embarrassed to undress in front of her husband. When I convinced her that her love life would improve and her orgasmic capability would return with the loss of weight (not to mention greater energy, health, and self-acceptance), she decided to follow my advice and make an appointment with a weight specialist. Within nine months I received a letter telling me that she had seen improvement in four months and that her love life was now back to normal. She had lost sixty of those demotivating pounds.

Losing weight is hard work. I know that personally, for I've been working at it all my adult life, but it is well worth the effort spiritually, mentally, physically, and emotionally. Most overweight Christians must realize that their problem is not overweight, but overeating (the Bible calls it gluttony). Many of us seem more concerned over the penalty for this sin (being overweight) than the sin itself (overeating). Such people must come to realize they can never indulge in eating all that the appetite craves. Stop eating so much and trust God to give you a joy in knowing you are obeying Him; allow Him to make you more attractive to yourself and your mate.

One thing I have learned that has been beneficial not only for keeping the weight down but also for producing better health is recognizing that what you eat is as important as how much. By cutting down on fat grams and eating less beef and more fish or chicken, you can avoid going through life hungry all the time. Also, substituting fruit for desserts is a simple but beneficial habit to get into. I recommend to those with a weight problem to get a booklet that lists the fat content of foods and keep track of everything they eat for one month. By that time they will be familiar for life what each food item costs them. For example, I formerly loved a double Big Mac hamburger with cheese until I found it had 56 fat grams—an entire allotment for four days! Four good salads may not seem as tasty at first, but they are certainly more healthful.

Choleric Dominance

10. *Sexual surrender vs. choleric dominance.* The very nature of the act of marriage involves feminine surrender. For most women this comes naturally in the early stages of marriage, because they love their husbands and enjoy giving them pleasure. After they learn the art of orgasmic fulfillment, it is a small price to pay for such an ecstatic experience. But to a strong-willed, choleric woman, surrender in any way is difficult. Consequently she will often subvert her sex drive and responses to avoid surrender. I have found that only when her marriage and family are threatened with collapse will she seek help.

Married to a passive, easy-going husband and the mother of four lovely girls, a choleric woman came into my office with a rather unusual symptom that led to the discovery of a common problem. "I just can't stand to have my husband fondle my breasts," she began. "He likes it very much, and for years I let him, but I can't take it any more. Instead of exciting me, it just turns me cold." Upon further questioning, she revealed that she had never reached an orgasm and really didn't enjoy lovemaking. The more she withdrew from her husband (cholerics are quite transparent and cannot hide their feelings), the more he crawled into his passive shell. Mistaking his quietness for acceptance, she erroneously assumed that everything was all right. Then one day he quietly said, "I'm leaving you next Saturday." To her question why, he responded, "It's obvious you don't love me anymore, and I can't take a sexless marriage." That's what motivated her to visit my office.

Typical of many choleric women, she resented being a woman. She liked to lead, make decisions, and

dominate everything. It was difficult for her to understand why God had made her a woman instead of a man.
Only after facing the sin of self-rejection was she able to
gain God's forgiveness. Then we talked about her need
to accept her femininity. When she finally accepted herself as a woman, she could accept her breasts as a vital
and exciting part of her sexual apparatus, regardless of
whether she thought they were too small or too large.
Gradually she learned to experience orgasmic fulfillment
and saw her husband's love return. As an interesting
sidelight to her recovery, her passive husband became
more aggressive and thus easier for her to respect and
admire. Her sexual self-acceptance made it possible to
find his lovemaking exciting, which in turn transformed
his self-acceptance.

Dr. Marie Robinson explained it well:

> The ability to achieve normal orgasm can
> be called the physical counterpart of psycholog-
> ical surrender. In most cases of true frigidity it
> follows on a woman's surrender of her rebellious
> and infantile attitudes as the day the night. It is
> the sign that she has given up the last vestige of
> resistance to her nature and has embraced
> womanhood with soul *and* body.

> The achievement of orgasm, usually, is the
> last step in the process of growing up. If one
> reviews in one's mind the actual orgastic expe-
> rience it is not difficult to see why this is so.

> For a woman orgasm requires a trust in
> one's partner that is absolute. Recall for a
> moment that the physical experience is often so
> profound that it entails the loss of consciousness
> for a period of time. As we know, in sexual inter-
> course, as in life, man is the actor, woman the

passive one, the receiver, the acted upon. Giving oneself up in this passive manner to another human being, making oneself his willing partner to such seismic physical experiences, means one must have complete faith in the other person. In the sexual embrace any trace of buried hostility, fear of one's role, will show clearly and unmistakably.

But there is even more to the psychic state necessary for orgasm than faith in one's partner and readiness to surrender. There must be a sensual eagerness to surrender; in the woman's orgasm the excitement comes from the act of surrender. There is a tremendous surging physical ecstasy in the yielding itself, in the feeling of being the passive instrument of another person, of being stretched out supinely beneath him, taken up will-lessly by his passion as leaves are swept up before a wind.[19]

One wise woman commented, "A woman is the only creature that can conquer by surrendering."

11. *Weak vaginal muscles.* In the next chapter we will investigate in detail what has recently been recognized as one of the most common causes of orgasmic malfunction. It is estimated that two-thirds of the women who cannot achieve orgasm have this problem. Interestingly enough, the remedy is very simple, inexpensive, and achievable in a relatively short time. So far every woman to whom I have suggested the Kegel exercises to cure this problem has gone on to orgasmic fulfillment.

Dr. Paul Popenoe of the American Institute of Family Relations has advocated this technique for several years. He reports that 65 percent of the sexually unsatisfied women gained relief, and almost all were helped. He further states, "It is a rare woman who cannot heighten her sexual adequacy through this understanding and technique, usually to a considerable extent. We now try to give the information to every woman we see professionally. We believe that this is a key to good sexual adjustment."[20]

Another comment comes from one of the world's foremost authorities on the diseases of women, Dr. J. P. Greenhill, professor of gynecology at Chicago's Cook County School of Medicine and editor of the *Yearbook of Obstetrics and Gynecology*: "In all the reports on the use of the Kegel technique there has never been any question of its safety for any woman. And for surprising numbers of women, its benefits, both sexually and medically, are likely to be great indeed."[21]

Any woman not receiving the ultimate satisfaction in the act of marriage will probably find the next chapter the most helpful material she has ever read on feminine sexuality.

Notes

1. William H. Masters and Virginia E. Johnson, *Human Sexual Response* (Boston: Little, Brown and Co., 1966), 138.

2. Ronald M. Deutsch, *The Key to Feminine Response in Marriage* (New York: Random House, 1968), 24–25.

3. Herbert J. Miles, *Sexual Happiness in Marriage* (Grand Rapids: Zondervan, 1967), 139.

4. Marie N. Robinson, *The Power of Sexual Surrender* (New York: Doubleday, 1959), 25–26.

5. Ibid., 11.

6. David Reuben, *Any Woman Can* (New York: David McKay, 1971), 37–38.

7. David Reuben, *How to Get More Out of Sex* (New York: David McKay, 1974), 37.

8. Deutsch, *Feminine Response*, 46.

9. Ibid., 39.

10. Miles, *Sexual Happiness*, 66–67.

11. Robinson, *Sexual Surrender*, 68.
12. Reuben, *Any Woman Can*, 53–55.
13. Ibid., 61–62.
14. Ibid., 62.
15. Deutsch, *Feminine Response*, 20–23.
16. Reuben, *Any Woman Can*, 30–31.
17. Deutsch, *Feminine Response*, 4–5.
18. Ibid., 93.
19. Robinson, *Sexual Surrender*, 157–58.
20. Deutsch, *Feminine Response*, 14.
21. Ibid.

Ten

The Key to
Feminine Response

It isn't often that a special key is found to open the solution to an almost universal problem, but the Kegel exercises have provided such an opportunity for countless married couples. The many women who have been guided to orgasmic fulfillment through the Kegel method consider it undoubtedly the greatest sex breakthrough of the century. Amazingly enough, it was discovered quite by accident. Ronald M. Deutsch, a foremost writer on medicine, tells the story in his book *The Key to Feminine Response in Marriage.*

In 1940 Dr. Arnold H. Kegel, a specialist in female disorders, was visited by a patient named Doris Wilson. Although her basic health was good, after the birth of her third child Mrs. Wilson developed an embarrassing problem that her doctor called "urinary stress incontinence." He assured her that as many as one woman in twenty was troubled with this problem and that at certain times, when the bladder was full, "a laugh, a cough, a sudden movement" would cause an uncontrolled urinary leakage. For safety Mrs. Wilson was forced to wear a protective pad.[1]

Dr. Kegel told Mrs. Wilson that her problem was probably due to a weakened muscle, but before they resorted to surgery, which often provided only temporary relief, she should learn to exercise the weak muscle. He explained that

> this muscle ran between the legs, from front to back, like a sling. It was wide and strong. In fact, it formed the floor of the pelvis, the lower trunk. It was the base of support for the bladder, part of the rectum, the birth canal and the womb.
>
> In women, three passages penetrated this muscle to empty outside the body—the rectum, birth canal and the urethra, or urinary canal. Kegel believed that, since the birth canal passed through the muscle and was firmly attached to it, childbirth could damage the muscle. And since the urinary passage was supported by the same muscle and kept closed by it, a weak muscle might mean poor urinary control. The muscle might be strong enough to hold back urine ordinarily. But with extra stress, some of the fluid would push through. Kegel also believed that this muscle might be strengthened.
>
> Mrs. Wilson was one of several stress-incontinence patients who agreed to try special exercises. In less than two months, the distress and embarrassment had ended.
>
> Today these exercises, known as the Kegel exercises, are standard technique in cases of stress incontinence. For most patients, they succeed and make surgery needless.

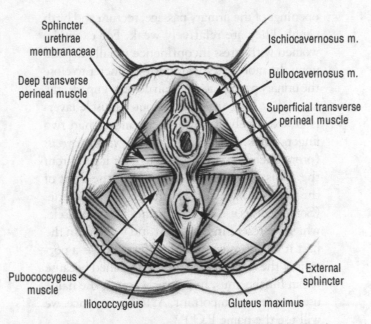

Sphincter urethrae membranaceae

Deep transverse perineal muscle

Ischiocavernosus m.

Bulbocavernosus m.

Superficial transverse perineal muscle

Pubococcygeus muscle

Iliococcygeus

External sphincter

Gluteus maximus

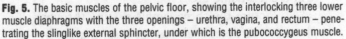

Fig. 5. The basic muscles of the pelvic floor, showing the interlocking three lower muscle diaphragms with the three openings – urethra, vagina, and rectum – penetrating the slinglike external sphincter, under which is the pubococcygeus muscle.

Shortly after Mrs. Wilson had gained urinary control, she confided to Dr. Kegel that something else had happened. For the first time in fifteen years of marriage, she had reached orgasm in intercourse. She wanted to know if this could be associated with the exercises.

Kegel was skeptical. But then he heard the same thing repeatedly from women given instructions for the exercises. He wondered about a possible mechanism.

To understand Kegel's reasoning, one must know something of the pelvic floor muscles. They are composed of several layers. The outermost layer is made up mainly of sphincters, ring-like closing muscles. These muscles close the outer openings of the urinary passage, rectum and birth canal. They are relatively weak. For example, women with stress incontinence usually depend upon the more external urinary sphincter to close the urinary passage, a job it can do only imperfectly.

But lying inside these outer muscle layers is an extremely strong muscle, more than two fingers thick. It is known as the *pubococcygeus* (pronounced pyoobo kok-sijeus), for it runs from the pubis, the bony prominence at the front of the pelvis, to the coccyx, the end of the spine. (Some doctors use different names for this muscle, which is present in both men and women. In the past it has been commonly referred to as a portion of the *levator ani*, which is so called because it can lift the anus. In practical terms, the name used is not very important. As a convenience, we will use the name P.C.)

Picture the three canals passing through the muscular floor. Each passage is surrounded by a net of interlocking muscle fibers from the P.C., for a length up to about two inches. The fibers run both lengthwise along each canal and surround each as sphincters. Thus, the rings of muscle around each passage can be squeezed shut at will.

It is the sphincteric action of that part of the P.C. surrounding the urinary passage which fails in stress incontinence; the P.C. cannot squeeze the passage shut. Exercise gives it strength enough to function properly.

What has this to do with sexual satisfaction? Kegel knew that the P.C. surrounded the vagina in the same way. And he began to find that a surprising number of women had P.C. weakness.

In fewer than one of three women the muscle had relatively good tone, making a rather firm straight platform and performing well. Among these women, urinary incontinence was a rarity. (It should be added that the disorder can have causes other than muscle failure.) Childbirth was easier for them. The birth canal seemed rarely to be damaged in delivery. And sexual responsiveness tended to be good.

But in at least two of three women the P.C. was relatively slack and weak. It sagged much like a hammock; and organs sagged which it was meant to support. Among these women, childbirth was more likely to be difficult. Birth-canal injuries were more common. Incontinence appeared after children were born, and sometimes as early as their own childhoods. Sexual satisfaction was unusual.

Oddly, the strength of the P.C. seemed unrelated to the general muscular strength of the

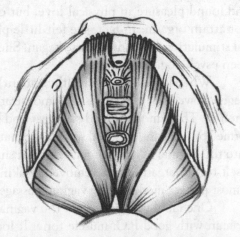

Fig. 6. The pubococcygeus (P.C.) muscle seen from above after removal of some of the more superficial muscles. Note how the fibers surround each of the openings interlocking with other muscle fibers of these organs. Firm P.C. muscle tone produces support to those organs, slack muscles give little support. These muscles are responsive to proper exercise.

patient. Female athletes might have poor, slack P.C. musculature. Some frail, sedentary women had good tone. The explanation was that the P.C. was suspended between two fixed bony structures. Therefore, it was unaffected by the use of other muscles. It stood alone.

Gradually Kegel developed a way to exercise and strengthen the P.C. In 1947 the USC School of Medicine established a clinic in which he could continue his work, and in 1948 his work won the annual award of the Los Angeles Obstetrical Society.

Though Kegel's primary interest had not been in sexual problems, he felt obliged to pursue the sexual component of his findings. At his clinic, he began to accept referrals from the American Institute of Family Relations of women who failed sexually.

... [One] patient had been affectionate and found pleasure in physical love, but could not attain orgasm. In fact, she felt little physical stimulation once intercourse began. She had been psychologically normal.

When he had examined [the patient], Dr. Kegel showed her two molds to demonstrate his findings. These molds, called *moulages*, had been formed by inserting a special soft plastic material into the vagina. When the material had shaped itself to the organ, it was removed, making an almost perfect model of the vaginal passage.

One mold was made from the vagina of a woman with good P.C. muscle tone. It looked something like a squeezed tube. Wide at the opening, it narrowed for a space of about two inches, then widened again. The narrowing showed the squeezing action of a strong P.C.

Throughout the narrowed portion, the mold rippled slightly, the ripples made by the pressure of tightening muscle bands, row on row. These bands were the spreading fibers of the P.C. They made the vagina a strong, muscular organ.

The second mold was made from the vagina of a patient who had never experienced true orgasm. It looked rather like a straight-sided funnel, broadening steadily from its opening toward the top. Its walls were virtually unmarked by muscle pressure. Clearly the P.C. was weak. The organ had poor support and little strength.

"The second mold," the doctor told [her], "approximates your own condition. You can see that the vagina from which this mold was made cannot exert the pressure which is an essential for good sexual function."

Why is the ability to exert pressure important? The answer to this question explains to many experts the ancient puzzle of how the vagina can provide sexual satisfaction when it appears to contain almost no nerve endings.

The solution is explained this way by Dr. Terence F. McGuire and Dr. Richard M. Steinhilber of the Mayo Clinic: "According to current data, the muscles beneath the vagina mucosa (the lining of the vagina) are well supplied with proprioceptive endings (nerve endings of the type sensitive to pressure, movement, and stretching). These are adequately stimulated during intercourse, and could well represent the primary ... sensory apparatus. ... It would appear that vaginal orgasm is a reality."

In other words, the muscle which surrounds the vagina is rich in sensitive nerve endings.

Doctors failed to find these endings because their search was limited to the lining of the vagina.

Since these nerves are outside the vagina, it takes firm pressure from within to stimulate them. In a wide, slack vagina, the male organ makes poor and infrequent contact with the walls of the passage, thereby stimulating nerves in the surrounding musculature very little.

If the vagina is narrowed to a tight, firm channel by the contraction of surrounding muscle, the male organ will press and push these muscles, giving strong stimulation. Stimulated, the muscles will respond with an automatic contraction which increases the contact, thus helping to build the tension which leads to feminine climax.

This phenomenon had long been suspected by some observers. As early as the turn of the century, Dr. Robert L. Dickinson reported that he could identify women likely to fail sexually by examining them. He wrote, "The size, power, reactions and rhythm of contraction of the pelvic floor muscles give information concerning vaginal types of coital orgasm (orgasm during intercourse).

In one of his early case records he noted: "Levator is not very good. Taught her to use the muscle." And he adds, "It seems very important that many women are able after instruction to get something which they call orgasm, when they failed before instruction."

Some primitive and Oriental people have observed the need for such muscular control and strength and teach young women accordingly. In one African tribe, no girl may marry until she is able to exert strong pressure with the vaginal muscles. Other cultures have noted that sexual performance is often poorer after childbirth because of the stretching or injuring of the birth canal. In some Moslem countries women actually follow the appalling custom of packing the vagina with rock salt after giving birth, in order to make it contract.

After their study of sexual response in many societies, Ford and Beach concluded: "There is considerable evidence to support the belief that distention of the vaginal walls resulting from insertion of the penis is an important factor."

Widespread reports now confirm this conclusion. Dr. Donald Hastings, of the University of Minnesota, comments: "The exercise and contraction of the voluntary muscles which form the pelvic floor and surround parts of the vagina are important for ... enhancement of sexual pleasure." He adds, "Some of the 'secret' sexual practices of other cultures depend upon the strength and cultivation of the vaginal muscles."

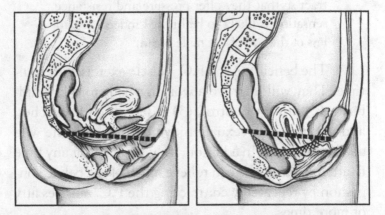

Fig. 7. (Left) Side view showing *good* P.C. muscle tone. Note how the vagina is in proper position; (right) The P.C. muscle with weak tone hangs loose and low, permitting sagging of the female organs due to poor support. Childbirth may be more difficult for this woman; she may be susceptible to backaches; menstruation may be harder and coitus less stimulating to both her and her husband.

And Dr. John F. Oliven, of New York's Columbia Presbyterian Hospital, reports in his textbook on sexual problems for physicians and other professionals: "The most important hypesthesic [lack-of-feeling] syndrome occurs in connection with vaginal over-relaxation. To the patient herself this may appear to be a matter of insufficient contact between penis and vaginal walls. However, there is evidence that relaxed walls are hypesthesic walls, because the sub-mucosal 'deep-touch' nerve endings, which are responsible for the greater part of so-called vaginal sensation are minimally represented if their vehicle—chiefly the pubococcygeus—is hypotrophic [weak through underdevelopment or degeneration]."

Oliven ends by saying, "Thus, probably no degree of 'bulk immission' can completely overcome these women's diminished sensation." In other words, when the vaginal walls do not contract so that they offer pressure and resistance, sensation is likely to be limited indeed, regardless of the size of the male organ.[2]

The benefits of the P.C. muscle exercises are multiple. They will improve a woman's body for (1) childbirth, (2) urinary control, (3) reduction of backaches, and (4) increased sexual enjoyment for both the wife and the husband. In addition, if she is unable at any time to attain orgasm, she can relieve much of the pelvic congestion by repeatedly contracting the P.C. muscles fifty or more times.

Considering the benefits from the exercises, Deutsch continues,

The exercises which strengthen the P.C. muscle are safe, simple and not fatiguing. Aside from the sexual benefit they seem to provide, they improve the support given to the organs of the pelvis. Such support has been found by experts to reduce the number of the childbirth injuries to the mother and to shorten the time of delivery, thus increasing safety for the child.

Proponents of natural childbirth see such exercise as essential. And even many doctors who are not in favor of natural childbirth feel that this muscular training is valuable. Instructors who teach the Y.W.C.A. classes in preparing for childbirth give the exercises to the pregnant women they train. And the International Childbirth Education Association has made the exercises part of its programs of instruction.

But for the vast majority of the many thousands of women who have now learned the exercises, there is meaning beyond health and safety....

Many women can contract the P.C. on conscious command by merely learning it exists. And Dr. Kegel has pointed out that some women can achieve satisfaction for the first time just by being made aware of the muscle and its role in the sex act.

But if the muscle is weak, as it is in most women, awareness is unlikely to be enough. Not only must the woman learn conscious control of the muscle; she must strengthen it with exercise. "And it is a rare woman," says Dr. Kegel, "who cannot benefit from increased strength of the muscle."

Gaining control, however, can be difficult without guidance. Most women, when they are asked to contract the vaginal muscles, begin by

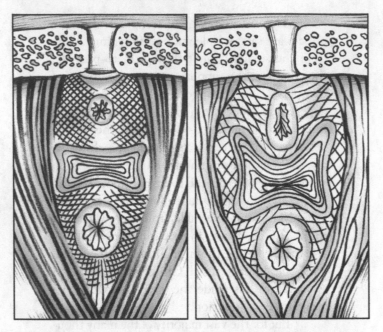

Fig. 8. (Left) An artist's conception of the vagina, seen from above, showing good muscle development. The heavy lines indicate strong muscle fibers, which are exaggerated here to suggest the thickness and resistance of the pubococcygeus muscle, which make possible better vaginal perception; (right) An artist's conception of the vagina, seen from above, showing poor muscle development. The lines indicating muscle here are lighter and sparser, suggesting the thinness and lack of the resistance of the pubococcygeus muscle usually accompanied by poor vaginal perception. Note how much wider are the poorly supported vaginal and urinary passages.

trying to contract the smaller, weaker, *external* muscles instead. This may be seen in a kind of pursing of the vaginal opening.

Asked to try again, and reminded that this is internal muscle, many make greater and greater efforts, contracting muscles of the abdomen, the lower back, the hips and thighs. These muscles have no link to the P.C. And, in fact, one may be certain that the exercise is done incorrectly if one experiences muscle fatigue.[3]

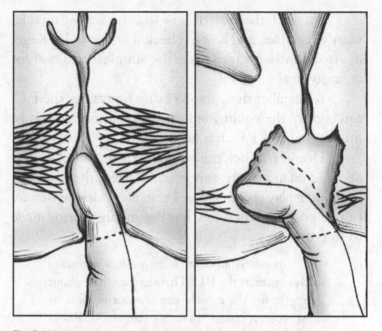

Fig. 9. How the doctor examines the pubococcygeus muscle. (Left) When the muscle has good tone, resistance is felt in all directions; (right) When the muscle has poor tone, the vagina is roomy and the thin walls feel as though detached from surrounding structures.

The Kegel Method of Exercises

The best method of exercising the P.C. muscles to provide maximum muscular control and strength was devised by Dr. Kegel and used by him and his associates on hundreds of women. The fame of its near-unanimous success and improvement of sexual response in patients who diligently fulfilled the six-to-eight-week program spread until it was adopted by many doctors throughout the world. Although the exercises demand concentration and consistency, they are really quite simple and well within the capability of most women. One doctor has said, "Nearly all women could be taught to contract the muscle."

To teach the patient how to contract the muscle, what it feels like, and how to check it at home, Dr. Kegel devised another way. This is the simplest and best for an individual.

Remember that, among other functions, the P.C. can control the voiding of urine. So if urination can be interrupted, the P.C. has been contracted.

However, since the weaker external muscles can also shut off urine flow, except under stress, these must be kept out of play. To do so, the knees are widely separated. In this position, once flow has begun, an effort is made to stop it.

In nearly all women, this effort automatically contracts the P.C. This signifies little about strength, for the muscle can stop urine flow in most women unless there is extra stress. But it teaches the feeling of a P.C. contraction. After a few trials, most women can recognize the sensation and can repeat the contractions at any time, anywhere, using the occasional interruption of voiding only as a check. Each contraction exercises the muscle surrounding the vagina.

There is little physical effort, though concentration is needed at first. "Once the contraction is learned," says childbirth educator Dr. Mary Jane Hungerford, "it takes little more effort than to close an eye. In fact, it can be done as rapidly as you open and shut an eye, though when exercising, the contraction should be held for about two seconds."

Once control of the P.C. is learned, women are instructed to begin exercise with five or ten contractions before arising in the morning. The contraction seems to be easier at this time.

Six Week P.C. Exercise Chart

	Sunday	Monday	Tuesday	1st Week Wednesday	Thursday	Friday	Saturday
10 contractions per session							
				2nd Week			
15 contractions per session							
				3rd Week			
20 contractions per session							
				4th Week			
30 contractions per session							
				5th Week			
40 contractions per session							
				6th Week			
50 contractions per session							

Each day on this six-week chart is divided into six blocks. These blocks represent six P.C. muscle exercise sessions. On the left of the chart is the suggested number of P.C. contractions to be done during each of the six sessions per day. Write in the block the number of contractions achieved per session.

And at first, the exercises should also be tried whenever urine is voided. "With good control," says Dr. Hungerford, "urine can be released a teaspoon at a time."

How much exercise is needed? The plan can be varied widely, but a usual recommendation is for some ten contractions in a row, made at six intervals during the day. This makes sixty contractions in all. Though it may sound laborious, each contraction need take no more than a second. Each group of ten contractions might take ten seconds. Six such sessions in a day would make a total of one minute.

Gradually, the number of sessions and the number of contractions made in each can be increased. For example, twenty contractions in a session would bring the six-session total to a hundred and twenty a day. Dr. Kegel suggests that each voiding of urine be an opportunity for exercise. If this is done three times a day, adding exercise before arising, when retiring and at one other time, the initial program is completed. (However, Dr. Kegel often suggests that the day's exercise be done in three twenty-minute periods.)

This program should then be stepped up, for the contraction becomes almost effortless. Many women find that thirty contractions in a session is a comfortable number, and can be done in a minute once training is under way. There is no rush to increase, but eventually most women find that two hundred and three hundred contractions a day are easily achieved, spaced throughout the day at convenient times. This would make a total of three hundred contractions in the day's exercise. Dr. Kegel says most patients reach a total of about three hundred a day in some six weeks. By this time, control of voiding is usually very good, though in some women with especially weak musculature ten weeks might be needed. Most women can note sexual and other changes within three weeks, but nevertheless are urged to continue.

How long? After six to eight weeks, when the three hundred-a-day pattern has been reached, further exercise is usually not necessary. One reason is that the normal state of the P.C. is not full relaxation. To do its job of pelvic support, it stays in a state of partial contraction and tends to maintain its strength. Without such partial contraction, for example, urine would not normally be retained. The P.C. relaxes completely only under anesthesia.

The exercises strengthen this steady state of contraction. After a few weeks, a mold of the vagina shows a markedly changed shape. Moreover, sexual activity helps preserve the new muscle tone in several ways.

First, it appears that the steady-state contraction is heightened during intercourse. Second, sexual stimulation seems to produce mild reflex contractions of the vaginal muscles. Third, many experts counsel women to make occasional conscious contractions as a technique of intercourse, as we shall see in greater detail. Finally, in sexual climax, the P.C. contracts involuntarily, strongly and rhythmically, from four to ten times, at intervals of about four-fifths of a second. (The feeling of release and the disappearance of tension follow this contractile burst.)

Women who have difficulty in determining whether or not they contract the P.C. are taught to do so at first only while voiding urine. Other women, who seem to have little sense of the position and existence of the muscle, may need a doctor's help in learning to exercise.

At the American Institute of Family Relations, women are counseled to use the new contractile ability in intercourse consciously at first, squeezing firmly and slowly. In fact, a series of conscious contractions are recommended before the entrance of the male organ. This is thought to help set the stage for the function of the muscle as an automatic reflex. And it appears to heighten sexual tension, which is desirable, since it is the buildup of such tension which, reaching a summit, seems to trigger the orgasm....

Participation by the woman is among the most important of modern concepts of successful physical love. Speaking of this, Dr. Charles Lloyd, a leading sex authority, comments that in our society "adult women are often incapable of sexual aggressions and assume an inactive role during marital intercourse. Frequently they do not experience clear-cut orgasms. Societies in which there is training for the sexual role," he points out, "usually produce a higher degree of aggressiveness in sexual activity with vigorous participation by the woman and much more regularly complete and satisfactory orgasm."

The use of the P.C. muscle provides a clear mechanism for such participation. It offers a concept of the vagina, not merely as a passive receiver of action, but as an actor.

Some forty years ago, Van de Velde described this concept: "The whole structure [of the female organs] accentuated by the working of the ... muscles ... is an apparatus for gripping and rubbing the male sexual organ, during and after its insertion or immission into the vagina, and thus to produce the ejaculation of seed or sperm-cells, in the culmination of excitement, and at the same time, by pressure and friction, to ensure this orgasm, or some of pleasure and ecstasy, in the woman also."

How intrinsic in intercourse is this pattern? Some reports indicate that it occurs through simply an awareness and strengthening of the vaginal musculature.

According to Dr. Hungerford,

"In childbirth education we teach the contraction exercises in order to strengthen the birth canal, and to help the canal distend more easily so that pain and injury for the mother can be avoided. At first, in teaching the exercises, I made no mention of the sexual value. I taught them only in terms of childbirth.

"But within weeks after I began teaching, one woman took me aside before class to say she had experienced orgasm in intercourse for the first time. The same thing has happened repeatedly. Many women seem to think this was the most important thing they got from the courses and report they have taught others with the same result.

"Some years ago a marriage-counselor colleague, a woman of sixty, observed my class and listened as I taught the exercises. By now I was explaining the sexual importance, and the counselor questioned me about this. When I saw her a month later, she threw her arms around me and said that for the first time in forty years of marriage, she had experienced a full orgasm."

The exercises seem able to restore sexual adjustment which has been lost, apparently through the extreme stretching of the P.C. during childbirth. As Dr. John Oliven explains: "If it [the P.C.] is constitutionally predisposed to weakness, it may not regain normal tonus, even following relatively normal childbirth, and especially after several childbirths in succession." . . .

Some doctors recommend that their patients exercise during pregnancy to give the walls greater strength and tonus. Like other muscles, the P.C. actually thickens with exercise. For similar

reasons, doctors also use the exercises restora-
tively, after delivery.

If, as Dr. Kegel suggests, perhaps two-thirds
of American women have P.C. muscle weakness
enough to interfere with sexual function, one
would expect that childbirth injuries associated
with weak muscle, along with other medical groups
of P.C. weakness, would be common indeed.
There are indications that this is the fact. . . .

The prevention and restoration afforded
by exercise of the P.C. muscle are said by many
experts to make the exercises valuable to most
women at some time in life, especially for women
who bear children. Good tone of the muscle is
accepted widely as medically desirable. And exercise to achieve that tone is certainly harmless.

Sexually, the strengthening of the muscle
and an understanding of how it functions have
relieved many cases of inadequacy. And the understanding has further implications. Together with
other new scientific knowledge, the concept has
considerable effect on what has been believed
and is now known of the art of physical love.[4]

Occasionally I have encountered resistance to
these exercises from Christian wives. In one such case,
a mother of five and married almost twenty-five years
said, "Pastor, it all seems so unnatural to me. If God
wanted those vaginal muscles strong enough for me to
get more sensation during lovemaking, He would have
made them that way." I explained to her that He did
originally, but her five births and natural aging process
had so relaxed them that they were of little help to her,
and the older she grew, the more she would need them
toned up through exercise.

Quite reluctantly she went home to try, but admitted she had little faith it would work. Still, she did her exercises diligently, and as she reported later, "Within one month I experienced sensations I had never felt before. Within five weeks my husband, who had been experiencing a little trouble maintaining an erection, noticed the added dimension of excitement in our love life. Now we both think our next twenty-five years of love will be more exciting than the first twenty-five."

Some women who refused to try it for their own benefit were prevailed upon to attempt it for the sake of their husbands. Before the eight weeks were up, several of them acknowledged their first orgasmic fulfillment in many years of marriage. Eight weeks really isn't very long for an experiment that may bring lifelong benefits. Try it—the chances are good that you'll like it.

NOTE: Many doctors, gynecologists, sex counselors, and marriage counselors recommend a unique gynetic exerciser called "Femogen" that was designed to enhance and simplify the performance of the Kegel exercises. It is inexpensive and is said to shorten the time of the exercises and has proven extremely successful with women. Results are guaranteed. For a free descriptive brochure write to Family Services, P.O. Box 9363, Fresno, CA 93792.

An Update on the Kegel Exercises

Twenty-two or more years since the original edition of this book was published and literally hundreds of inquiries and testimonials later, it would be appropriate here to give a brief update on the Kegel exercises. I am still quite enthusiastic about them as a means of enriching the love life of married couples by improving the muscle tone of many women and increasing the sensitivity of the genitalia. Particularly is this true of women who have had several babies. As we mentioned, everyone knows that pregnancy stretches a woman's reproductive system way out of its original form. Most of her organs return to normal within six months after childbirth. Unfortunately, the muscles in the vagina may be left permanently relaxed unless she exercises them. (This is also true of her abdominal muscles.) Her muscle tone may recover enough to maintain good sexual relations, but not quite as tight as before. When she has had three or four children, the problem can become acute. Later in life, as a woman goes through menopause, many of her muscles begin to relax just a little, making sexual feeling for both her and her husband less stimulating.

The Kegel exercises seem to be the procedure of choice for many therapists. I have noted new devices on the market that may prove helpful, but all are based on the Kegel exercises. From the messages we have received from women who have read this book, they are still very effective. In fact, a recent letter came from a frantic woman who had given birth to three boys within five years. She was twenty-seven years old and had lost much of her sexual sensation. She was a bit upset with me because she had tried the exercises faithfully for four weeks and still had not experienced an orgasm. But by the time her letter had worked its way to me and I found time to respond, I received her second letter saying, "It finally happened, I am becoming a new woman!" This is not an uncommon response, for we all want success right now.

We are now convinced that a woman should not quit her exercise program after she achieves her desired results, even if she continues for twelve weeks. We think it wise to plan to do them at least three times a week for life. If she does, she will be assured of maintaining the good results of her efforts for life. Most physical fitness experts tell us that even the most conditioned athletes will lose their muscular buildup if they stop exercising altogether. Exercising three or more times a week as a lifetime habit is a small price to pay for the pleasure you gain for yourself and the man you love.

Men Can Benefit from Kegel, Too

One of the things we have learned about the Kegel exercises is that most men, particularly those over fifty, can benefit from doing them also. As a man matures in life, his muscles also begin to relax, and he may have trouble maintaining an erection or at least as rigid as he did in his youth. In addition, he may begin to have difficulty controlling his urinary drip. In both cases researchers have discovered that faithful exercise of the sphincter muscle as outlined in this chapter for women is a tremendous help to men. Again, it is persistence that pays off.

Notes

1. Ronald M. Deutsch, *The Key to Feminine Response in Marriage* (New York: Random House, 1968), 52–53.

2. Ibid., 53–66.

3. Ibid., 68–73.

4. Ibid., 74–81.

Eleven

The Impotent Man

Convalescing after surgery in a famous medical research center, a doctor was seated in the office of a medical school colleague who was then the head of the hospital. He asked, "Do you find any medical problems increasing today?" Without hesitation his friend replied, "Yes. Male impotence! Hardly a day passes that some man does not come in and worriedly exclaim, 'Doctor, I'm afraid I am becoming impotent.' I have seen many of them burst into tears." This book would not be complete without a careful examination of the increasing problem of impotence.

After his fortieth birthday a man's most important sex organ is his brain. The size of his genitalia has nothing to do with sexual capability, but what he thinks of himself does. If he considers himself virile and effective—he is. If he deems himself inadequate—he is. The old adage "You are what you think" is particularly true of a man's sexual capability.

I first encountered male impotence after a Family Life Seminar lecture on "Physical Adjustment in Marriage." A forty-eight-year-old husband asked if I thought there was any hope for a man who had been impotent for eight years. Inwardly groaning at this unnecessary tragedy, I asked how his wife took it. He replied, "She has learned to live with it." How sad! Ignorance had cheated them both out of many lovemaking experiences.

Why Some Men Become Impotent

Research shows that impotence is increasing at an alarming rate. But we predict it will get worse unless men learn something about themselves, and their wives discover what they can do to help.

The sex drive in a man reaches its strongest peak between ages eighteen and twenty-two; from that time on, it begins to taper off slowly—so slowly, in fact, that most men fail to notice it until their mid or late forties, and many do not detect it until their sixties. The first time a man has difficulty maintaining an erection or is unable to ejaculate, his malady soon runs out of control. Within an amazingly short time he has convinced himself that he is losing his manhood, and the more he thinks in this manner, the more likely he is to undergo other bad experiences.

A forty-five-year-old man who enjoyed a beautiful relationship with his wife decided to get a vasectomy. Three doctors assured him that it was perfectly safe and would not lessen his sex drive. He waited the six weeks after the operation as instructed and then had a disastrous experience trying to provide a semen sample for the doctor to test. The catastrophe fell on the same day he was to leave town on a week's business trip. His plane was scheduled to depart at 3:00 P.M., so he went to the office in the morning after determining with his wife that they would make love in the afternoon in order to obtain the semen sample. She was to drop it off at the doctor's office on the way back from the airport. Unfortunately he arrived home later than he intended, packed his clothes furiously, and then hurriedly initiated lovemaking, only to find that his erection was not hard enough to prove enjoyable to his wife and that for the first time in his life he could not ejaculate.

Although he told his wife, "It doesn't make any difference," it did. With a week to think negatively about his sexual failure, he returned convinced he was impotent. He loved his wife enough to seek help, however, and when he learned more about the function of his reproductive system, he regained confidence in his sex drive. The first good experience with his wife led to another, and finally all thoughts of impotence vanished. Today they enjoy a very fulfilling love life.

Ninety times out of a hundred, impotence can be cured. We are reminded, "As [a man] thinketh in his heart, so is he" (Prov. 23:7 KJV). The heart is often used to describe the emotional center of the brain, which is the primary motivator of *every organ* of the body. If a man *thinks* he is impotent—he *feels* impotent; if he feels that way—he *is* impotent. A formula would express the problem this way: Impotent thoughts + impotent feelings = impotence. Research indicates that almost all male impotence can be cured.

Copulatory malfunction is often the first step toward impotence. For any one of several reasons a man may find it impossible to ejaculate after years of successful experiences. After that first malfunction, his fear of another will convince him, "I'm running out of gas!" or "I'm getting too old," and that fear may bring on subsequent malfunctions. Although he may not have had trouble maintaining an erection before, you can be sure that unless he resolves his fear, similar problems will follow.

Limp penis is the most common form of impotence and until the last two decades was primarily a problem of middle-aged men. Now, because of the overemphasis on sex in our emotionally pressurized society, it is unfortunately afflicting many younger men today. This kind of impotence cannot always be traced to a single problem but is usually the result of a combination of difficulties.

A rigid penis is absolutely essential for satisfactory consummation of the act of marriage. The male afflicted by limp penis, either before entering the vagina or after, may be completely unaware of its cause. He may have a desire to make love to his wife but experience difficulty in getting his penis hard enough for entrance. He may make a good entrance, moving them both excitedly toward orgasm, when suddenly his penis refuses to cooperate by going soft. It is biologically almost impossible for him to ejaculate while having intercourse unless he can maintain an erection. However, a man's wife can massage and manipulate him to orgasm with a limp penis, and this may sometimes provide temporary relief of sexual tension.

What Causes Male Impotence?

It is difficult to target a single cause of male impotence, for it usually results from a combination of several factors. Whatever the cause, it produces great emotional torture for any man. The problem is worth careful consideration because an overwhelming number of cases can be cured if the husband and wife are willing to work at it. The first step toward curing this malady is to understand its most common causes.

1. *Loss of vital energy.* Few professional football players remain active players after their fortieth birthday, and, in fact, most of them drop out of the game in their early or mid-thirties. Bones become more brittle, muscles take longer to heal, and their youthful vigor begins to wane. Such men, of course, do not cease being men. Most proceed into other professions and live productive lives.

In similar fashion, a man suffering from male impotence because of a loss of vital energies must not view his malady as a kind of castration. Merely lacking the same intensity of sex drive in his late forties and fifties that he maintained in his twenties should not suggest that he is "sexually all washed up." Admittedly, somewhere around his forties or fifties he probably will not require the frequency of intercourse he did in his twenties, his penis may not remain as rigid as in previous years, and he may malfunction occasionally—but by no means does that signal *he is through.* In fact, with proper help and understanding from a loving wife, he can learn to experience some of the most satisfying lovemaking experiences of his life.

2. *Anger, bitterness, and resentment.* For years I have directed one leading question to impotent men: Is there anyone in your life whom you dislike? An airline pilot, scarcely thirty years old, came in and, after several embarrassed attempts to tell me his problem, blurted out, "I'm impotent!" Looking at this handsome specimen of humanity built like an athlete, I could hardly believe it.

To my question, "How are things between you and your mother?" he replied with a snarl, "Do we have to talk about her?"

"Since you put it that way, we had better," I responded.

He proceeded to inform me about "this witch" who masqueraded as his mother. Humanly speaking, he had every right to feel that way, for if she was guilty of only half of what he accused her, she must have been a fiend.

Not until that young man got down on his knees and confessed his bitter hatred for his mother was he able to function normally with his wife. Somehow such hatred is transferred subconsciously from the mother to the wife, totally suppressing a normal sex drive. Impotence is a high price to pay for such bitterness.

Domineering mothers are not the only ones who can effect impotence through hatred. A boss, a neighbor, a father, and of course a wife can spark the same response. Such sinful thoughts and emotions will not only stifle a man's natural sex drive and cheat him and his wife out of many thrilling expressions of love, but it will also keep him a spiritual pygmy all his life. Our Lord said, "For if you forgive men when they sin against you, your heavenly Father will also forgive you" (Matt. 6:14). Dealing spiritually with extreme bitterness provides the only therapy we know that is effective. Someone has sagely said, "Love or perish."

3. *Fear.* Men are seldom really what they appear to be: confident, controlled, and manly. Beneath that façade may be a fear of becoming impotent. As stated previously, the male ego is closely tied to his sex drive. Some men have induced impotence by the fear that they

cannot satisfy their wives. For that reason a wise woman goes out of her way to let her husband know how much she enjoys his lovemaking.

Researchers in this field almost invariably report that fear of castration is a universal problem with men. Most men give it only a fleeting thought, but with some it becomes a phobia. Since it lurks in the subconscious mind of every man, one can really appreciate why the first middle-age malfunction is mentally magnified out of proportion and leads to additional problems of impotence. Once this fear of failure grips a man, only with great difficulty can he shake it off; however, by prayer, education, and tender loving care it can be dispelled. Just as surely as a piece of metal falling across a high-voltage line can short-circuit the normal flow of electricity, so fear can short-circuit a man's sex drive.

When a throbbing, rigid penis suddenly goes limp for no apparent reason, we may suspect that the brain is the culprit. Fear has done it again!

In spite of the bravado he maintains and the "sexually all wise" image he likes to project, a man is regularly plagued with five great sexual fears.

(a) *The fear of rejection*. Depending on his temperament and the past responses of his wife to his advances, a man often approaches his wife with a deep-rooted fear that he will be rejected. Naturally there are times when she really is "too tired" or "not feeling well tonight," but it is important that she be very honest. If her husband is a sensitive man, she had better make sure she convinces him that the problem lies with her, not with him, lest his subconscious fear of rejection cause him to interpret her refusal to mean that she does not find him sexually stimulating. A man cannot accept being unattractive to his wife. Nothing is worse for his male ego. Wives have confided that such rejection has turned their husbands off for weeks.

(b) *The fear that he will not be able to satisfy his wife.* Recent studies indicate that a man finds it very frustrating when his wife is not satisfied in the act of marriage. This likewise seems to threaten his manhood. A wise wife will verbally make her pleasure known to her husband, as well as informing him in other subtle ways.

(c) *The fear of being compared with other men.* This basic masculine fear should never be a problem for Christians, since the Bible clearly teaches virtue and chastity before marriage. If you violated that standard, or if you were previously married, *never* let yourself express such a comparison. (Even a mature Christian has a difficult time completely forgetting this violation of God's perfect plan.) One man I know hounded his wife until she finally admitted that her deceased husband was more sexually satisfying than he. But that confession caused inexpressible heartache, and they finally ended up in my office for counseling.

(d) *The fear that he will lose his erection.* To a large degree, satisfying lovemaking is dependent on the husband's ability to maintain an erection. A limp penis is unsatisfactory to both partners and humiliating to the husband.

(e) *The fear of not being able to ejaculate.* Until he has experienced his first ejaculatory malfunction, no man ever dreams this could happen to him. That first experience is so devastating that recurring fear may create a neurosis that can render a perfectly normal man impotent.

4. *Ridicule.* A man simply cannot accept ridicule— and a wise woman will never subject him to it. Particularly is that true of anything associated with his

masculinity, and even more so his sex apparatus. It is a strange quirk of nature, but almost every engorged penis is the same size (six to eight inches), no matter how large the man. However, the soft penis will measure anywhere from two inches to eight inches in length. Research has yet to explain adequately why some shrink more than others, but one can be certain that if a man is small when soft, he fears being inadequate. However, the male organ need only be two to three inches long to do a superlative job of lovemaking, for the only part of the inner vagina that is sensitive to touch or pressure extends from the outer lips to approximately two to three inches inside.

In all probability no man has ever really been too small, yet millions regularly *fear* that possibility. Therefore, it can be devastating for a wife to joke about her husband's organ, for she could well negate his normal function. One husband was so humiliated that he could not express to his wife how her simple statement "Are you man enough to take me on tonight?" devastated him. Unhappily, she meant no ridicule, but was nervous herself in talking about lovemaking and never dreamed he would find it offensive. You can no doubt guess the effect on another husband when his wife, not aware that he was having his first sexual malfunction, said, "What's the matter, big boy? Aren't you the man you once were?" Ridicule is a weapon of children. When used by a wife, it is akin to murder.

5. *Guilt*. A subject that modern psychology overlooks today in its humanistic attempt to solve human problems independent of God is the reality of conscience. For that reason psychologists seldom if ever clarify that free love and promiscuity before or during marriage can

produce severe guilt that results in impotence. It is well known that women frequently develop such strong guilt feelings after marriage, because of weak moral standards prior to marriage, that their ability to enjoy sex after marriage is severely diminished. The same thing can happen to men. One young man, reviewing his encounter with impotence the first year after the wedding, summed it up by saying, "I had more sex drive when we were living together than after she became my wife." Another stated, "Ever since I had an affair with my best friend's wife, I go limp each time I enter our bedroom." A door-to-door salesman admitted to his first bout with impotence shortly after he was enticed into a housewife's bed (he claimed) and was caught by her husband. The one thing these men all had in common was guilt.

The merits of virtue and chastity are many, the greatest being a clear conscience. One of the saddest cases that has come to our attention concerned a young minister who left his wife, his children, and the ministry for a woman he "loved so much he couldn't give her up." After ten years of feeling guilty he complained of impotence at age thirty-seven. Finally he admitted, "Every time I walk into the house and see my wife, I think of the first wife I left. Whenever I enter our bedroom, I am reminded of my unfaithfulness. Every time I pass a church, I think of the ministry I once enjoyed. Now on top of my guilt I am impotent. My lack of attention threatens my wife, she presses me for marital relations, and everything gets worse."

The Bible warns, "The way of the unfaithful is hard" (Prov. 13:15). In addition, "A man reaps what he sows" (Gal. 6:7). Fortunately there is a remedy for a guilt complex—accepting Jesus Christ as your Lord and

Savior and confessing your sins in His name. "If we confess our sins, he is faithful and just and will forgive us our sins and purify us from all unrighteousness" (1 John 1:9). Although our Lord forgives instantly, I find that it takes much longer for one to forgive oneself. For that reason, guilt-produced impotence will not vanish overnight.

6. *Unreasonable expectations*. It is important for a man to understand that God made him so that his sex drive will peak between eighteen and twenty-two years of age. During that time his reproductive organs will produce an unbelievable amount of testosterone, semen, and sperm cells. The reason is obvious: God intended man to marry and begin fathering children while he is young. During these years some men can experience from one to five ejaculations a day. As we have previously noted, that desire and proficiency tends to diminish shortly after twenty-two. When a man becomes aware of this lessening drive and intensity, he magnifies the problem by comparing his performance with his youthful capabilities. Most men fail to consider that God never intended him to compare his fifty-year-old potency with that of a twenty-two-year-old. We may likewise need to be reminded that a fifty-year-old man has a greater capacity for love, emotional expression, and sharing than an immature man. There is much more to lovemaking than the explosion of the glands, and most men eventually come to realize this fact; but some unfortunately let an occasional malfunction rob them of years of enjoyment. A mature husband is willing to sacrifice some quantity for well-appreciated quality.

Frankly, the man who accepts the fact that at certain times during his maturing process (quite different for each individual) he can experience a weekly quota of one to four or more meaningful experiences with his wife—depending on the pressure of circumstances, workload, rapport with his wife, and several other factors—will prepare himself mentally for hundreds of lovemaking experiences in the later years of life. The man who unrealistically demands that he retain the marathon capability of youth is kidding himself and invariably predisposing himself for impotence.

Research indicates that many men have engaged in lovemaking all their married lives—not so frequently in their eighties as in their seventies, of course, but hundred-year-old men have fathered children. After one Family Life Seminar a seventy-four-year-old woman asked, "How old does a man have to be before he stops wanting sex? My husband is after me every day." Her husband was eighty-one.

Research in this area has revealed that couples who are lifetime lovers have only one thing in common: not the size or shape, good looks or apparent virility of a partner, but a positive mental attitude. The man who starts making love to his wife expects to see it through to completion; one who anticipates failure will invariably confront it. Someone has said, "There are two kinds of people, those who think they can and those who think they can't—and they are both right." This is particularly true of male potency.

7. *Obesity.* There is nothing glamorous about obesity, either to others or to the overweight man himself. Rolls of fat do nothing to stimulate self-confidence, which is essential for potency. When a man lets himself get severely overweight, he loses self-respect, is embarrassed to see himself undressed, and even more important, is usually ashamed to let his wife see him that way. The

more he rejects his appearance, the more he assumes that his wife finds him repugnant. Instead of calling her "honey" or "sweetheart," he begins to use such epithets as "mamma" or "mother," and lovemaking drops to zero.

Spencer, a fifty-five-year-old man thirty pounds over his normal weight, complained of a "lack of sex drive." Besides showing him the need for more discipline in his spiritual life (more faithful church attendance, regular Bible study, walking in the Spirit, and learning to share his faith in Christ), I recommended that he visit his family doctor and commence a weight-reduction program. When he came in two weeks later, he brought his wife. Already he showed improvement. He had lost seven pounds and proudly told of "taking his belt up one notch," but he still had not tried lovemaking. During that session I quickly detected that he called his wife "mother"; they had raised three sons and Spencer explained that he had just "gotten into the habit."

Most people underestimate the importance of words. Scientists tell us that language establishes mental images that affect the subconscious mind. The word *mother* in our culture conveys dignity, respect, honor, purity, and many wholesome thoughts. However, it almost never is sexually stimulating. In my opinion one of the worst habits a middle-aged man can initiate is to call his wife "mother." In marriage it does nothing to ignite either the wife or the husband. Although it may be the result of a subconscious habit of many years standing, it nevertheless puts the husband in the role of son instead of head, leader, provider. I am convinced that if a man calls his wife "mother" long enough, eventually he will subconsciously begin to think of her in that role—and she will come to envision herself that way. I always recommend that a husband return to the use of those endearing titles for his wife that he used during courtship days. It frequently returns an excitement to what has developed into a "comfortable relationship."

By the third interview Spencer reported "a miracle in our marriage. We have made love twice!" Obviously it wasn't a world record, but after almost five years of "nothing," it was a good start. Do not rush things when seeking to overcome impotency. Like other organs or muscles of the body, the sexual organs build up a capability to work in proportion to repeated and effective exercise. It is better to enjoy one fulfilling experience per week at first, since one success leads to another. One accomplishment out of two attempts may be improvement, but it doesn't do nearly so much for the subconscious mind as a string of weekly successes. Besides, a week's anticipation after a successful ejaculation helps make it easier to achieve the next time.

The last time I talked to him about his love life, Spencer (now in his sixties) not only has lost most of his extra weight, but admitted, "I feel great, and our love life is better now than it has been in fifteen or twenty years." When I asked if he had suffered any recurrences of impotence, he replied, "Once in a while, but now I realize it is just one of those things that happen, so I don't become discouraged. I just try to concentrate better the next time." A psychiatrist couldn't have said it better.

Any man fifteen pounds or more overweight ought to see his doctor and inaugurate a weight-reducing program. When he realizes that excessive weight could (though it doesn't always) interfere with his potency, he will be more motivated to stay on a diet. Obesity lowers all vital energies and is hazardous to the health, so normally it will reduce a man's natural sex drive.

8. *Poor physical fitness.* God told Adam, "By the sweat of your brow you will eat your food" (Gen. 3:19). In Western countries today life is often too sedentary. As people become more experienced and skilled at their jobs, their work becomes less physical and more mental. Consequently sweating is not so common as it once was, and people do not get the physical exercise they need. When a man loses his muscle tone, he forfeits vital energies and self-confidence. We have already seen how that produces a loss in sex drive. Every healthy man should stay fit, but that takes discipline—and discipline demands motivation. Many men have reported that regular jogging, exercise, or other forms of physical conditioning have improved their sex drive. Just that possibility ought to motivate a man.

9. *Heavy smoking.* Some years ago an issue of *Reader's Digest* carried an article entitled, "Is Your Sex Life Going Up in Smoke?" According to Dr. Alton Ochsner, senior consultant to the Ochsner Foundation Hospital in New Orleans, who is quoted in the article, "It is estimated that tobacco use kills about 360,000 people a year in this country." Some German doctors discovered that smoking lowered the level of testosterone production, making fertilization more difficult. In fact, childless men have fathered children after giving up smoking. The article further quotes Dr. Ochsner:

> "I've had literally dozens of patients tell me, almost as an afterthought, that after they quit smoking, their sex lives improved." He likes to tell about a 73-year-old man, a heavy smoker for 45 years, who had a lung abscess removed. "I

told him he had to stop smoking, so he did. Two months later, the lung had healed completely. Before he stopped smoking, he told me, he's had sexual relations once every four to six months. Now it's three to four times a week."

Joel Fort, M.D., director of San Francisco's Center for Solving Special Social and Health Problems, which helps people both to overcome the cigarette habit and to deal with sexual maladjustments, automatically counsels smokers who complain of impotence to enroll in the center's stop-smoking clinic. The overwhelming majority of men who do so, says Dr. Fort, report their sex lives markedly improved. He gives the same advice to women who complain of lack of interest in sex.

Dr. Fort theorizes that smoking impairs sexual performance in two primary ways: the carbon-monoxide intake reduces the blood oxygen level and impairs hormone production; the nicotine intake constricts the blood vessels, the swelling of which is the central mechanism of sexual excitement and erection. Dr. Fort also cites secondary effects of heavy smoking: lung capacity is reduced, cutting back on stamina and the ability to "last" during intercourse; nicotine discolors the teeth and taints the breath, reducing the smoker's sexual attractiveness.[1]

In conclusion, the article makes another statement by Dr. Ochsner.

"The ironic thing is that many men don't recognize they have a libido problem until after they quit smoking, and then they realize what they've been missing. It just seems sad to wait until you're 73 to make this discovery."[2]

10. *Mental pressure.* Many men are single-minded. Their brains seem capable of only one job or interest at a time. For that reason, thinking of the mental pressures at work can interrupt their concentration at a crucial moment, causing the penis to go limp. If the truth were known, we would probably find that just such a break in concentration at a time of fatigue is the primary cause of that first bad experience with impotence. From then on, all it takes to wipe out a man is fear that it will recur.

A Spirit-controlled Christian should not have this problem. He learns to "cast all his anxieties" on the Lord, not take them to his marriage bed. God intends for His children to "lie down ... in peace" (Ps. 4:8). A relaxed mind is far more conducive to lovemaking than one filled with the anxieties and cares of the world. This accounts for the fact that many an impotent man has performed nobly by just taking his wife to a motel for a weekend vacation.

11. *Depression.* Counselors agree that depression is the emotional epidemic of our times. One writer has labeled the seventies "the Decade of Depression." In my book *How to Win Over Depression*,[3] I noted that one of the symptoms of depression is a loss of sex drive. A man who encounters frequent periods of depression should read carefully through that book, for I am convinced no one need succumb to depression. Once he is rid of depression, his normal sex drive will return.

12. *Drugs and alcohol.* Since the 1950s the use of drugs has risen at an alarming rate. Somehow people have the misconception that anything can be solved by chemistry. What few realize is that while they treat one symptom, another problem often arises. It is no accident that impotence and drug use have increased during the

same period. Only recently have researchers been will-ing to face the fact that they can be related. "Uppers" or "downers," appetite-control pills, marijuana, and heroin may make a person feel better for a time or even be a help to him in one area of life, but they can also have an adverse effect on the sex drive. The problem may not surface in youth, but several middle-aged men have indi-cated that their first sexual malfunction occurred when they were taking drugs. A frequent problem stems from overuse of diet pills or tranquilizers prescribed by a doctor.

The harder drugs produce even harsher results. Some Vietnam veterans who had been heroin addicts remained completely impotent long after withdrawal from the drug. Psychiatrists indicate, however, that after a reasonable time the problem is more psychological than physical. The impotence of drug users among the young has been well publicized, and thousands of men in their twenties are needlessly impotent. The wife of a converted drug addict in his mid-forties, freed from drugs for several years, indicated that her husband had made love to her only "a handful of times in the last eight years, and he hasn't touched me in the last five." It is difficult for those who enjoy lovemaking to under-stand why a person would sacrifice the ecstasy of the act of marriage for a trip on drugs. That alone would make it "a bitter pill to swallow."

A great deal of confusion exists concerning the effects of alcohol on a person's sex drive. Some consider it a stimulant, because it removes inhibitions and moral restraints. My view from the counseling room suggests that this is more true in women than in men. However, alcohol chemically is always a sedative, never a stimu-lant. It may increase a man's desire for sex but decrease or destroy his ability to maintain an erection. Two other factors are involved: the amount of alcohol consumed and the variety of its effects on the individual. Some people react one way, others quite another. It seems to me that heavy drinking frequently leads to impotence. I have yet to deal with a male alcoholic with a normal sex drive.

Several years ago I was pleading with a successful young banker to accept Christ, but he refused. His beautiful wife was a dedicated Christian and did her best to win him, but she lost the battle to the bottle. As he rose in influence at the bank, he was exposed to more and more social drinking; today he is a regional vice president at fifty years of age and a thorough-going alcoholic. His wife confided, "At his request we sleep in separate bedrooms. We have not had relations for more than ten years." His love for alcohol has made him a loser in this life and ostensibly in the life to come.

An attractive woman who attended my Bible study class in Washington, D.C., confided that her husband, who owned his own auto body shop, had not made love to her in eight years. Now at fifty-eight he is completely addicted to the bottle. It is really humiliating for a woman to realize that her husband finds alcohol more appealing than she. Her experience is not rare today as more people are losing the battle to alcohol and drugs, which are definitely sexual demotivators, particularly in men fifty and over.

Sometimes certain medications prescribed by a doctor will produce impotence as a side effect. When a man's first problem with impotence has been preceded by a newly prescribed medication, he should consult his physician.

As men grow older it is not uncommon for their blood pressure to go up. Their doctor will usually prescribe an appropriate medication for this. Unfortunately, however, one of the side effects of the most common blood-pressure medicine is a lessening of men's sex drive. This usually comes at a time in life when their sex drive may already be getting tentative, and in some cases they may begin having trouble maintaining an erection. (And one thing absolutely necessary for good sexual relations is a rigid penis.) Unless the blood pressure is dangerously high, it might be better for men over fifty (when this malady becomes most common) to be honest with their doctor about the side effects and urge him to prescribe a weight-reduction program if necessary. He should also begin an exercise program (with his doctor's approval) and consult some of the many nutritional aids that are available in health-food stores. Often, when middle-aged men notice the first signs of impotence, they are motivated to begin a drive to improve their general good health. I have seen men who never maintained any semblance of self-discipline in their lives do so for the first time when they are motivated by the desire to lengthen their years of enjoyable sex.

One of my close friends is among the nation's leading specialists on physical fitness. He agrees that far too many men, because of poor nutrition and lack of physical fitness, accept impotence long before necessary. After long conversations with him on the ski slopes and talks with other doctor friends, I am convinced that the human body is a living, breathing machine. If you put junk into it and neglect to exercise it properly, you will experience an early decline in many of its important functions.

Recently I had my annual physical exam at the Aerobics Center in Dallas, Texas. When I came out to my car, I noticed someone's bumper sticker that read, "Joggers do it longer." Maybe that's why so many men are jogging these days. If so, it's worth the effort!

13. *Masturbation.* One of the first questions I ask when a man consults me about the problem of impotence is whether or not he masturbates. Not surprisingly, many who rarely make love to their wives use this infantile method of sexual gratification, and a great deal of literature in recent years condones this psychologically damaging habit. I can understand why humanistically oriented psychologists and psychiatrists may endorse it, but it is difficult to comprehend why some Christian counselors are willing to regard it as a blessing instead of a potentially psychologically harmful habit actuated by sinful thought processes.

Until about forty years ago, masturbation was regarded as harmful to one's health. Young boys had nightmares over the suggested evils that would befall them for indulging in this practice. Now that medical science has proved that it is not harmful physically, popular opinion tends to accept it as a legitimate sexual function. But this does not take into account either the guilt that almost always follows it or the fact that a husband is defrauding his wife contrary to the Scripture (1 Cor. 7:5). Moreover, the Bible says, "It is better to marry than to burn with passion" (v. 9), not "It is better to masturbate than to burn with passion." Masturbation is a thief of love. A married man should never cheat his wife and himself out of the mutual blessing of sexual union because of masturbation. This is particularly true for the man having problems with sexual malfunction;

he requires all the help he can get to recover his sexual confidence. The last thing such a man needs is to drain off his sex drive with this childish method of self-gratification.

Any man who can successfully masturbate is not impotent. The fact that he can masturbate at least proves his capability. True, he won't fear rejection, and it may be easier to bring himself to orgasm because he knows his most sensitive erotic areas—but it is still wrong. Actually, it is a cop-out, an action of selfishness. A woman needs to be assured of her husband's love. If he showers his attention on himself, it is always at the expense of his wife. Instead of demonstrating his love for his wife in the God-ordained act of marriage, he shows his love for himself through masturbation.

Through the years I have counseled couples in which the unfulfilled wife has openly accused her husband of masturbating instead of making love to her. In several instances it was a too forceful wife and a too sensitive husband who could point to times he did approach her only to be rebuffed or rejected. Most men find it difficult to accept sexual rejection, and some resort to bitterness and some to masturbation. It has been my policy to excuse the wife at that point and explain to the husband that as he grows older his reproductive system slows down. When he was younger, masturbating an hour or so before having sex may have been beneficial in solving his premature ejaculation problem, but after fifty he should save all his sex drive for his wife.

Then I ask for a private chat with the wife and urge her to be more sensitive to her husband's needs and try to be more seductive in the bedroom. I suggest to her things a loving Christian wife can do in the sanctity of their own love life that her husband will find sexually exciting, so that together they can work on the problem.

Now it is possible for you to learn many of those suggestions from this book.

14. *A sagging vagina.* In the previous chapter we dealt at length with the problem of an excessively relaxed vagina. Any woman who has given birth to children could have this problem. The muscles around the vagina that keep it firm and sensitive begin to sag and relax around the midpoint in life, just as do other muscles in the body. Instead of being firm and sensitive against the glans penis during lovemaking, the sagging or weakened vagina does not maintain sufficient contact to provide stimulation to produce ejaculation—and often at the stage in life when the husband needs more friction instead of less. This problem explains why some men can masturbate who cannot ejaculate during lovemaking.

There are two basic remedies for this problem— the exercises recommended in the previous chapter and a relatively new form of minor surgery that is becoming increasingly popular. In either case, when a couple suspects that a sagging or weakened vagina has created a problem in their love life, the wife should see a gynecologist for an examination. However, it is advisable to try the Kegel exercises diligently for at least three months before consenting to surgery.

15. *Passive wife.* Practically every man has dreamed of having a sexually aggressive wife. No matter how lofty his ideals of womanhood, a husband often fantasizes his wife as a sexual ball of fire in bed. Unfortunately most women maintain a mental image of their role as passive. One wife said, "I've always thought he would lose respect for me if I did anything sexually aggressive." To

be truthful, a man finds it ecstatically stimulating when his wife approaches him. It makes him think she wants and needs his lovemaking. That helps to inflate his male ego, whereas passivity leads to boredom, and boredom to impotence.

Few sexually vigorous wives have impotent husbands. The only exceptions I have found are those who became aggressive only after their husbands began to encounter impotence problems. The fact that they cannot have normal intercourse may increase their aggression, but this tends to create resentment in the husband, who vividly recalls the many times he approached his wife earlier in marriage only to find that she either rejected him or was so passive that he felt she was "just going along with the wifely ritual." Most of the time men enjoy being the aggressor in love, but no man wants to make love to a "cadaver," and at times he likes to know that his wife enjoys it as much as he does.

16. *Nagging.* Nothing turns a man off faster than nagging! That overworked art does nothing for a relationship—except destroy masculinity and sex drive. It absolutely must be avoided! Some women have to guard against this habit more than others. Those who reflect a melancholic temperament doubtless have to watch their tongues, because melancholic people are perfectionists and naturally find it easy to criticize the actions of others. A man's passionate emotions can be turned to ice in a moment through nagging and criticism.

A doctor friend once reviewed an extreme case of nagging. The husband he counseled was impotent at the age of thirty-six. The only clue he could find was the wife's habit of chattering during lovemaking. She had little difficulty reaching an orgasm, after which she would start talking—usually making some minor critical observation, something that would distract him—and he would lose his erection. Fear of another failure made it more likely that he would malfunction. All it took to solve their problem was for her to be aware of his needs at that moment.

17. *Feminine dominance.* Next to nagging, nothing is less pleasing to a husband than a domineering wife. (It turns children off too.) There is just nothing feminine about a domineering woman. Choleric women (who often marry phlegmatic men) particularly need to beware of this problem. They frequently mistake the husband's quiet acquiescence for agreement; if he is slow of speech, he will usually give in rather than fight or argue. This creates resentment, and we have already traced the results of that response. Any wife with a problem of this kind needs to pursue a Bible study on Ephesians 5:17–24 and 1 Peter 3:1–7, then ask God to give her submissive grace.

The next two problems are not, strictly speaking, forms of impotence. But they are often dealt with in relation to impotence problems, and it seems best to include them in a discussion of the subject.

18. *Premature ejaculation.* Described as the inability to withhold ejaculation long enough to bring one's wife to climax 50 percent of the time, this difficulty plagues young men more than the middle-aged. Simply stated, it involves ejaculating too soon. Men afflicted with this problem are poor lovers and usually have unsatisfied wives. They tend to ejaculate with the slightest friction of the glans penis either before or just after entering the vagina. This form of impotence can often be traced to heavy petting as a teenager, which may end in ejaculation

with clothes on or may culminate in hurried intercourse in a by-the-hour motel or in a parked car where there is fear of interruption. (See also pages 141–3.)

The Cure for Premature Ejaculation

The most common remedy for premature ejaculation is for the husband to avoid any unnecessary friction on the glans penis immediately after entrance. This of course takes great self-discipline, because at that high point of excitement his instincts motivate him to a deep thrusting action. This instinctive movement is nature's method of depositing the male sperm deep into the vagina where the possibility of its fertilizing the female egg is greatest. Actually that seemingly universal instinct is not the best method of producing female satisfaction, for recent studies seem to indicate that it actually works against it. That is, a woman tends to respond more to very gentle movements than to deep thrusting. Some women, for example, find that their tension buildup drops off after their husband's thrusting action starts, but again begins to build when he slows down and moves from side to side. In fact, if she develops her P.C. muscles, she can actually bring herself to orgasm by contracting these muscles several times on his motionless penis.

Therefore, if the husband will maintain a motionless position for about two minutes *immediately* after entrance, he will gain a degree of control that will retard his ejaculation. And if the wife will pinch his penis with her P.C. muscles during this motionless period, her emotional tension will build toward climax while his is dormant. Then, when her husband gains control of his ejaculation, they can begin the thrusting that will bring them both to climax.

It is also helpful if the husband avoids rough, forceful penetration and remembers that the first two to three inches inside the vagina constitute his wife's primary sensitive area. Once the penis goes beyond that point, it can become uncomfortable to the wife rather than stimulating. Men have a tendency to think that deep thrusting is exciting to their wives because it is to them—but that is not generally true unless at the same time they use other more gentle motions that stimulate the wife's clitoral area. Concentrating their motion closer to the opening of the vagina, then, has two advantages over deep penetration: it is more exciting to the wife and less exciting to the husband, further helping him to control his ejaculation while she builds toward orgasm.

One husband's reaction to this suggestion is rather typical. "I thought it was essential for my penis to maintain a close contact with the clitoris." Although the clitoris is the most sexually sensitive organ, the first three inches of the vagina contain sensitive tissue, and besides, that position continues the friction and pulling of structures against the clitoris. This method makes use of both sensitive areas together. Another advantage of this method is that when the husband realizes he is approaching his point of no return, he can easily slip his penis out momentarily, continue caressing the clitoris and in other ways petting his wife, then return the penis into her vagina after regaining his control. If he is deep-thrusting when the "no return" point is reached, the friction caused by withdrawal may trigger his ejaculation.

The concentration it takes to learn this technique—providing the husband with the degree of control he needs while at the same time building the wife's tension through muscular vaginal pinching of the motionless penis—pays big dividends in mutual pleasure. Most men fail to remain motionless for two full minutes at that point of excitement. Once he is inside the vagina, a man's instincts cry out for motion, but this drive must be resisted until he gains self-mastery. After the first motionless period, the husband can experiment as to how long subsequent pauses are needed to control ejaculation, but this technique can help him learn to resist his ejaculation almost indefinitely. During some tests men have claimed such self-mastery for over two hours, though this would almost never be necessary to please his wife.

In May 1994 a report given at the American Urological Association meeting in San Francisco indicated that some medical help may be available to retard ejaculation for men who have this problem. According to an article in *U.S. News and World Report* (June 26, 1995) in fifteen couples aged twenty-three to fifty-six, clomipramine delayed ejaculation as much as fivefold. If true, any man afflicted with the problem of premature ejaculation should consult his urologist.

19. *Retarded ejaculation.* The opposite of premature ejaculation, this problem confronts a man who has no difficulty maintaining a rigid penis, but cannot proceed to ejaculation. This is frustrating to both husband and wife. Although the wife of such a man has little trouble achieving an orgasm (some have as many as four or five in one session), she finishes the exercise worn out, and he is frustrated. This form of sexual failure can result from a number of things, two of which are fear of pregnancy, because of uncertainty about the birth-control measures used, and guilt induced by promiscuity prior to marriage. This problem is rare. When a man reaches his sixties or seventies, he may not ejaculate every time

during intercourse, but doctors tell us this is normal. Both partners must understand this and simply enjoy each intercourse without feeling any pressure to force an orgasm every time.

The Cure for Retarded Ejaculation

No mechanical device or technique will cure the man who faces the problem of retarded ejaculation. Although quite rare, it is nevertheless a source of unhappiness to both the overwrought husband and his worn-out wife when, after an hour or two of intercourse, the husband cannot relieve his tension by ejaculation. Since this malady is caused by the mind, it must be cured there. Psychologists suggest that the problem is created by a subconscious resistance to giving his sperm to his wife. This can be a form of selfishness and probably indicates that the man is not generous in other areas of his marriage. If such is the case, he needs to repent of his selfishness and concentrate on the joy of giving pleasure to his wife instead of trying to gain it only for himself. Another cause of this problem could be a resentment toward women because of a bitter spirit toward his mother. The cure for this mental sin has already been suggested under guilt removal.

These nineteen factors are the main reasons for male impotence. Only occasionally is the problem caused by one of these factors singly, but it takes little imagination to understand how several of them occurring at once can create it. Before a man gives up on the blessing of sexual union that God intended him to enjoy most of his life, he should objectively examine his relationship;

if he is suspicious that even one of these conditions exists, he should work toward its elimination.

Did you notice something missing in the above list? We said almost nothing about physical or biological causes. They are so rare that they are scarcely worth considering, even though they constitute the excuse most frequently given. Doctors, ministers, counselors, psychiatrists, and especially formerly impotent men believe that most impotence exists in the head—not in the glands! If the problem persists, however, see your doctor. Some men have developed a hormone deficiency that may cause impotence; it responds very well to male hormone shots, so it is well worth investigating.

Is There a Cure for Impotence?

Male impotence is not new, for it has doubtless plagued some men and their wives ever since the fall of man. However, the cure for this malady is new, primarily because today greater understanding and greater willingness to face the problem work wonders. No difficulty can be resolved without honesty and frankness. Having faced it with candor, we can then review the numerous potential cures and expect one of them to effect complete renewal. Naturally some work better than others, and the cure should be tailored to the cause.

The Remedy for Guilt

We have already seen that guilt, fear, anger, depression, and an unforgiving or bitter spirit can contribute to impotence. If any one of these is the cause, you should not seek relief through new methods or physiological techniques. Instead, turn to God through His Son Jesus Christ to gain the forgiveness He offers to sinners. The first step is to confess your sins in the name of Jesus Christ. First John 1:9 tells us, "If we confess our sins, he is faithful and just and will forgive us our sins and purify us from all unrighteousness." The next step is to walk under the control of His Spirit as a means of overcoming these negative emotions. This removes the roadblocks to emotional expression and will contribute greatly to satisfying love experiences with your spouse. Once you have resolved your spiritual problems, you are ready to find a cure for the others.

We have cited the remedies for each of the various causes of impotence. Study carefully those that particularly pertain to you and follow the corrective steps suggested.

Anticipate Success

In almost every case a man can guarantee a cure for his impotence if he changes his mental attitude toward the problem. Instead of thinking he is "the same as dead," he needs to recognize that his experiences are basically normal and *will be overcome*. He should first consult with his doctor, who will probably give him a good physical examination. Once assured that nothing is organically wrong, he can more readily anticipate success. The expectation of accomplishment is absolutely essential! The man who considers himself impotent is going to remain impotent. The man who visualizes himself potent will be capable of performing well.

The next step is for a man to have an honest talk with his wife, sharing his problem with her. Most wives will be very understanding and cooperative. One man who "had not made love in five years" was amazed at his wife's reaction. Having mistaken his disinterest as lack of love for her, she changed after their discussion from a nagging, insecure wife to a sexually stimulating partner. Men commonly underestimate their wives' ability to accept such a problem maturely. Ignorance of the problem, however, does nothing but complicate matters.

What Can a Wife Do to Help?

Next to changing his own mental attitude toward impotence, a man can find in his wife the most powerful medicine available. Among other things, a wife can—

—Accept the problem as a challenge that takes two to overcome. She should never do or say anything to aggravate her husband's sexual fears as previously outlined, suggesting that he is inadequate, inept, or undesirable. She must be careful about jokes or kidding that might accentuate his fears. Someone has sagely said in this regard, "A man's sense of humor quits at his belt buckle."

—Become sexually aggressive. For most of their marriage, a woman has expected her husband to "carry the ball"; now it is time for her to hurry onto the playing field and call some of the plays. If sexual inhibitions make it difficult for her or cause it to seem degrading, it is because she is more interested in herself than in her husband. Two things usually happen when a wife becomes more uninhibited in her sexual expression: she is transformed into a more exciting and stimulating partner to her husband, and she increases her own enjoyment in the relationship.

After a few months of marriage most lovemaking becomes much too routine. The partners begin the same way, assume the same positions, make the same sounds, and share the same experiences. It is time to get out of those ruts and become aggressive. What man will remain impotent who enters his bedroom to find the lights down low, soft music playing, an open bed, and a scantily clad wife whose every movement indicates her eagerness to get her hands on him? If you really want to turn him on, help unbutton his shirt and clothes. Let him sense your excitement. I know, some who read this will ask, "But isn't that hypocritical?" Not at all! You may be accustomed to letting your inhibitions squelch your real desires and thus hardly know how to react naturally. That is worse hypocrisy, and you have probably been doing it for years. If you really love your husband, you will thoroughly enjoy the reaction you get from him. When you are aggressive toward him, he will interpret it to mean that you find him sexually attractive. And when he considers himself attractive to you, it is easier for him to believe in his sexual capability.

A loving, middle-aged wife whose husband had started to battle the problem of impotence noticed that when she was sexually aggressive, her husband had little trouble ejaculating. "However," she admitted hesitantly, "even though I enjoy it, I feel guilty." I explained that her guilt was misplaced; God approves such loving behavior. She responded, "But I didn't think a lady would act that way." To this I replied, "She wouldn't—in church or in a parked car—but the sanctity of her own bedroom is quite different." One of the advantages of my being a pastor as well as a counselor is that I can more easily dispel such unfounded cases of unnecessary guilt. A minister is often regarded as a spokesman for God—which he is if his words are based on biblical principles. In chapter 1 we dealt extensively with the matter of a woman's sexuality; remember that 1 Corinthians 7:1–5 clearly says a husband's body belongs to his wife.

Accordingly, she can do with it as she wishes. That should certainly include exciting him sexually.

A thoughtful wife should keep in mind that a man tends to find a sexually passive wife somewhat demotivating, whereas he finds an aggressive wife terribly stimulating. More than one wife has discovered that she can arouse her husband by artfully stroking his skin and massaging his body, by very lightly touching his genital organs. Even the limp penis will often respond to a wife's tender loving strokes, especially at the scrotum and inner thighs. Remember to use light, teasing, gentle caresses, which stimulate the imagination.

Probably the best service a wife can perform for an impotent husband is to concentrate on the vaginal exercises outlined in the previous chapter. Once he begins to encounter difficulty in maintaining an erection or ejaculating, he should not have to compound his problem with a wife who lacks strong vaginal muscles. He requires an increase of friction, not a decrease. When she develops these otherwise lazy muscles to such a point that she can crimp down on his penis once he is inside, she will greatly contribute toward keeping that organ hard. In addition, the increased friction can well be the "little bit extra" in their lovemaking that turns failure into success. As we have seen, a few successes will make him anticipate more of them, and when that happens he is practically cured.

Admittedly these efforts on a wife's part in helping her husband overcome impotence will take concentration, hard work, and sometimes the adoption of a new role, but if she loves him, she will pay the price—and both will share the dividends.

The Husband Is the Key

No woman can cure her husband's impotence alone. She can provide assistance, as indicated above, but this is uniquely a male crisis that he can resolve only through earnest effort. Here are some things a husband can do in addition to those previously mentioned:

1. Pray about it, preferably with your wife. The Bible says, "In all your ways acknowledge him, and he *will* make your paths straight." God has led man in amazing ways to find help for this problem. Let Him aid you.

2. See your doctor and follow his advice.

3. Talk it over honestly with your wife.

4. Read everything good that you can find on the subject. Nothing magnifies fear like ignorance, but nothing reduces fear to life-size as does knowledge. As Christians we frequently disagree with the theories and conclusions of humanistically oriented authorities, but we can uncover many helpful recommendations in their writings. Remember that all truth is God's truth. Regardless of its source, truth is truth. Einstein's theory of relativity should not be negated because the author was a humanist. In the same manner, a liberal medical treatise read with spiritual discernment may furnish prompt solutions. Unfortunately most Christian writers on human sexuality have not dealt clearly with the problem of impotence.

5. Begin a physical fitness program in accord with the advice of your doctor. Several of my friends claim that jogging increases their virility. Tests indicate that it heightens all vital energies, so their observations may well be accurate.

6. Pursue a weight-reduction program if necessary.

7. Avoid making love when you are tired. Most people fall into one of two categories: they are either "nocturnalists" (people who work best at night, but come to life around 10 A.M.) or "early birds" (those who wake up with the birds but conk out about 8 or 9 P.M.). Whichever you are, attempt lovemaking when you are wide awake, for you get the most out of your glands at that time.

8. Don't rush lovemaking. The longer you anticipate it before entrance, the easier it will be to ejaculate.

Several therapists suggest that men tend to have less difficulty maintaining an erection while lying on their back during intercourse. Somehow it aids in the blood flow to their pelvic area. Consequently, if a husband and wife use the wife-above position, his erections will remain more rigid and last longer, which, of course, is the main key to mutual satisfaction. One position a couple may enjoy during much of their marriage is that of the husband on top and rising up on his knees. (This can be most pleasurable to them both). However, it may become necessary to discontinue this position and let the wife take the top position if the husband develops difficulty maintaining an erection. This is particularly true after age sixty or seventy.

9. Don't give up! Expect success. A medical doctor, David Reuben, has spent many years in the field of sexual relations and has written several best-selling books on this and related subjects. In one he sums up the problem of impotence by saying,

> *Almost* any man can overcome his impotence. There is a minority whose problems are basically physical and there is a small group who wear impotence like a badge—and wouldn't give

it up for anything. But for the majority, restoration to vigorous satisfying sexual performance only depends on their personal decision. With determination, hard work, and the love of a devoted woman virtually any man can become *and remain* dramatically potent to the age of seventy, eighty, and beyond. Most men, if they had the choice, would want it that way. The good news is: most men *have* that choice—all they have to do is exercise it.[4]

Is There Sex After Sixty?

It is obvious from the above quote by Dr. Reuben that millions of married men do indeed enjoy a normal sex life right on into their later years. Some men have fathered children in their nineties. Admittedly, not many. But good and satisfying sex is possible in the later years of life; however, as we pointed out earlier, it will not be as frequent.

Actually, satisfying sex in marriage is as frequent as the two lovers desire it. God has given us a natural sexual clock that races in our twenties and thirties, slows gradually in the forties and fifties, then slows even more in the seventies and eighties. My opportunities to interview eighty-year-olds on this subject has been somewhat limited, but the one universal comment is that, though the frequency level slows to one to four times a month, the satisfaction level tends to increase. Perhaps it is the anticipation or scarcity that makes it more enduring and valuable. Seniors tend to put higher meaning on quality whereas their juniors tend to evaluate the experience more on the basis of quantity. The important thing is that healthy married seniors, like healthy juniors, tend to get all the sex they want.

If couples have a problem in later life, usually the husband has the difficulty. One doctor friend of mine is a nutritional enthusiast who believes that because our farming soil is so depleted of its natural life-giving nutrition men over fifty should take zinc supplements regularly. He also recommends Yohimbe bark or extract for those who enjoy low blood pressure. One thing is clear, any man who has experienced difficulty maintaining an erection should go to his local health-food store and make a personal study of what nutritional helps are available to mature men whose testosterone production has slowly declined through the years. It is a subject he should discuss openly with his wife and his nutritionally informed doctor. Otherwise he may bypass years of pleasure for both his wife and himself unnecessarily. As with almost every other subject, lack of sexual pleasure is a high price to pay when a little self education, proper diet, regular exercise, and nutritional support can provide great improvement. It won't turn you into a thirty-year-old again, but it could well give you hundreds of satisfying lovemaking experiences during your golden years.

Notes

1. Genell J. Subak-Sharpe, "Is Your Sex Life Going Up in Smoke?" *Reader's Digest* 106 (January 1975), 106–7.

2. Ibid., 107.

3. Tim LaHaye (Grand Rapids: Zondervan, 1974).

4. David Reuben, *How to Get More Out of Sex* (New York: David McKay, 1974), 176.

Twelve

Sane Family Planning

A striking young couple spoke with me following a Family Life Seminar in a southern city. After introducing themselves as the full-time directors of a local youth ministry, they asked, "Is it wrong for us to avoid having children? We are so involved in the Lord's work that we don't have time for children." I responded, "Do you expect this to be a permanent or temporary condition?" They indicated that it was permanent.

The attitude of these two young people is not rare, and their kind are increasing in number today for a very simple reason. Modern science has put into the hands of humankind for the first time in history an almost foolproof method of family exclusion. In city after city, after my lectures I am set upon by the younger generation because I advocate having a family of four or five children.

In Chicago a couple attending the University of Chicago's graduate school made it very clear that I was

256

"Neanderthal" in my approach to family planning because I reaffirmed God's first commandment to humans, "Be fruitful and increase in number; fill the earth and subdue it" (Gen. 1:28). They had been so brainwashed by the humanistic family planners of our educational system that they considered avoidance of a family a patriotic service. However, I was suspicious (as I told them personally) that the real reason largely reflected selfishness. At that point the wife's anger erupted, and she revealed the extent of her humanistic brainwashing by parroting the women's libbers' line, "What do you think I am, a baby factory? I want to pursue a career."

A young minister, educated for the most part in secular schools, insisted, "Genesis 1:28 is no longer in force; the world is already overpopulated. You should be urging people to cut down on the size of their families." To this I replied, "Who says Genesis 1:28 is obsolete? God is the only one who can nullify His commands, and I know of no verse in the New Testament that negates Genesis 1:28."

Still others offer the excuse that "the day in which we live is so immoral and the world situation is so grim that we have no right to bring children into the mess we have created." That is the cry of unbelief. People who use that argument do not realize that the moral conditions of the first century under the tyranny of Rome and the Corinthian culture of the Greeks were worse than ours. Those first-century Christian children made it, and so will ours, but we must live before them the precepts by which we train them: to be obedient to the principles in God's Word and to be filled with the Holy Spirit.

Personally we do not accept responsibility for the mess this world is in. The principles of God to which we have given our lives have not created the problem; our nation's leaders' rejection of them is at fault. Not an acceptance of our Lord and Savior, but our rejection of Him has left humankind in despair. Humanistic man has repudiated God's plan for his life and for the destiny of nations; therefore he must accept full responsibility for the ensuing degradation.

Reasons for Raising Children

Before considering the rationale and methods for limiting a family, we would like to present four reasons why Christian couples should, if at all possible, have children.

1. *Children are a unique gift of eternal creativity.* God has granted to a husband and wife a unique ability, unshared by any other creature in the universe: to create another human being with a free will, an eternal soul, and the capability of passing on that unique gift to their children. Reduced to the barest of terms, a husband and wife have the ability to create an eternal person. Where that person decides to spend eternity is entirely up to him or her. In a practical way, when a Christian couple decide not to have children, they exclude a potential child from the potential blessing of eternal life as God planned for him or her. Fulfilling God's command in Genesis 1:28 solves that problem.

2. *Children provide a lifetime blessing.* The psalmist says, "Sons are a heritage from the LORD, children a reward from him. . . . Blessed is the man whose quiver is full of them" (Ps. 127:3, 5). People sometimes look on children as a "responsibility," an "expense," or an "accident," but the Bible calls them a "blessing." We would be the last to overlook the problems and sorrows involved in raising a family: we have raised four and

lost one. In the process we confronted sickness, failure, financial pressure, and almost every dilemma children and young people can create. But after forty years of marriage, we can honestly say that the joys and blessings of our children *far* outweigh any sacrifices we may have made. In fact, my wife and I agree that we encounter no greater joy than to know that our children are walking in the truth (see 3 John 4). They and our grandchildren are without question our greatest human blessings.

Someone has suggested that according to Jewish tradition, a "quiver" of arrows (Ps. 127:5) numbered five. If that is true, could it suggest that the blessing God is speaking of here included at least five children? When I performed a wedding recently, the bride told me she wanted six children: "I come from a family of six, and it was such fun growing up, I'd like six of my own."

3. *Children are a tangible expression of your love.* Far more is involved in begetting children than biology. When married partners become "one flesh," they combine their genes in a God-given way and produce a one-flesh person that merges both of them. It was God's plan, then, that children be an expression of their parents' love. Fortunate indeed are children who are regarded so by their parents; they are a "heritage" that provides a "blessing." Only parenthood enables us to see certain traits of the one we love mixed with our own in another human being.

4. *Children fulfill the psychic design of your mind.* God never commands people to do anything that does not cooperate with the function of their mind. The best way to deduce the human psychic mental mechanism is to study the commands of God in the Bible.

For He put the human mind into its psychic pattern, so that it would function best when one obeys His commands. We call that "natural." It is "natural" to marry, beget children, and become grandparents. A person's mind has to be severely warped to feel "unnatural" about fatherhood or motherhood. God has given certain instincts to the mind that function in accord with His commands—and these produce that "natural" feeling essential to a happy life. Parenthood is such an instinct. "God's grace is sufficient" for those couples who find it impossible to procreate; but the natural desire of humankind for family loving will result in a lifetime void and a lack of fulfillment for those who selfishly refuse to have children.

The chief enemy of personal happiness is self-interest. Nothing forces people to mature beyond the limitations of selfishness like being entrusted with an infant of their own. The fact that some adults never mature and even brutalize their babies does not alter the fact that, for most people, children are a blessing needed to fulfill, not only their destiny, but their lives.

One of the healthy signs of humanity in our present decaying culture is the fact that so many childless couples are actively seeking to adopt one or more children. It is a beautiful sight when a parentless, unwanted, or fatherless child, born to a teenager much too young for parenthood, is adopted by a Christian couple who have been praying for a child. We have assisted many such couples, and in every case it has resulted in the child's becoming a Christian. The right adoption experience is a life-changing experience for both the parents and the child. We enthusiastically recommend it.

Planning Your Parenthood

In view of what we have said, the reader may conclude that we reject all family planning, but this is not the case. The Bible says nothing about the number of children one should have in a given lifetime. God leaves that decision up to each couple. Personally we don't believe He is against restricting the size of one's family, but we do believe He is opposed to excluding a family altogether.

Almost all Christians today seem to believe in limiting the size of their families. Why do we say this? According to medical science, a normal woman unhindered by any form of birth control is capable of having as many as twenty children during her childbearing years. Since we have yet to meet a Christian family with twenty children, we suspect that they have utilized some method of reducing that potential number. Realistically speaking, each couple should prayerfully and thoughtfully bring into the world the number of children they can properly train to serve God, welcoming each child as a gift from Him.

For the past twenty-five years we have traveled this country, holding over eight hundred two-day Family Life Seminars in civic halls, churches, schools, and anywhere people will listen to biblical principles on family living. Over one million people have attended these seminars and other millions have read our many books on marriage and family relations, including this one. We are convinced that it is still possible to raise children to love and serve God, even in this day of graphic moral decline. But every prospective parent should realize that to do so will take more priority time and effort than it did in their parents' generation. For if they spend only the time and effort raising their children that their parents spent on them, they will not succeed as well as their parents.

Our reason for saying this is that parents of the past generation had a positive or at least a neutral culture that influenced their children. Today our official institutions like education, the media, and the entertainment industry have unprecedented access to our children's minds; and everyone knows these institutions are not controlled by those who share the traditional values of America that two generations ago were essentially based on the Bible. In fact, a good case could be made that many leaders of those agencies, based on their own products, have no moral commitment whatsoever but enjoy destroying our once-great culture. However, although the resultant hostile culture makes raising good children today more difficult, we are convinced it still can be done. That is, if the parents are willing to use the ministry of a Bible-teaching church to uphold and proclaim those moral principles that every child needs to be trained in to prepare him or her for life. Many of these principles will be found in our book *Against the Tide: How to Raise Sexually Pure Kids in an "Anything Goes" World*.[1]

All of this brings us back to the all-important question, "How many children should you have today?" Currently the national average is 1.8 children per family. Christians tend to have slightly larger families than the general population. One reason for this is that we believe children are "a heritage from the Lord" and that it is not just a matter of biology, but the two lovers are permitted by God to create another eternal soul. That is an awesome responsibility. Every couple should make up their own minds how many children they should have. We think a Christian couple should have all the children they think they can reasonably have, and with God's help raise them to love and serve Him. It is at least a twenty- to thirty-year commitment, but it can be the most enjoyable and satisfying two or three decades of life.

Methods of Birth Control

Most young couples plan some form of birth control, beginning right from their wedding night. The wise bride will select a date for her wedding day that does not coincide with her period or her highest fertility week, which is ten to fourteen days after her last period. Some young women are very regular and can set their wedding date months in advance. Others are not so fortunate and find their body cycle changes after the invitations are sent out. Generally speaking, she will find that her safe days are one week before her period until five days afterward. During the rest of her monthly cycle she is vulnerable to pregnancy.

Today most young couples prefer a few months to become more familiar with each other before starting a family. Others, because of educational or other such considerations, may want to delay even longer. Unfortunately, the tendency in our day is for couples to wait until the wife is beyond the physically ideal years for childbirth, which are usually eighteen to twenty-seven. That does not mean that women cannot safely have children after the age of thirty and even forty, of course. But as your doctor has probably told you, if complications arise in the birth process, they are more likely to appear if you delay childbirth. We are convinced that God intended *young* adults to bear children when their bodies and nerves are best able to cope with them. We could, of course, be biased in that assessment since all four of our children were born before Beverly was twenty-nine years old. The benefits are that we were young enough to be able to enjoy them and their children. Our grandchildren like to brag to their friends that they can still snow ski and water ski with both their parents and grandparents. Such are only some of the blessings of young parenting.

Birth control is a very personal decision, one of the first a young couple should have settled before their wedding day. Some people, for religious reasons, do not believe in contraceptives. We respect that and feel each couple should be convinced in their own minds what is the best plan for them. We recommend a joint visit to the doctor and the self-study necessary for the couple to become fully informed on the subject. If they do nothing, they will likely become early parents—and, as we have implied above, that can be a great blessing.

Ours is one of the first generations that has had near failure-proof means of limiting family size. As early as the 1500s, attempts were made to sheathe the penis to keep the semen from surging into the vagina on ejaculation. This concept was not popular because the sheaths used were so thick they almost eliminated sensation. In the twentieth century many advances were made, particularly the use of rubber condoms, which is probably the most common form used today.

New methods are continually being developed and sold as preventions of conception. However, some forms of "contraception," such as the IUD and RU486, are actually abortifacients; that is, they do not prevent conception, but rather destroy life after conception. We, of course, cannot recommend such procedures. In addition, there are two kinds of birth-control procedures that should be considered—reversible and irreversible. We definitely do not believe young couples should consider irreversible procedures until they are absolutely certain they have all the children they feel led of God to raise to serve Him. The following are listed in the order we recommend them.

1. *The Pill.* The most effective is the pill—between one and five pregnancies for every thousand users.

It is estimated that fifteen to twenty million women in the United States are on the pill. When it first came out, the number of adverse side effects reported made many women reluctant to use it. But modern research has reduced many of these by discovering that a milder dosage is just as effective and is safer for use over a long period. Statistically the pill is less hazardous to life and health than smoking, driving, or swimming.

About one-fourth the size of a standard aspirin tablet, the pill must be prescribed by a physician. Different kinds require one tablet daily for twenty, twenty-one, or twenty-eight consecutive days each month. When the tablets are taken as directed, it is believed that they control ovulation, for no egg has ripened. Thus sperm may freely enter the oviducts without the possibility of conception occurring. In this way the oral tablet provides the advantage of protection at all times.

Because of its safety and simplicity, we consider the pill the preferred method for a new bride in the early stages of marriage. Then, after she and her husband have both learned the art of married love, she may decide on some other method. We suggest that she see her doctor at least two months prior to her wedding and follow his advice carefully.

2. *Condom with cream or foam.* When used in conjunction with a contraceptive jelly, cream, or foam, the condom has produced less than ten pregnancies per thousand women and is quite inexpensive.

The condom, often referred to as a prophylactic, pro, sheath, or rubber, is the world's most often used artificial method for conception control.

The condom has many advantages. It is available at drugstores without a medical prescription, it is free from side effects, visible proof of effectiveness is available immediately after intercourse, it is simple and easy to use, and it places the responsibility for birth control on the husband, which some wives consider a distinct advantage.

Certain drawbacks are normally ascribed to the condom. First, it may reduce sensation to the penis, but for many couples this is an advantage in helping to delay the husband's ejaculation; second, it is an interruption to sexual foreplay, but this objection can be easily overcome with the right attitudes when the wife lovingly places the condom on her husband's penis as an erotic part of sexual foreplay; third, there is discomfort to the wife without some lubrication, but this may be resolved through the purchase of lubricated condoms hermetically sealed or the use of contraceptive jelly for lubricating, which serves a double purpose by affording added safety. Do not use petroleum-base lubricant, for this may be harmful to rubber. It is usually good to put a small amount of the lubricant inside the condom to provide lubrication directly to the head of the penis. There is the possibility of having a defective device, perhaps a minute, undetectable pinhole in the condom. However, even with such a pinhole, there would be less than one in three million chances for a pregnancy resulting from this small imperfection.

Many couples do not know that they may purchase a high-grade latex rubber condom and reuse it many times by simply washing it thoroughly with soap and water, drying with a towel, then powdering it with talcum powder or cornstarch and inspecting it thoroughly by blowing it up like a balloon and holding it up to a good diffused light. If no flaws appear, slip the condom onto the first and second fingers and, with these fingers spread apart, roll it up just as it was originally.

In summary, the condom continues to be the world's most widely used and universally understood method of contraception. When properly used, it is quite effective—but not perfect even when used correctly. It has been estimated that three out of one hundred wives who use condoms properly for one year get pregnant. Assuming two lovemaking experiences a week during that time, that would mean three pregnancies for over ten thousand uses—admittedly, a pretty safe procedure *if* used correctly. Unfortunately, many couples use a combination of *coitus interruptus* and the condom. That is, to assure sensitivity and feeling, they wait until they have almost reached orgasm, withdraw, and then slip on a condom. What they do not realize is that even before ejaculation the penis can secrete seminal fluid containing some sperm. The husband may dutifully withdraw, place the condom on his penis, and not realize that some sperm may already be on its way to his wife's fallopian tubes, where she can be impregnated. Obviously, such a procedure, which is more common than most people think, is not the fault of the condom but of the user. In addition, even when done properly the man must be careful afterward to make sure he grips the mouth of the condom to assure that no semen gets into his wife's vagina. Sperm cells are incredibly active.

3. *Diaphragm.* The vaginal diaphragm is a strong, lightweight rubber cap somewhat smaller than the palm of the hand. It was the first medically accepted contraceptive, developed over eighty years ago. The thin rim of the diaphragm is made of a ring-shaped, rubber-covered metal spring. Because the spring is flexible, the whole diaphragm can be compressed and passed easily into the vagina. It is then released in the upper widening canal of the vagina, where it covers the cervix like a dome-shaped lid.

The distance from the back wall of the vagina to the pubic bone varies from woman to woman. For this reason, diaphragms are made in a variety of sizes. During a pelvic examination that offers no discomfort to the woman, the doctor must measure this distance in order to select the proper diaphragm for her. As properly instructed by the physician, the diaphragm must be inserted prior to intercourse, preferably several hours before intercourse. If the diaphragm fits properly, neither mate should be aware of its presence.

The diaphragm acts as a barrier or deflector, preventing sperm from entering the uterus, but to be effective, it must be covered on the side next to the cervix with a spermicidal jelly or cream made for this purpose. If extra lubrication is desired during intercourse, choose a jelly; if extra lubrication is not needed, select a contraceptive cream. The spermicidal preparations are placed on the diaphragm to kill all sperm on contact, and we must emphatically warn you that the diaphragm is almost worthless without a spermicidal preparation.

You may be able to use the same diaphragm for many years if you find no flaws in it.

The diaphragm is a well-established, proven method that affords many women the security of the physical barrier in addition to the spermicide. The diaphragm has no effect on future fertility.

4. *Vaginal foam.* Vaginal foam, containing spermicides, has been used for over sixty years. It allows about seventy-six pregnancies per thousand women and costs very little.

Spermicidal products used by themselves for the control of conception contain chemicals that, when placed in the vagina, will kill sperm without harming the delicate vaginal tissue. These products, available in three forms—foams, cream, and a synthetic gel—are applied with a slim, plastic vaginal applicator that automatically measures the proper amount. They are so effective that only one application is required before each act of intercourse, and the woman need not douche after its use. In fact, she should wait at least six hours if she douches at all. Foams are significantly more effective than rhythm, withdrawal, suppositories, or douching. Many women have found this method to be safe, effective, and reliable.

5. *Rhythm method.* The oldest and now least effective method of birth control is the rhythm method. It produces about 140 pregnancies per thousand women. We often jokingly note in our family lectures that "the people who use the rhythm method are called parents." The cost of the rhythm method is upwards of $1000 per pregnancy, but it yields the wonderful blessing of children. We suspect that it is so ineffective because couples

find the self-control required to follow it almost impossible to maintain.

The rhythm method for controlling conception requires abstinence from intercourse during the days just after ovulation. It attempts to avoid conception by permitting sperm to be present in the woman only when the ripened egg is thought to be absent. No product is used in this method.

Ovulation may be predicted in two ways. The first is called the temperature technique, in which the wife takes her temperature before arising each morning. A slight drop in temperature, followed by a substantial rise, usually indicates that ovulation has occurred about the time of the decrease. This procedure must be carefully followed for many months, for only after a series of consecutive months of recorded body temperatures can a fairly valid prediction of the time of ovulation be made.

The second method for predicting ovulation requires a record of the wife's menstrual cycles for at least eight months or, ideally, one year. This means that she must keep track of her menstrual flow on a calendar—thus the appellation "the calendar technique." A formula can then be applied to this information to determine the days on which ovulation is most likely to take place.

Ovulation most often occurs about two weeks prior to the beginning of the menstrual period. A woman with a regular twenty-eight-day cycle will therefore ovulate about the fourteenth day. Allowing three days before and three days after ovulation to include the time when both the egg and the sperm are still alive, the fertile or unsafe days would last from about the eleventh through the eighteenth days. From the eighteenth day on, no egg would be present to be fertilized, and thus conception would not normally take place. The days before the eleventh day are also believed to be safe, but this is much less certain because of the length of time the sperm cells may remain alive within the woman.

From the recorded menstrual cycle information, eighteen is subtracted from the number of days in the shortest cycle and eleven is subtracted from the number of days in the longest cycle. The days between are considered fertile, or unsafe days.

The discipline of adhering to abstinence on certain days is the least of the problems presented by this method. The crucial problem is to know when abstinence is indicated. Unfortunately this cannot consistently be determined with accuracy for a specific woman because the menstrual cycle is often irregular and is never so reliable as it may appear on the calendar. If a woman's periods are irregular, the safe and unsafe days will likewise be irregular. In addition, illness, shock, or other physical or emotional changes can disturb the menstrual cycle and upset the calculations of the time of ovulation.

For a practical, one-sentence suggestion on how to use the rhythm method effectively without resorting to unbearable self-control, you may consider it quite safe not to use contraceptives one week before your period, during your period, and for about five days after your period, but otherwise use them faithfully.

6. *Coitus interruptus.* Abstinence and coitus interruptus are two of the least commendable popular methods. We know that abstinence from intercourse is not a meritorious practice in preventing pregnancy, for 1 Corinthians 7:3 tells us, "The husband should fulfill his marital duty to his wife, and likewise the wife to her husband." In this passage of Scripture (vv. 3–5), every husband and wife

are absolutely commanded to do that which satisfies their marriage partner. No other permanent option is offered.

Another frequently used but meritless method of birth control is "coitus interruptus," or the withdrawal method. This is generally considered a weak practice, because it imposes great restrictions on both partners at the very time each should feel the most free in the act of love. Also, it fails to take into account that some sperm are usually present in the lubricating fluids secreted from the penis during sexual excitement before ejaculation or climax. Only *one* sperm is needed to fertilize the egg, and that one may be well on its way before ejaculation occurs. Another reason we do not recognize this as a good procedure is that it is almost impossible for a wife to reach orgasm regularly this way. It is *not* recommended by most marriage counselors.

Irreversible Birth Control

Now let us consider the most popular irreversible method of birth control—vasectomy. It is a simple operation on the husband that is usually performed in the doctor's office.

In chapter 5 we described the small tube called the vas deferens, which proceeds from the testicle upward toward the seminal vesicles near the prostate gland. This tube is about the size of the ink reservoir of an inexpensive ball point pen. If a husband will grasp the loose skin of his scrotum between his testicle and his body, he will be able to roll this little tube between his thumb and fingers.

During the operation the doctor grasps this little cordlike tube between his fingers and then, catching a loop of the tube with a sharp grasping instrument, makes a small (about one-half inch) incision in the skin of the scrotum, bringing a loop of the tube to the outside. This skin incision is usually small enough that it does not require sewing up after the operation, largely because of the looseness of the skin of the scrotum.

A section of this cord is then removed, from one-half inch to two inches long. For an older man who is absolutely certain he will never want to consider a future repair of the tube (an attempt to be capable again of releasing sperm), he may suggest that his doctor take out an extra-long section. The length of the section removed determines, more than any other single factor, the success of the operation, which can fail only if a new channel develops through the scar tissue between the two cut ends. The doctor may also cauterize or burn each cut end of the vas to help decrease the opportunity for recanalization.

Certain medical articles suggest that a reversible method of vasectomy can be accomplished and in some cases has been successful. But we would advise any husband considering a vasectomy to regard it as an irreversible operation and not pursue it until he and his wife prayerfully consider that they *never* again wish to have children. One man had such an operation before his wife passed away. When he married a second time, they could not share the joys of children, much to the sorrow of his new wife and himself. No Christian couple should ever take this operation lightly or rush into it without careful consideration.

Summary

Every couple must prayerfully decide their attitude toward children and family size. It is best to have a plan; God will guide you to one as you seek His will. Make sure you are not unduly influenced by the humanistic philosophy of our day but seek the basic will of God as revealed in His Word. We feel every Christian family should plan on having children, if at all possible. How many they have should be based on the number they think they can adequately care for and train for a dedicated life of service to God.

Notes

1. Portland, Ore.: Multnomah Press, 1993.

Thirteen

Sex Survey Report

Until recently it has generally been assumed that Christians or very religiously inclined couples were so rigid or confused about sex that they regarded it more for propagation than for pleasure. As counselors we knew differently. For several years it has been our conviction that married Christians enjoy a sex life that is as good as or, in many cases, better than that of the average couple. Even though many of the people we counsel reflect problems in this matter, we know a great majority of others who do not need counseling; their occasional comments and visible treatment of each other betoken a very fulfilling love life. Because most Christians do not have an obsession with sex, they do not need dirty stories, pornography, or artificial stimuli to motivate them toward each other. They simply continue year after year enjoying their love, as God intended they should.

A number of factors make us confident that believers do enjoy happier sexual relations. A Christian's relationship with God produces a greater capacity for expressing and receiving love than is possible for a non-Christian. The fruit of the Spirit (love, joy, peace, patience, kindness, etc.—Gal. 5:22–23) removes the specter of resentment and bitterness that devastates an exciting bedroom life. In addition, people who genuinely love each other will strive harder to please one another, become better informed, and treat each other more unselfishly. This will naturally enrich their love life.

Those who believe the distorted notion that "Victorian ideas" about sex were spawned in Christian circles are totally misinformed. In actuality, the "Victorian morality" was not shaped by enlightened Bible students but became a cultural reaction in a day of biblical ignorance. Thus Christianity cannot be blamed for the sexual barrenness of many couples due to the Victorian influence, for the Bible has always viewed married love as a sacred and vital part of a happy marriage.

A primary consideration in writing this book was to take a sex survey to prove or disprove once and for all our thesis that Christians maintain a higher enjoyment level in the intimacy of their love life than the population in general. Since we had access to the names of thousands of couples from around the country who have attended our Family Life Seminars, we wrote them telling about our survey and asking them to return a card if they would be willing to respond to such a frank and intimate test. We acknowledged that the results would be computerized for use in doing the needed research for this book. Twenty-three hundred couples volunteered to take the survey, but the final number that were completed and returned totaled 3,377—1,705 women and 1,672 men.

It was a gargantuan job to prepare the responses. When the survey was coded and fed into a computer, we finally received sixteen pounds of data on large computer sheets. Now for the first time we possessed factual information about the intimate lives of a sufficient number of Christians to establish a general norm. We were delighted with the results, not only because they confirmed our assumption, but because they provided valuable information that will probably be used by researchers in this field for years to come.

While we were compiling the data for this chapter, *Redbook* magazine published their survey of 100,000 women who took a similar test. Doubtless, theirs is the largest ever compiled on this subject, and it too confirms that "the strongly religious woman seems to be even more responsive than other women her age."[1] Their conclusion was extremely interesting: "A positive religious approach to sexual pleasure, which links sex and marital fulfillment, is likely to have considerable effect on women for whom religious authority still serves as a sanctioning force in life."[2] The reason is clear—if a woman really understands the biblical teachings on lovemaking, she will suffer few inhibitions and openly enjoy her husband's expressions of love.

In comparing our survey with that of *Redbook*, we can draw many interesting conclusions. The *Redbook* survey was derived from both "religious and nonreligious" people, but we had almost no "nonreligious" surveys with which to compare our data until theirs was published. Ninety-eight percent of those who took our survey profess to be born-again Christians. Those labeled "strongly religious" by *Redbook* include 20 percent Catholics and 80 percent Protestants, but there is no way to determine how many of these had experienced a personal relationship with Jesus Christ. The women in our survey reported a 10 percent higher degree of sexual enjoyment, greater frequency in lovemaking experiences per month, and a more active part in coitus than their "strongly religious" counterparts, likewise scoring much higher in these same areas than the average "nonreligious" women in the *Redbook* survey.

After carefully studying the first *Redbook* article, we discovered that their findings stood in basic agreement with our own. The only variations were percentages that can be explained by the religious difference between their mixed clientele and our predominantly Christian group.

On the strength of these two surveys we now feel even more confident that our original presupposition is true—that Christians do enjoy the sublimities of the act of marriage more than others in our culture—but we invite you to study the results of the following questions taken from our survey and see for yourself. At the end we will offer a few comparisons and analyses relevant to various groups and the *Redbook* report. (We purposely deleted those questions that did not relate specifically to this subject.).

The whole survey consisted of ninety-five questions regarding sexual involvement of both husbands and wives. Listed here are their comparative answers to some of the most relevant questions. These percentages will not always total 100 percent because some participants did not respond to every question.

Family Life Seminars Sexual Involvement Survey

		WIVES	HUSBANDS
1. Participants		1,705	1,672
2. Ages	Average	mid-30s	late 30s
	20–29	25%	14%
	30	42	44
	40	22	30
	50 or over	10	12
3. Years married	Less than 1 yr.	1%	1%
	1–6 yrs.	20	18
	7–15 yrs.	37	41
	16–25 yrs.	31	25
	26+	11	12
4. Average number of children		2.5	2.5
5. Pray together (weekly)	Never	33%	30%
	1–2 times	31	43
	5 or more	36	27

6. Years of education: 67% of the women and 80% of the husbands attended at least two years of college, while 38% of the wives and 61% of the men completed four years. 10% of the women and 37% of the husbands went to graduate school.

7. Wife employed outside home: 40% worked regularly full- or part-time, while 60% did not.

8. Husbands' vocations: 64% were professional or managerial, 29% skilled or clerical, and 7% semi-skilled.

9. Length of courtship	6 mos.	10%	9%
	6–12 mos.	27	27
	12–18 mos.	15	12
	18–24 mos.	14	14
	2–3 yrs.	19	17
	3–5 yrs.	14	18
	over 5 yrs.	1	3

10. Main source of sex education before marriage

None	13%	18%
Parents	13	9
Minister	1	1
School	14	11
Reading	53	47
Other	6	14

11. What books on marriage have you found most meaningful? (They are listed in the order of the frequency mentioned.)

1. How to be Happy Though Married
2. The Christian Family
3. Bible
4. Sexual Happiness in Marriage
5. Total Woman
6. Fascinating Womanhood
7. Letters to Karen/Philip
8. Heaven Help the Home
9. Sex Without Fear
10. Sex in Marriage

12. Feelings about sex before marriage

Apprehension	20%	13%
Anticipation	68	82

13. Leader in your (childhood) home

Father	51%	61%
Mother	32	27
Neither	8	8
Fought for leadership	9	4

14. Impression of parents' sex life

Fulfilling	36%	36%
Casual	28	34
Cold	28	20
*Other	8	10

*Didn't know, or only one parent most of time.

15. Did you have any unpleasant sexual experiences in childhood?

None	81%	90%
Indecent exposure	7	3
Molested	7	1
Rape	5	—
Homosexual	—	5

16. Were you ever divorced?

No	92%	91%
Yes, before accepting Christ	5	6
Yes, after accepting Christ	3	3

17. Did you discuss sex with your partner before marriage?

Never	15%	15%
Some just prior to marriage	29	28
Periodically after engagement	56	57

18. Did you engage in premarital intercourse?

No	59%	46%
Once	10*	9*
Occasionally	20*	32*
Frequently	11*	13*

*Among those who did engage in premarital intercourse, 29% indicated they had not yet received Christ as their Lord and Savior at the time of that relationship; 38% noted that they had previously accepted Christ. The remaining 33% did not indicate the time when they began the premarital relationship.

19. Which birth-control methods do you prefer?

Pill	37%	38%
Diaphragm	13	12
Condom	12	12
IUD	10	5
Foam	9	1
Rhythm	5	4
Contraceptive jelly	3	2
Douche	2	—
Withdrawal	2	3
*None	7	7

*Although this may be listed as a personal preference for a few, many noted that no artificial birth-control method was required because of a vasectomy or hysterectomy.

20. Did you go on a honeymoon?

No	16%	14%
Yes, 1–2 days	14	11
Yes, 3–4 days	19	25
One week	31	31
Two weeks	20	19

21. Did you see each other undressed the first night?

Yes	76%	71%
No	24	29

22. Did you attempt intercourse the first night?

Yes	79%	69%
Yes, but could not make entrance	12	22
No	9	9

23. Did you reach orgasm the first night?

Yes	26%*
No	74
Of these:	
No, but did within 1 week	22
No, but did within 2–4 weeks	17
No, but did within 3 months	9
Never	5

*This figure includes 14% who indicated they had premarital sex.

24. Frequency of orgasm now

Regularly or always	77%
Periodically	11
Never or seldom	10

Note: 2% of the women indicated they did not know what an orgasm is.

25. Does husband know when wife reaches orgasm?

Regularly or always	82%	85%
Periodically	7	8
Never or seldom	3	7
Don't know	8	—

26. Does wife attain orgasm during sexual intercourse?

Regularly or always	64%	60%
Periodically	10	14
Never or seldom	24	23

27. How often do you reach orgasm by clitoral manipulation before penile entrance?

Regularly or always	31%
Periodically	17
Never or seldom	51

28. How often does wife require clitoral manipulation as the only way to reach orgasm?

Regularly or always	45%	33%
Periodically	10	16
Never or seldom	41	49

29. Does husband manipulate wife's clitoris orally?

Yes	68%	67%
Never	31	33

30. If yes, how often?

Regularly or always	19%	13%
Periodically	20	21
Seldom	29	33

31. How does the wife feel about being orally manipulated, and how does the husband think the wife feels about it?

Enjoys it	54%	43%
Neutral	13	15
Dislikes it	33	42

32. How does the husband feel about orally manipulating his wife, and how does the wife think he feels about it?

Enjoys it	78%	69%
Neutral	9	18
Dislikes it	13	13

33. How often does wife reach orgasm before husband?

Regularly or always	38%	31%
Periodically	16	22
Never or seldom	45	46

34. How often do you and your partner reach simultaneous orgasms?

Regularly or always	13%	19%
Periodically	44	40
Never or seldom	41	41

35. How often does the wife experience multiple orgasms?

Regularly or always	11%
Periodically	14
Never or seldom	71

36. Minutes from beginning of foreplay to orgasm

Less than 10	6%	7%
10–20	51	55
20–30	31	26
30 or more	12	12

37. Has the husband ever had difficulty ejaculating?

Never or seldom	93%
Periodically	6
Regularly	1

38. How often has husband verbally told wife what stimulates him?

Never or seldom	31%	29%
Periodically	21	30
Regularly or always	45	39

39. How often does wife tell husband what stimulates her?

Never or seldom	34%	41%
Periodically	28	24
Regularly or always	36	33

40. On the average, how often do you have intercourse per week?

0–2 times	61%	61%
3–6 times	36	37
7–9 times	3	1

41. How often do you desire intercourse per week?

0–2 times	48%	27%
3–6 times	49	62
7–9 times	3	11

42. To what extent have you been satisfied with intercourse?

Regularly or always	73%	90%
Periodically	19	6
Never or seldom	8	3

43. How often does the husband have trouble maintaining an erection, and how often does the wife think he does?

Never or seldom	96%	92%
Periodically	4	6
Regularly or always	—	2

44. How often does wife help husband achieve orgasm by oral stimulation?

Regularly or always	11%	8%
Periodically	15	15
Never or seldom	73	76

45. Self-acceptance of personal appearance

	Totally	20%	33%
	Mostly	62	54
	Provisionally	13	11
	Minimally	3	1.2
	Reject	2	0.8

46. How mate accepts my appearance

	Totally	37%	34%
	Mostly	55	57.6
	Provisionally	6.4	6
	Minimally	1.2	2
	Reject	0.4	—
	Don't know	—	0.4

47. How do you rate your love life?

	Above average and very happy	81%	85%
	Average	10	13
	Below average	9	12

Chart I

Sexual Satisfaction Chart

Wives	81%	10%	9%
Husbands	85%	3%	12%

☐ Very Happy Above Average   ■ Average   ▨ Below Average

Based on answers to the following question: Using a scale of 0 to 100, how would you rate your general marital love life?

Chart II

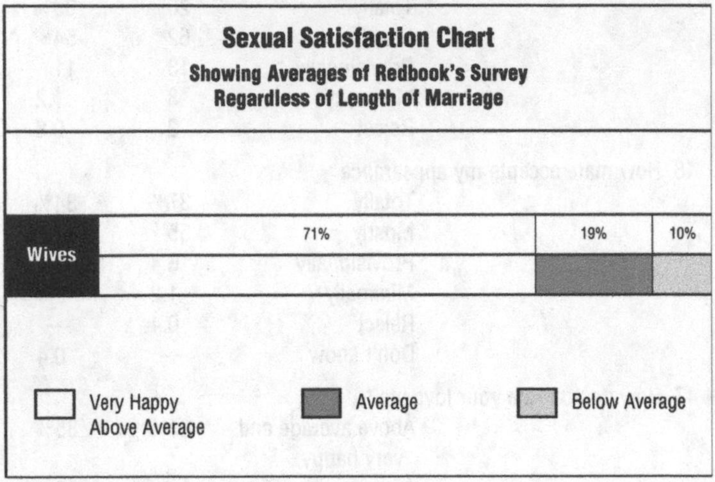

Sexual Satisfaction Chart
Showing Averages of Redbook's Survey
Regardless of Length of Marriage

Wives	71%	19%	10%

☐ Very Happy Above Average	■ Average	▨ Below Average	

Chart III

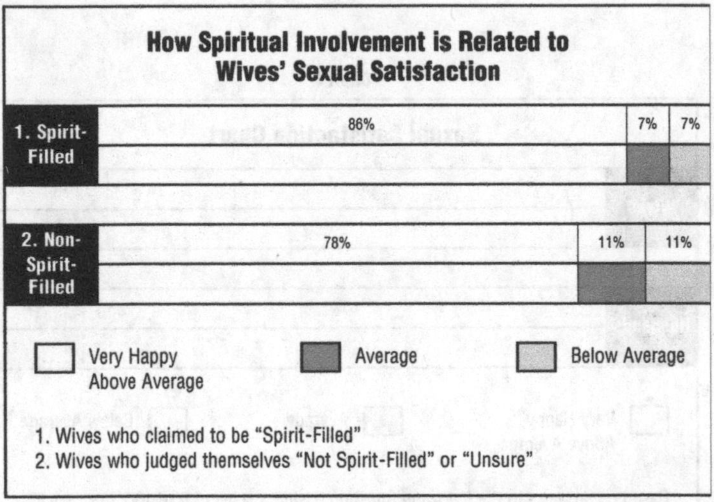

How Spiritual Involvement is Related to
Wives' Sexual Satisfaction

1. Spirit-Filled	86%	7%	7%
2. Non-Spirit-Filled	78%	11%	11%

☐ Very Happy Above Average	■ Average	▨ Below Average	

1. Wives who claimed to be "Spirit-Filled"
2. Wives who judged themselves "Not Spirit-Filled" or "Unsure"

Based on a comparison of these three charts, it is reasonable to conclude that Christians are considerably more satisfied with their love life than non-Christians, and Spirit-filled Christians tend to record a somewhat higher degree of enjoyment than even the average believer. This should not come as a surprise, however, since the first fruit of the Spirit is "love." The more love an individual has from God to give to his partner, the more fulfillment he will give and receive in marriage. Hopefully these statistical facts will cause both the Christian community and secular counselors to recognize that a person's relationship with God will improve his relationship with other people, beginning with his partner.

Additional Interesting Comparisons

As we analyzed the results of our survey, we made a number of fascinating discoveries—far too many, in fact, to include in this book. We would, however, like to draw your attention to some of these we consider most important and have drawn charts to visualize the data.

The following chart was compiled by averaging the responses of both the husbands and the wives in their respective age groups and indicates the highest level of sexual satisfaction of all surveys that we are familiar with. The graph showing the satisfaction level for those in their fifties may indicate that what we discussed under male impotence, but what few men over fifty admit freely today, is true: as their vital energies decline, some do in fact begin having problems in their sexual performance. It is worth noting that 81 percent do not indicate such a decline, and hopefully by studying chapters 10 and 11 (the Kegel exercises and male impotence), many of those who do will be able to resolve their difficulties.

Chart IV

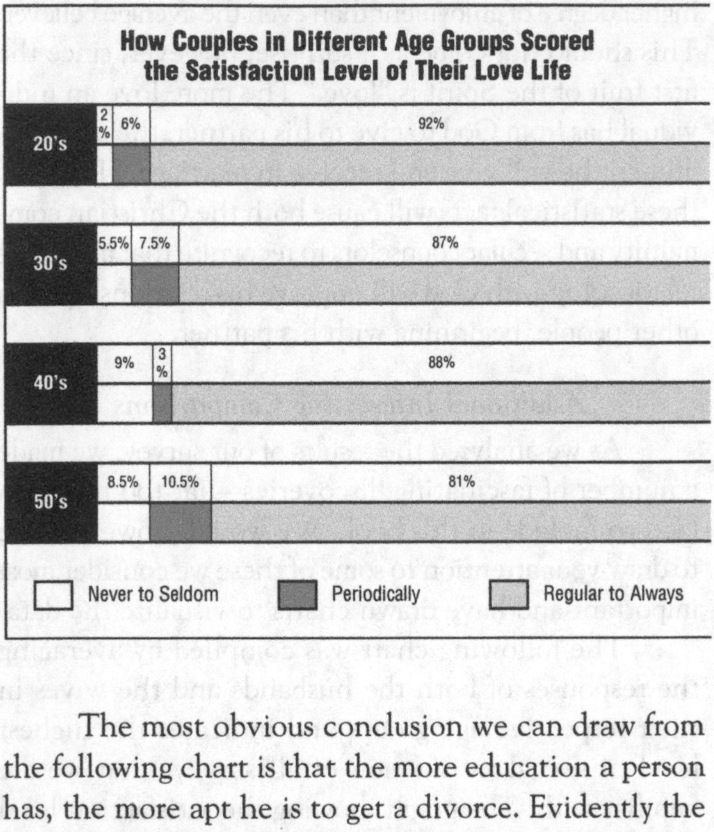

How Couples in Different Age Groups Scored the Satisfaction Level of Their Love Life

20's 2% | 6% | 92%

30's 5.5% | 7.5% | 87%

40's 9% | 3% | 88%

50's 8.5% | 10.5% | 81%

☐ Never to Seldom ▮ Periodically ▮ Regular to Always

The most obvious conclusion we can draw from the following chart is that the more education a person has, the more apt he is to get a divorce. Evidently the humanistic philosophy of higher education, which often tries to destroy the permanency of marriage, makes inroads even into the thinking of Christians. This figure would probably be much higher but for those who attended Christian colleges. Unfortunately no differentiation was sought in the survey. However, over half of those who divorced did so *before* becoming Christians, so it is safe to assume that the majority of the divorces occurred among those who attended secular colleges or universities.

Chart V

Divorce Rate at Various Levels of Education		
Among those who had divorced:	**Wives**	**Husbands**
High School Only	5%	5%
Two Years of College	10%	13%
Four or More Years of College	20%	14%

Children Are a Blessing

The Bible, in Psalm 127, calls children a "heritage from the Lord" and further states, "Blessed is the man whose quiver is full of them." We were rather surprised to find that those taking our survey had an average of 2.5 children per couple. Although this is somewhat above the national average, we had expected a higher number of children in Christian families. In addition, it was interesting to observe that couples who had never attended college had 2.8 children, whereas those with two years' college registered 2.5, those with four years of college scored 2.4, and those who went on to graduate school recorded a 2.3 rate.

Young couples today often acquire the impression that children are a hindrance to sexual enjoyment. Some are so convinced of this fallacy that they use it as an excuse for not starting or enlarging their families. Our survey and *Redbook*'s refutes such an idea. As researcher Levin stated, "The major point that emerges from the statistics is that women with children are just as likely to be satisfied with sex as married women without children, and women with two or more children are as satisfied as women with just one child. In other words, when it comes to sexual satisfaction in marriage, *children make no appreciable difference.*"[3]

Chart VI

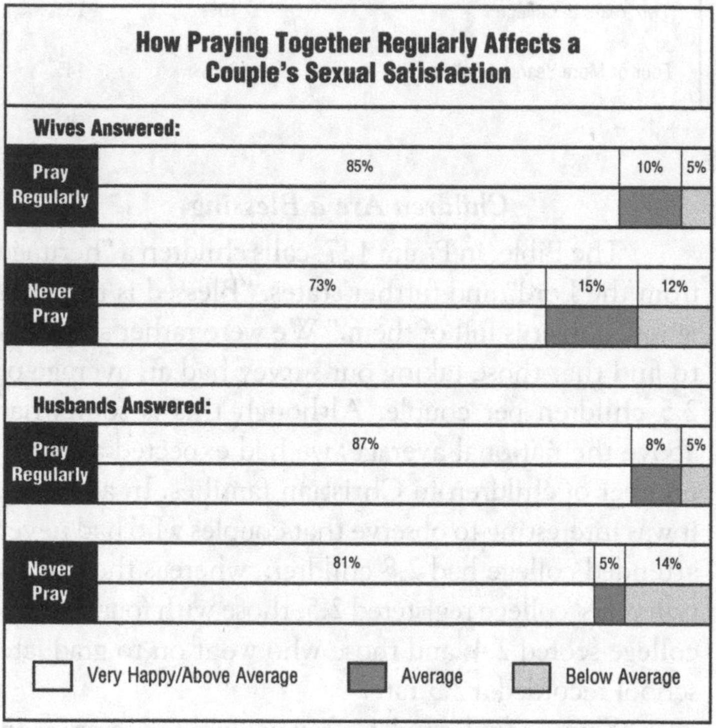

How Praying Together Regularly Affects a Couple's Sexual Satisfaction		
Wives Answered:		
Pray Regularly	85%	10%	5%
Never Pray	73%	15%	12%
Husbands Answered:		
Pray Regularly	87%	8%	5%
Never Pray	81%	5%	14%

☐ Very Happy/Above Average　■ Average　▨ Below Average

Prayer Still Changes Things

It was encouraging to discover that 67 to 70 percent of the Christian couples we surveyed prayed together one or more times a week. After preaching for years that prayer changes things, we were excited to find that such an experience even includes improving sexual satisfaction in marriage.

The Big Lie About Premarital Sex

For years now, amoral advocates of premarital sex have encouraged young people to gain sexual experience as an aid to future marital adjustment. We who believe the Bible and its timeless principles for happy living have advised that such a practice is harmful. Our survey indicates quite clearly that premarital sex is *not* necessary and, according to statistics, may hinder sexual adjustment.

Chart VII

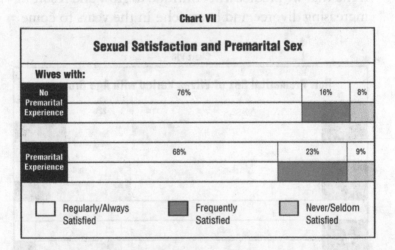

The reason for the difference in the satisfaction level indicated above is unknown, for we did not ask that specific question. We did, however, inquire, "If you had your life to live over again, what one thing would you do differently?" The most popular answer by far was, "I would not have engaged in premarital sex." No wonder the Bible calls it a "sin against your own soul." Whether or not the trend to premarital promiscuity is increasing can be deduced from Chart VIII.

During the past thirty-five years, modern sex educators have inundated junior high, high school, and college young people with massive doses of sex education without the benefit of moral principles or guidelines. We are not surprised that the most alarming increase in those who admitted to giving up their virtue before marriage occurs within that group. We must keep in mind, however, that the group in our survey is predominantly church oriented and was exposed to moral principles. Doubtless the statistics would be much higher if we surveyed the population as a whole. This indicates a tragic trend that we predict will continue to grow and result in increasing divorce and heartache in the years to come.

Chart VIII

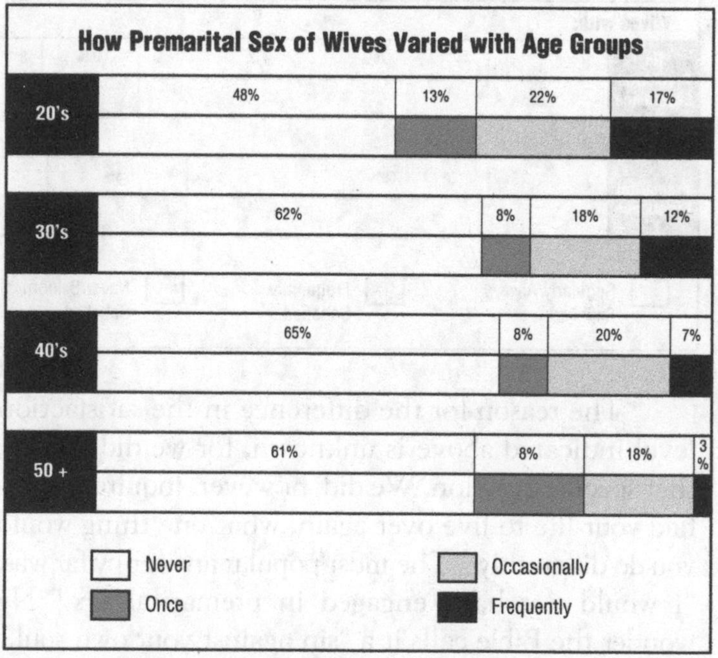

How Premarital Sex of Wives Varied with Age Groups

Age Group	Never	Once	Occasionally	Frequently
20's	48%	13%	22%	17%
30's	62%	8%	18%	12%
40's	65%	8%	20%	7%
50 +	61%	8%	18%	3%

Legend:
- Never
- Once
- Occasionally
- Frequently

Oral Sex on the Increase

It is readily apparent from Chart IX that oral sex is on the increase today, thanks to amoral sex education, pornography, modern sex literature, and the moral breakdown of our times. These figures are considerably lower than those revealed in the *Redbook* report, which claims that "among those 20–39 years of age it is 91%."[4] Of these 91 women out of 100, "40 engage in it often" (compared to our 23), "45 engage in it occasionally" (25 in ours) and "5 tried it just once. . . ." "Only 7 women out of 100 have never experienced it. . . ."[5] In our survey, 27 twenty-year-olds and 25 thirty-year-olds never tried it; the statistic jumped to 39 and 43 for forty- and fifty-year-olds. Obviously the Christian community has not unanimously accepted oral sex. Most Christian counselors are reluctant to condemn or endorse the practice, leaving that decision to the individual. However, there still seems to

Chart IX

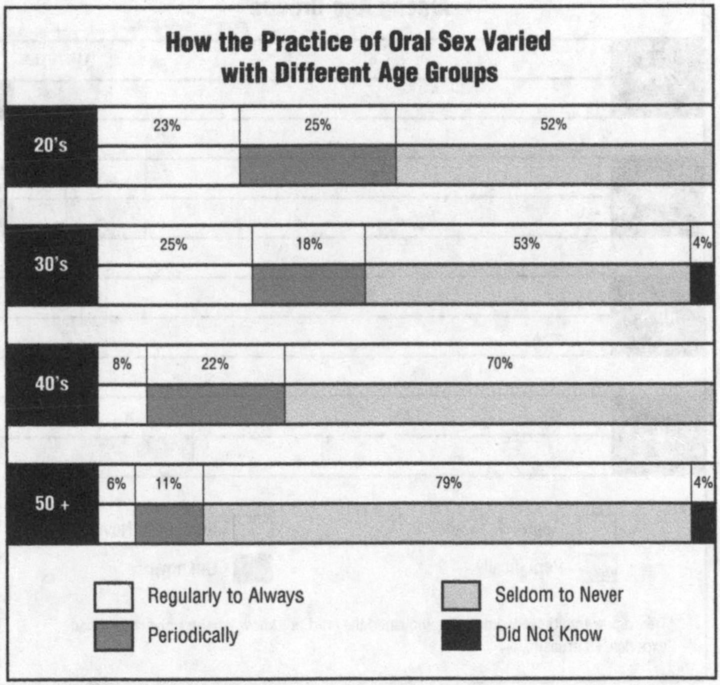

How the Practice of Oral Sex Varied with Different Age Groups

Age	Regularly to Always	Periodically	Seldom to Never	Did Not Know
20's	23%	25%	52%	
30's	25%	18%	53%	4%
40's	8%	22%	70%	
50 +	6%	11%	79%	4%

□ Regularly to Always   ▨ Seldom to Never
■ Periodically   ■ Did Not Know

be a large number of Christians who enjoy a fulfilling and exciting love life without engaging in this practice.

We are not convinced that oral sex is as popular on a regular basis as most modern sexologists would have us think. Even the *Redbook* report acknowledged that only 40 percent practiced it regularly, and the other 60 percent ranged from occasionally to never. What makes that particularly interesting is that their statistics were drawn from those between twenty and thirty-nine years of age and that, admittedly, the older women did it less frequently. The article did not offer statistics for these women, but our survey showed that 70 percent of the

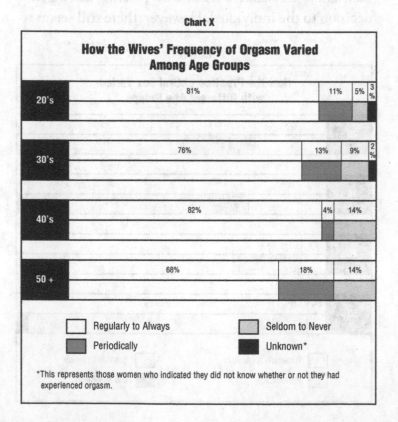

Chart X

How the Wives' Frequency of Orgasm Varied Among Age Groups

Age	Regularly to Always	Periodically	Seldom to Never	Unknown*
20's	81%	11%	5%	3%
30's	76%	13%	9%	2%
40's	82%	4%	14%	
50 +	68%	18%	14%	

☐ Regularly to Always   ▨ Seldom to Never
▨ Periodically   ■ Unknown*

*This represents those women who indicated they did not know whether or not they had experienced orgasm.

women between forty and forty-nine years of age seldom or never engaged in oral sex, and those fifty and over abstained at a rate of 81 percent. We conclude from all this that cunnilingus and fellatio have in recent years been given unwarranted publicity, causing far more couples to experiment than had previously been in the habit of doing so. But the majority of couples do not regularly use it as a substitute for the beautiful and conventional interaction designed by our Creator to be an intimate expression of love.

We are confident that nothing will ever replace the traditional act of marriage as the favorite method of expressing sexual love between married partners.

For centuries most married women did not experience orgasms frequently, and many never knew what orgasm felt like. In spite of that, no feminine revolt arose against man or marriage; women just didn't know what they were missing. Even today, many nonorgasmic women testify that they enjoy the closeness, excitement, and affection that lovemaking provides and that sex is pleasurable without orgasm. But in recent years women in increasing numbers have come to expect their marriage bed to ring all the bells frequently and culminate in a woman's ultimate sexual experience—orgasm.

Chart X indicates that the vast majority of Christian women experience orgasm most of the time; only a small percentage do not. The above figures indicate that 81 percent do most of the time, and another 11 percent frequently. That means 92 out of every 100 Christian women in their twenties who took our survey indicate that they have experienced orgasm at least "frequently." That is the highest figure reported in any surveys known to us, further suggesting that Christians enjoy the sublimities of sexual union more than anyone else in our society.

Chart XI

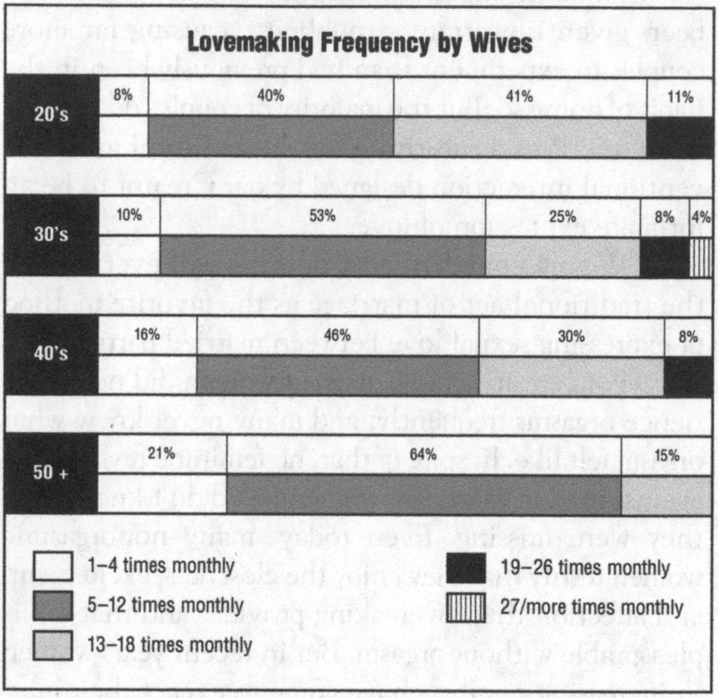

Lovemaking Frequency by Wives

Age	1–4 times monthly	5–12 times monthly	13–18 times monthly	19–26 times monthly	27/more times monthly
20's	8%	40%	41%	11%	
30's	10%	53%	25%	8%	4%
40's	16%	46%	30%	8%	
50 +	21%	64%	15%		

Legend:
- 1–4 times monthly
- 5–12 times monthly
- 13–18 times monthly
- 19–26 times monthly
- 27/more times monthly

The Sexual Numbers Game

No study of sexual responses would be complete without considering the frequency of intercourse. As *Redbook* says, "When it comes to making love, Americans seem particularly preoccupied with numbers."[6] We have already observed that frequency depends on many things—age, health, immediate pressures (business, social, family, financial), resentment, guilt, inability to communicate about sex, and a host of other things. Both surveys, however, indicate that frequency is not nearly so important as satisfaction. We are convinced that it is much more important to bring sexual satisfaction to your partner with almost every lovemaking experience than it is to run a bedroom marathon.

There is no set "normal frequency" pattern. Each couple should find the frequency level at which they feel comfortable and enjoy each other. Even that level will vary at times. However, both our survey and *Redbook*'s indicate that most wives in their late thirties and forties desire more lovemaking than they receive. Most husbands would be advised to leave their vocational problems at the plant or office so that they may spend more time loving and enjoying their wives.

Chart XII

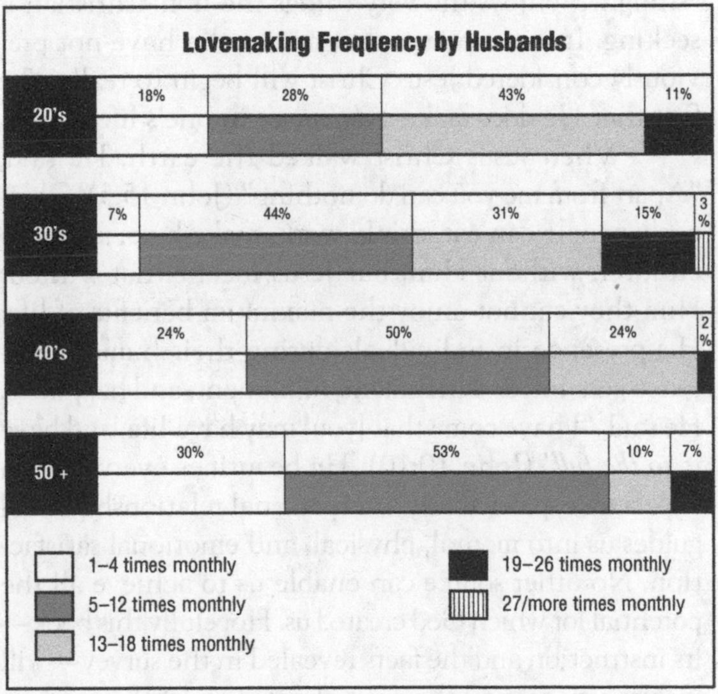

Lovemaking Frequency by Husbands

20's	18%	28%	43%	11%
30's	7%	44%	31%	15%	3%
40's	24%	50%	24%	2%
50 +	30%	53%	10%	7%

Legend:
- ☐ 1–4 times monthly
- ▨ 5–12 times monthly
- ☐ 13–18 times monthly
- ■ 19–26 times monthly
- ▥ 27/more times monthly

Summary

We are quite satisfied that our survey has established that over the long years of matrimony Christians do indeed experience a mutually enjoyable love relationship and that they engage in the act of marriage more frequently and with greater satisfaction than do non-Christians in our society. This will not really come as a surprise to those who know and obey biblical principles, because the scriptural keys to happiness require that we learn and obey the principles of God.

It is a sad paradox that so many of those who have rejected or neglected God in their pursuit of sexual freedom and happiness often live miserable lives, whereas the Christian, who is despised or ridiculed as being too "straight," enjoys the very things the non-Christian is seeking. It is our prayer that many who have not previously considered Jesus Christ will begin to realize the fact that He does make a *difference* in one's life.

When Jesus Christ walked the earth, He said, "Apart from me you can do nothing" (John 15:5). Obviously people can eat, drink, work, make love, and raise children without Him, but Jesus meant that without Him they cannot enjoy the maximum benefits of life. His presence in individuals during their human existence guarantees enrichment, fulfillment, and happiness. He said, "I have come that [you] may have life, and have it *to the full*" (John 10:10). He beautifies every human experience, particularly interpersonal relationships, and guides us into mental, physical, and emotional satisfaction. No other source can enable us to achieve all the potential for which God created us. Hopefully this book— its instruction and the facts revealed in the survey—will inspire you to read the next chapter and enhance your personal relationship with Him. If He is not presently in your life, we suggest that you permit nothing to hinder you from receiving Him. The Bible states repeatedly that when people came to Jesus, they "went on their way rejoicing." Do you enjoy the "abundant life" He came to give? Can you think of a better way to live?

Notes

1. Robert J. Levin and Amy Levin, "Sexual Pleasure: The Surprising Preferences in 100,000 Women," *Redbook* 145 (September 1975), 53.

2. Ibid.

3. Ibid., 55.

4. Ibid.

5. Ibid.

6. Ibid., 57.

Fourteen

The Missing Dimension

The human person is a four-part being: body, emotion, mind, and spirit. The present-day humanistic philosophy that has reduced man to body, emotion, and mind is, in our opinion, one of the greatest causes of marital disharmony in the world today.

It is our belief that the spiritual part of every person, often the missing dimension, is the most significant of the four. To illustrate its influence on the others, we should examine all four individually.

1. *Physical.* We are all aware of the physical part of our nature. It involves our bodily functions and is of vital importance when considering the art of marital lovemaking.

2. *Emotional.* The motor of a human being is the heart, out of which proceed "the issues of life" (Prov. 4:23 KJV). The heart is the seat of all emotions, both good and bad—love and hate, joy and bitterness. If our

emotions function properly, we will have no problem functioning physically.

3. *Mental.* The mind is the most complex mechanism known to humanity. Some have called it the most complicated computer in the world. The memory bank of the mind registers the lifetime impressions that influence our prejudices, likes, and dislikes, thus indirectly producing our feelings. For example, those who display a continuing distaste for sex are not reflecting a bodily malfunction, but a mental distortion that inhibits their emotional feelings and prohibits normal physical expression. Incompatibility, for instance, hardly ever starts in the body; it almost invariably begins in the mind. For that reason, mental misconceptions replaced by good mental images usually unstop the flow of good emotions and enable the individual or couple to experience proper physical responses.

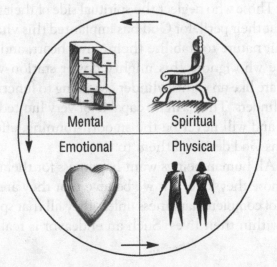

4. *Spiritual*. The least recognized side of a person's nature is the spiritual. One ancient philosopher recognized the significance of this aspect when he declared that the "God-shaped vacuum" in the heart of every person can be satisfied by none other than God Himself. Unless that God-shaped vacuum is filled by a personal relationship with God, human beings are condemned throughout their lives to an endless treadmill of activity in an attempt to fill it. Some try to educate it out of existence, others attempt to ignore it, and still others seek a variety of self-gratifying experiences—but all to no avail. By ignoring the reality of that spiritual side of their nature, they compound the problem by violating the laws of God, which activate the conscience and heighten the recognition of futility and emptiness. Interestingly enough, this dilemma increases with age. It is no wonder that many in our culture resort to drugs, alcohol, and a host of other unproductive routes of escape from their own miseries.

Those who neglect the spiritual side of their nature do so at their peril, for God has implanted this vital part of their nature to stabilize their mind, heart, and body. People who ignore this mighty power station within them are like an eight-cylinder car trying to function on six cylinders. They will be capable of very limited operation and will never be the smooth-running, effective persons God designed them to be.

All human beings want happiness for themselves and those they love, but we believe that they are incapable of complete happiness unless they fill that spiritual void within their lives. Such an endeavor is really not difficult for them if they want it. Let us note five keys that make possible the filling of that void and the resultant happiness everyone desires.

 God loves you and has designed you with a spiritual side to your nature that has a capacity to enjoy fellowship with Him.

"For God so loved the world that he gave his one and only Son, that whoever believes in him shall not perish but have eternal life" (John 3:16).

Above all else, people should know that God loves them, regardless of what the circumstances of life seemingly indicate. The gift of His Son on Calvary's cross stands as a historical monument that God loves His human creatures. It is legitimate to personalize that fact and say that God loves *you*!

God also desires that we enjoy fellowship with Him. "God is spirit, and his worshipers must worship [fellowship with him] in spirit and in truth" (John 4:24).

As we have already seen, we are empty if we do not enjoy that oneness of fellowship with God. The following diagrams illustrate the two views of humanity:

Mankind's romance with intellectualism based on atheistic humanism pictures secular human beings in three parts as indicated in the diagram. The tragedy of this philosophy is that it limits mankind completely to human resources, producing a futility of life never intended by the Creator.

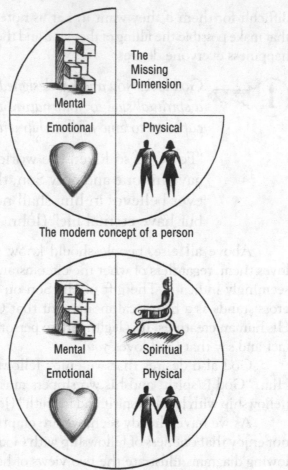

The modern concept of a person

People as God designed them

The self-will and sin of human beings have destroyed their spiritual life, separating them from God and making them miserable.

"For all have sinned and fall short of the glory of God" (Rom. 3:23).

In the spiritual quarter of a person's nature we have pictured a throne to clarify that, unlike animals, we humans were given a free will at birth to choose the ruler of our lives. We may wish to enjoy fellowship with God, or we may assert our free will and pride (as most do) and live independent of God. With this decision, consequently, a person's spiritual life dies, thus destroying his or her ability to produce lasting happiness.

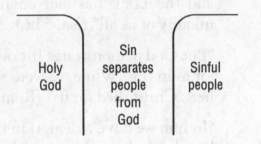

Holy God
Sin separates people from God
Sinful people

Human Beings Are Separated from God

"For the wages of sin is death" (Rom. 6:23). Since God is holy, the day-to-day sins that people commit when self is in control of their lives separate them from God. The Bible teaches that those who commit sins "will not inherit the kingdom of God" (Gal. 5:21).

People usually try to restore their fellowship with God by good works, religion, philosophy, or church membership. However, they are helpless to save themselves. "He saved us, not because of righteous things we had done, but because of his mercy" (Titus 3:5). The best efforts of people will never restore either their fellowship with God or their happiness.

Although many expressions of sin are described in the Bible, all are caused by self-will in opposition to the will of God.

Jesus Christ is God's only provision for your sin, and through Him you can again have fellowship with God and experience the happiness He has for you. The Bible teaches that Christ died in man's place.

"We all, like sheep, have gone astray, each of us has turned to his own way; and the LORD has laid on him the iniquity of us all" (Isa. 53:6).

"But God demonstrates his own love for us in this: While we were still sinners, Christ died for us" (Rom. 5:8).

"In him we have redemption through his blood, the forgiveness of sins, in accordance with the riches of God's grace" (Eph. 1:7).

Christ Is the Only Way to God

Jesus said, "I am the way and the truth and the life. No one comes to the Father except through me" (John 14:6). He also said, "I am the gate; whoever enters through me will be saved" (John 10:9).

God has provided the perfect bridge to bring sinful human beings back into fellowship with Himself: the cross on which His own Son was crucified for the sins of the whole world. "Christ died for our sins ... [and] was raised on the third day according to the Scriptures" (1 Cor. 15:3–4).

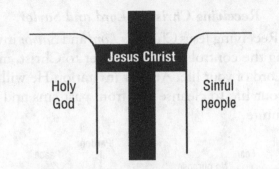

Holy God — Jesus Christ — Sinful people

4 *You must repent of your self-will and receive Jesus Christ as Lord and Savior by personal invitation to have that fellowship and happiness restored.*

The Three Steps to Receiving Christ

1. *Repent.* "Unless you repent [turn from self-will to God's will], you too will all perish" (Luke 13:3). Repentance means a willingness to turn from your own ways, your self-will, and follow God's ways. Some have mistakenly assumed that they must turn from their sins to be converted, but this is impossible until first they look to God. He then will turn you around and cause you to forsake your sins.

2. *Believe.* "Yet to all who received him, to those who believed in his name, he gave the right to become children of God" (John 1:12). The word *believe* literally means "to rest upon" or "to take completely at His word."

3. *Receive.* Christ said, "Here I am! I stand at the door [of your life] and knock. If anyone hears my voice and opens the door, I will come in and eat [fellowship] with him, and he with me" (Rev. 3:20).

Receiving Christ as Lord and Savior

Receiving Jesus Christ as *Lord* and *Savior* involves turning the control of your life over to Christ, making Him Lord of your life. At your invitation He will come into your life to cleanse you from past sins and guide your future.

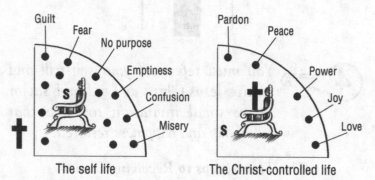

The self life   The Christ-controlled life

These diagrams clearly picture the two kinds of spiritual lives extant. The self life shows self on the throne making the decisions of life, with Christ symbolically pictured outside the life. This individual may be religious, irreligious, atheistic, or profligate; it really makes no difference. In all cases where self is on the throne, God is the missing dimension in that person's life, thus making him or her incapable of experiencing true happiness. Before a person has lived many years, he or she will begin to experience the misery, confusion, emptiness, purposelessness, fear, and guilt with increasing intensity—just as we have pictured it.

As we travel around the country and meet people from various walks of life, we customarily confront individuals with these five keys to happiness. When we demonstrate the empty results of the self-controlled life to people, they almost always agree with us. Indeed, I have never known a person of forty years or over to deny the fact that this was his or her personal experience. The only people who disagreed (and there have been only a few) were college-age youth whose idealism caused them to determine that they would be the exception. I am confident that the passing of time will dissolve that objection for them.

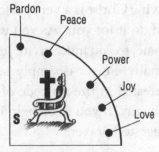

The Christ-controlled life

The Christ-controlled spiritual life is the result of an individual's receiving Jesus Christ as Lord and Savior by personal invitation. Note that we did not say accepting Christ "as Savior." The Bible repeatedly refers to the salvation experience as the result of accepting Christ as *Lord* and Savior. Romans 10:13 says, "Everyone who calls on the name of the Lord will be saved."

Whenever individuals are willing to recognize their self-will and call on Jesus Christ to save them from past sins and become Lord of their future, Christ comes into their lives to take control of the throne of their will. The self-will then becomes a servant to Christ. The *S* in the diagram no longer represents self; it now stands for *servant*.

Jesus Christ first brings into people's lives abundant pardon for past sins, producing in their hearts a peace that was previously unknown. Believers have the power of God resident within to begin overcoming their sins, bad habits, and weaknesses. Furthermore, they possess the joy of the Lord and the love of God to extend them abundantly to others. This is the Spirit-controlled spiritual life that produces happiness.

Receiving Christ Personally Through Prayer

Receiving Christ is a very personal experience. No one else can do it for you. As you would invite a guest into your home, so you must invite Jesus Christ into your heart personally. Prayer is simply talking to God, who is more interested in the attitude of your heart than in the words you say. If you need help in forming a prayer, here is a suggested prayer:

> Dear heavenly Father, realizing I am a sinner and can do nothing to save myself, I desire Your forgiveness and mercy. I believe Jesus Christ died on the cross, shedding His blood as full payment for my sins, and rose bodily from the dead, demonstrating that He is God.
>
> Right now I receive Jesus Christ into my life as personal Lord and Savior. He is my only hope for salvation and eternal life.
>
> Give me understanding and increasing faith as I study Your Word. I surrender my will to Your Holy Spirit to make me the kind of person You want me to be.
>
> I pray this in the name of Christ. Amen.

Does this prayer express the thoughts of your heart? If so, pray now to the heavenly Father; the Bible guarantees that Christ will answer your prayer and come into your life.

How to Know You Are a Christian

A Christian is one who has Christ in his or her life. If you sincerely asked Christ through prayer to come into your life, you can be sure He has. God cannot lie, and He promised to come in when invited (Rev. 3:20).

The Bible guarantees to you eternal life. "And this is the testimony: God has given us eternal life, and this life is in his Son. He who has the Son has life; he who does not have the Son of God does not have life. I write these things to you who believe in the name of the Son of God so that you may know that you have eternal life" (1 John 5:11–13).

Thank Him regularly for coming into your life.

How to Become a Strong Christian

When you were born physically, you needed certain things for growth—food, exercise, and knowledge. So it is spiritually. The following suggestions will help you:

1. *Read the Bible daily.* The Bible is God's message to you, but it will meet your needs only if you read it. It is advisable that you concentrate on reading in the New Testament, preferably the gospel of John, the first epistle of John, and the books of Philippians and Ephesians. Then read consecutively through the New Testament. It is impossible for anyone who does not regularly read God's Word to become a strong Christian.

2. *Pray daily.* God is your heavenly Father; He wants you to call on Him regularly (Matt. 26:41).

3. *Go to church regularly.* You will never become a strong Christian unless you consistently attend a Bible-teaching church where you can hear more of God's Word. You have only begun to learn about the many exciting things God has planned for you. You also need

to make Christian friends; church is the ideal place to do it (Heb. 10:25).

4. *Identify with Christ.* Make this identification public by following Him in believer's baptism (Matt. 28:18–20). Once you have been baptized, you should officially become a member of the church where you were baptized and seek to serve the Lord with that congregation.

5. *Share your new experience with others.* Relating what Christ has done for you will both strengthen you and help your friends to receive Christ (1 Peter 3:15).

6. *Study the Bible.* In addition, take advantage of the excellent Bible-study helps available today. Your church no doubt will be able to help you find such aids. If not, the Christian bookstore in your community has an ample supply.

 *Let Jesus Christ direct the daily decisions of your life, and you will enjoy inner happiness regardless of the circumstances around you.*

"In all your ways acknowledge him, and he will direct your paths" (Prov. 3:6 NKJV).

You have to invite Jesus Christ into your life only once, but to let Him control your life requires a daily commitment. He wants to help you make all the decisions of life so that you can experience the maximum happiness He has in store for you.

The Happy Life—A Christ-controlled Life

The only truly happy Christians are those controlled by Christ. Jesus said, "Now that you know these things [the principles of God found in the Bible], you will be blessed if you do them" (John 13:17).

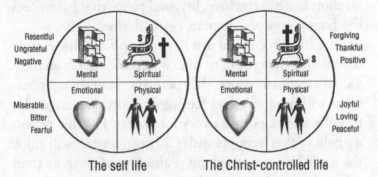

The self life   The Christ-controlled life

Happiness is not automatic for a Christian. Each of the diagrams above represents a Christian, but obviously one Christian is miserable, the other happy. The reason is clear. The person with the self-controlled spiritual life reveals that self is back on the throne and he is living independent of God. This is unfortunately a common state for many Christians, and it always produces unhappiness. In fact, many Christians who live this way are more miserable than non-Christians because, in addition to making a mess of their lives through selfish decisions, they also are increasingly convicted by the indwelling Spirit.

The Christ-controlled spiritual life pictured above shows Christ daily in command of the decision-making processes of life. These individuals, like everyone else, will have to make such decisions as to where they will work, how they will treat their families, who will be their friends, and where they will live. However, they will *inquire of the Lord* where they will work, how they will treat their families, who will be their friends, and where they will live. When Christ controls one's life, that person seeks to do those things and think those thoughts that please the Lord, who in turn will grant that person an abundance of the love, joy, and peace that guarantees the happiness every human being desires.

Christ in control of a person's spiritual life is truly the missing dimension to life. When He directs an individual's spiritual nature, that person's clean thought patterns will produce good feelings and in turn engender the physical responses everyone wants. For this reason we believe that a couple with Christ in control will enjoy the act of love over the long years of marriage more than other people. Good thought patterns and attitudes spark the good actions that all married couples need.

Love is the first of the "fruit of the Spirit" mentioned in Galatians 5:22–23. The person whose life is Christ-controlled will possess a greater capacity to love his or her partner. The best way to increase one's capacity to love is to bestow it on another.

God's Cure for Incompatibility

In recent years the most common excuse for divorce has been incompatibility. Because many have come into my office with this complaint, I have developed a basic technique for dealing with it. One typical couple will serve as an example.

After the wife had reported her sordid tale of woe, she exclaimed, "There is no hope for our marriage because Sam and I are no longer compatible." This meant that they no longer lived together in sexual unity, in this case avoiding intercourse for five months.

I asked Sara, "Has it always been this way?" Naturally she replied no. What couple would ever think of getting married knowing they were incompatible?

Some couples who complain of incompatibility were so compatible during their courting days that they couldn't keep their hands off each other. This indicates that they *learned* to be incompatible. Such discord has nothing to do with biology, physiology, or bodily function, but as we shall prove, it has everything to do with mental and spiritual sin.

Most couples today are attracted to each other on the emotional and physical levels because they are thrown together in a work or social environment. They notice that their body chemistry—or as I like to refer to it, biological magnetic attraction—sparks an emotional response. This is always an exciting experience for two red-blooded young people of the opposite sex. But if they lack a spiritual dimension to life, their first contact will produce additional associations that in turn fan their emotions and further spark their physical attraction. If they have been brainwashed by the free-love precepts of today's campus humanists, they may start living together and enjoy expressing their drives much as do animals. Many still wisely reserve their sexual expression for marriage, but in either case, after the novelty wears off, the couple discovers that a wealth of mental disagreement is producing conflict and incompatibility.

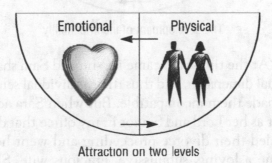

Attraction on two levels

Every couple is destined to discover after marriage that they are not so similar in their likes and dislikes as they had thought before marriage. Their backgrounds, intelligence, and education may be different, and they may find themselves strongly disagreeing on such vital issues as money, children, manners, family, business, and social events. If these differences can be faced unselfishly, they will not create incompatibility; but if self reigns on the throne of their will, they are going to indulge in thought patterns of ingratitude, revenge, and animosity. Such thoughts turn love, joy, and peace into bitterness and hatred—the very ingredients that produce incompatibility.

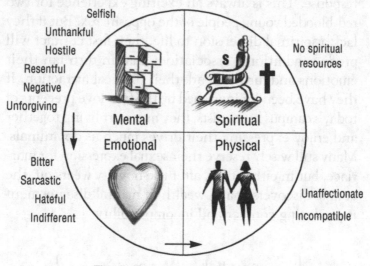

The development of incompatibility

At the time Sara came in, she and Sam shared no spiritual dimension, and thus their individual selfishness had made them incompatible. But when Sara accepted Christ as her Lord and Savior in my office that day, she canceled their divorce proceeding and went home to become a loving, submissive, gracious wife. She had become convinced that such attitudes were God's will for her life.

At my recommendation she did not tell Sam immediately about her new faith in Christ. Instead she waited until he noticed the obvious change in her. It did not take long. At the first spontaneous show of affection he was suspicious that she had been on a spending spree. Before long, however, he was forced to acknowledge her sincerity and candor. Within ten weeks Sam also came to a saving knowledge of Christ, and they have enjoyed a compatible relationship for many years.

If this were a rare experience, I would hesitate to cite it. One the contrary, I have found that making Christ the Lord of their life is a couple's best cure for incompatibility.

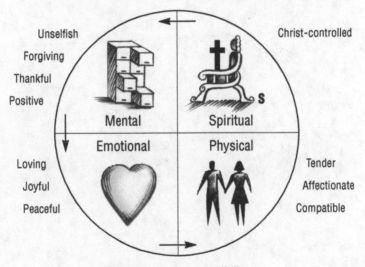

The cure for incompatibility

A compatible marriage is a happy marriage, producing the finest environment for raising children. Although every couple anticipates a harmonious marriage, few experience it because they have never considered the missing dimension, the spiritual side of their nature. When that part of marriage is right, everything else seems to fall into a proper perspective.

When Jesus Christ warned us that we can do nothing without Him, He knew we were unable to establish a truly happy marriage without His guidance. The first recourse of a couple who are not enjoying the ultimate blessings that God intended for them should be to let Jesus Christ take control of their spirits, minds, and emotions. This can occasion a miraculous improvement in the relationship between two people.

Fifteen

Practical Answers to Common Questions

Lovemaking is an intricate art that must be practiced by two people for them to enjoy mutual satisfaction. As in any activity that requires cooperation between two humans, a malfunction can be triggered by the inadvertent mistake of one or the other. We have tried to deal with the most important aspects of lovemaking, but to be exhaustive would make this book so long that no reader could finish it. Supplemental to these major areas we have selected the most frequently asked questions on sex and answered them briefly and specifically. This chapter contains such questions arranged alphabetically by subject. It is hoped they cover *your* most urgent questions.

During the past forty years we have conducted more than eight hundred Family Life Seminars throughout the United States and Canada, reaching nearly one million people. At many of these seminars we asked the participants to submit questions concerning family living.

More than 50 percent of these questions pertained to sexual adjustment. Our questionnaire, examined in chapter 13, contained a space at the end for important questions regarding sex, and almost every survey response included one or more questions. The obvious need for help on this score has greatly influenced us to write this book, particularly this chapter on sex questions.

Many of our answers will be different from those given by the popular sex writers of our day. We make no apology for this, because we are committed to the authority of the Bible, testing all problems and ideas by its principles. We believe that the key to happiness is to know the principles of God and do them (John 7:17). Secular writers are usually humanists who start with the fallacious premise that man is an animal and can satisfy his basic drives and passions in any way he desires as long as he doesn't hurt someone else. By contrast, we believe that man is a special creation of God and that the Bible is His manual on human behavior. Where the Bible speaks clearly on a subject, therefore, we will probably be 180 degrees in opposition to the humanistic viewpoint.

There are two reasons why we are convinced that obedience to biblical principles on this delicate subject produces far greater happiness than does the philosophy of humanism:

1. Biblical principles come from a loving, all-knowing God who understands what is best for the human race (His special creation).

2. We have seen so many miserable devotees of humanism switch to biblical principles and find happiness that we are convinced they work.

One thing should be kept in mind when a person finds answers to life's questions in the Bible: God's Word doesn't cover every single facet of married love in detail. Thus it is easy to be swayed by traditions or opinions that may or may not be grounded in Scripture but instead are carryovers from a past cultural practice or standard. We have tried to be fair in such matters and strip ourselves of unscriptural prejudices when answering these questions. Where the Bible speaks clearly, we speak positively; where the Bible is silent, we offer our opinions.

Abortion

Is it ever right for a Christian woman to have an abortion?

A crucial issue in today' society relates to the morality of abortion. Ever since the 1973 Supreme Court ruling granted a constitutional guarantee of privacy in such matters and left the decision to the individual woman during the first six months of her pregnancy, legalized abortions have increased at a catastrophic rate. Currently they are said to be 4000 per day or a total of 1.5 million per year. Many opponents of abortion had earlier warned that if it were made legal, it would result in promiscuity, infidelity, venereal disease, and guilt. Who can deny the accuracy of their forecast?

There are two kinds of abortions—natural and induced. Although medical science cannot tell why, some women abort their pregnancies naturally, which may be nature's way of dealing with birth defects or other prenatal complications. Induced abortions are medically simple if performed by a competent doctor in the early stages of pregnancy. There are two reasons for inducing an abortion: (1) to save the life of the mother when such action is necessary; this is called a "therapeutic abortion"; and (2) to serve the wishes of the mother, because she is either unmarried or does not want the child. In such cases those making such a decision must bear the moral responsibility for their actions.

Although abortion has been legalized by an overwhelmingly secularized court majority, such approval does not make it moral.

Most Christians oppose abortion with the sole exception of those extremely rare cases of saving the life of the mother. The abortion industry uses that exception as a smoke screen to try to justify their repugnant practice. Even President Clinton, in an attempt to justify the gruesome partial-birth abortion technique, which was opposed by both houses of Congress, tried to justify his veto because in some instances it would save the mother's life. In truth, most doctors acknowledge that if such were the case, the child could be removed through a cesarean section during the seventh or eighth month when both child and mother have an excellent chance to survive. Even pro-choice Senator Kay Bailey Hutcheson freely states, "The partial-birth abortion is not abortion, it is murder."

In recent years we have come to realize that even in rape cases there is no justification for abortion. All counselors, of course, should advise a "D and C" or other cleansing treatment by approved medical doctors immediately after such a traumatic experience *before* conception occurs. Such a procedure is therapeutically safe, and since life has not been "propagated" yet (or conceived, if you prefer), it is not murder.

To see the high regard for human life reflected in the Bible, read Exodus 21:22–23, which taught the children of Israel that the unborn child deserves the same protection as any other living human. For it instructs that if a pregnant women loses her child prematurely because a man happens to injure her, the man should be put to death. Obviously the Bible regards the unborn fetus as a truly living human being. We must do no less.

Abortion on demand has reached frightening proportions today. One report indicates that since the 1973 Supreme Court legalized such murder, over 40 million abortions have been performed in the U.S. Christians need to understand that the Bible, not the Supreme Court, is our basis for morality. We should all work for the defeat of any political leader who votes for abortion. He or she obviously does not have a sufficiently high regard for human life to represent the Christian community.

Many churches today that have traditionally been silent on political issues have become active in urging their members to be diligent in registering to vote, encouraging others to vote, and even considering running for public office. They have not ceased preaching the gospel, for that is their major thrust and commission, but they realize that the abortion carnage has become far worse than the holocaust of the '40s and must be opposed by all who have a high view of human life.

The Hidden Danger of the Abortion Issue

One of the best kept secrets of the abortion issue is that young women who have had an abortion are at higher risk of having breast cancer later in life than those who have not. In some cases the risk is almost two and a half times greater. This has been verified by several competent scientists qualified to make such an assessment. On her daily radio program Beverly interviewed Dr. Joel Brind, an endocrinologist at two prestigious medical institutions. He said, "There is a clear relationship documented in medical journals showing that women aborting their first pregnancy are at much higher risk of developing breast cancer than women who carry their pregnancy to term." For more information on this important subject call Concerned Women for America at 1 (800) 458–8797 and request their free brochure "Breast Cancer's Link to Abortion." You may also wish to order the excellent video *After the Choice*, which gives stirring testimonies of sixteen women who aborted their babies. Every young teenage woman or anyone considering an abortion should see this presentation.

When I was a teenager I had an abortion. Years later I became a Christian. Now I have a family, but I am still troubled by what I have done. Will I ever get over this feeling of guilt?

Pro-abortionists rarely discuss the enormous guilt that often follows an abortion. I well recall conducting a funeral for a twenty-one-year-old woman who had committed suicide after hers!

Thankfully, the Bible guarantees that the blood of Jesus Christ cleanses us from *all sin*, including abortion (1 John 1:7–9). I suggest two procedures that will help you to deal with your guilt: (1) do a Bible study on God's forgiveness; (2) after having asked God's forgiveness for that specific sin, thank Him by faith for His forgiveness each time you recall the experience. Gradually your feelings of guilt will fade away.

Adultery

Can a person truly be forgiven of adultery?

The sins of adultery, homosexuality, and murder were held as capital crimes in the Bible, as evidenced by the prescribed death penalty (Lev. 20:10). Clearly, human life is of prime importance in the Word of God, and these sins affect the perpetuity of life. In spite of that, Jesus Christ's sacrifice on the cross is sufficient to cleanse a person of these or any other sins (1 John 1:7, 9). Further evidence of God's pardon of this sin appears in Jesus' forgiveness of the woman taken in adultery (John 8:1–11) and the woman with five husbands who was living with still another man (John 4:1–41).

Can a Christian commit adultery?

Christians are potentially capable of committing any sin known to man, but if they are "born again," they cannot avoid the ensuing guilt that comes through the Holy Spirit (John 16:7–11). For that reason Paul challenges Christians to walk in the motivation of the Spirit, not in the motivation of the flesh (Gal. 5:16–21). If Christians harbor evil thoughts over a period of time, they will ultimately act out these thoughts. That is why Christ equated lustful thoughts with adultery (Matt. 5:28). In this day of abundant sexual temptation it is imperative to guard one's thought life.

How can I forgive my partner for his unfaithfulness?

There is probably no greater betrayal of trust than marital infidelity; consequently it is not uncommon for the offended partner to find great difficulty in forgiving his or her mate. But anguish and resentment must not be perpetuated, for though it is understandable, resentment is no basis on which to build a relationship. That is why many couples break up after an adulterous escapade, even when it is concluded with repentance and the offender discontinues such conduct.

Our Lord taught the necessity of forgiveness in Matthew 6:14–15; Ephesians 4:32; and many other passages. God never commands us to do what He will not enable us to do; therefore, if you *want* to forgive, you can. But if you wish to harbor bitterness and bear a grudge, you will probably never get over these destructive feelings. I challenged one offended wife with that problem, "Do you want to be happy the rest of your life or miserable? It's up to you!"

How can I forgive myself for being unfaithful to my partner?

Infidelity is among the most devastating blows to a marriage, creating a series of harmful results, not the least of which is the guilt that engulfs the transgressor. We have seen such guilt drive the offender to a nervous breakdown. The Scripture says, "The way of the unfaithful is hard" (Prov. 13:15); that is particularly true of sexual sins.

All self-forgiveness begins with God's forgiveness. Once the realization grips you that your confession of that sin in the name of Jesus Christ has cleansed you from *all* unrighteousness, you will begin to forgive yourself. Two things can hasten this: (1) get a Bible concordance and write down every verse in Scripture on the subject of forgiveness of sin, then read them over several times; (2) on the basis of 1 John 1:9, every time you remember your sin, pause long enough to thank God by faith that He has forgiven you. Gradually you will learn to accept forgiveness as a fact rather than condemn yourself for confessed sin.

I have confessed my sin of adultery to God and have no intention of repeating it. Should I tell my partner?

Although other factors must be considered that are not included in this brief question, we ordinarily do not recommend telling the offended partner in such cases when the following conditions are met:

1. Genuine repentance and confession of the sin to God;

2. Severing the illicit relationship and avoiding any contact with the other person;

3. The establishment of spiritual safeguards, e.g., a daily prayer and quiet time, regular church participation, and an honest talk with one's minister.

Once adultery has been committed, can you ever trust your partner again? Doesn't one offense make others easier?

This all depends on whether your spouse has repented of that sin, confessed it to God and to you, and has broken off all contact with the other person. If these have occurred, you would be wise to give your mate every chance to prove his or her sincerity by forgiving and forgetting the past. If these have not occurred and you tell your mate that you freely forgive the offense, you will only teach the offending person that he or she can "eat his cake and have it too."

This should be a time for you to evaluate your life honestly to search for ways to change your own attitudes and behavior so that, with God's help in applying biblical principles, you may become the best possible partner spiritually, emotionally, and physically. When a husband or wife is unfaithful, there is usually, but not always, some definite lack in the faithful mate in meeting the other's desires and needs.

In any marriage in which one or both partners is a Christian, the couple should exhaust all resources before deciding to obtain a divorce, even when one is an adulterer.

Divorce should always be the last resort after many sincere attempts at reconciliation.

Birth Control

Is it right for Christians to practice birth control?

Chapter 12 explains that virtually every couple practices some form of birth control, for otherwise families would be much larger than they are. If the partners do not use one or more of the scientific methods described in that chapter, they at least practice abstinence during the wife's most fertile time. However, this seems unfair to the wife, because that is the time when she would find lovemaking most enjoyable. Rather than cheat her out of the pleasure God designed for her to enjoy in marriage, it would be better to use a proven contraceptive. But as we warned in chapter 12, though we believe God does not oppose limiting the size of one's family to the number of children one can effectively raise to serve Him, we do think He never intended couples to use birth-control devices to exclude children. They are "a heritage from the LORD" (Ps. 127:3) and a great source of blessing that every couple should desire.

Doesn't God's displeasure with Onan in his spilling his seed on the ground indicate that He opposes birth control?

If that kind of reasoning were used in the slaying of Ananias and Sapphira in Acts 5, one could conclude that God opposes a person's selling his possessions and giving the return as an offering to Him. In both instances, however, God slew the people because they pretended to do one thing, but did another. In Genesis 38:8–10, we read that Onan cheated his brother out of his rightful heritage by refusing to father a child in his brother's name, as was the custom in his day. Thus it is wrong to use this isolated text to condemn the use of birth control.

Since the withdrawal method of birth control is the most natural, is it displeasing to God?

It is not wrong to use the withdrawal method (coitus interruptus), but doctors tell us it is not effective. Most men think that if their ejaculation occurs outside the vagina, their wife will not get pregnant. But that is not necessarily true. Preceding ejaculation, a man excretes a small amount of fluid that contains enough sperm to impregnate the average woman. For that reason the withdrawal method is not a recommended procedure. In addition, it is almost impossible for the wife to reach orgasm when coitus interruptus is used.

Please suggest Scriptures on birth control. I have a friend who is going to have her seventh child—her fifth baby in five years. Her husband does not believe in birth control (except the rhythm method).

There is no clear-cut scriptural reference advocating birth control, nor is there one condemning it. The attitude of Christians is changing on this subject, and thus birth control is gaining much more acceptance. The Bible was written long before such methods were developed; consequently its silence cannot be used to prove either point—as long as the couple does not refuse to have any children. We are inclined to believe that if the husband in question were to bear the eighth child, there probably would not be a ninth.

As a counselor I cannot help but comment on the abject selfishness of the above-mentioned husband. He obviously does not have loving regard for his wife's health, energy, interests, or person. There is certainly nothing wrong with a couple having seven or more children, even in our day, but it should be a *mutually* agreed upon decision.

The problem of sterilization for either man or woman—is this really trusting the Lord?

If you "trust the Lord," you will have children. That is His will, as attested by the way He has designed our bodies—for the propagation of the race. The question really is, When does one quit—after two, four, six, or more? Such a question all individuals must answer for themselves. We don't hesitate to have an infected appendix or gall bladder removed—is that "trusting the Lord"? We use modern science and medicine frequently; why shouldn't couples do the same with their reproductive organs once their families reach the size they feel they can raise effectively to serve Him?

Is it any greater sin to have a vasectomy than to use gel contraceptives?

Probably not, since both accomplish the same end. But a vasectomy in most instances is irreversible, so one must be absolutely certain he does not want additional children before submitting to such surgery. We do not recommend vasectomies for men under thirty-five or forty years old.

Communication
How can I learn to talk better to my husband about these things?

Sex is the world's most exciting subject, yet most people find it embarrassing to discuss. That is particularly true of married partners unless they begin immediately—

on their honeymoon or shortly after. Usually the longer you wait, the harder it is. Assuming that this question was asked by someone married quite some time, we suggest taking the following steps:

1. Pray for God's leading and direction.
2. Set a good time for your partner when you are not rushed and will not be interrupted.
3. Assure him or her of your basic love, then kindly state your true feelings—that you think something is missing in your love life and you would like to talk about it.
4. The giant step in working things out is for both partners to admit to a problem. In all likelihood, if you find sex difficult to discuss, you probably find it difficult to communicate about many things.
5. Try to get your partner to read this book and hopefully to discuss it with you.
6. Anticipate a solution—don't present an overly bleak picture; you *can* overcome this problem with God's help (Phil. 4:13).
7. If difficulties persist, make an appointment to consult your minister together.

How can I communicate what I like, as a wife, so that my husband understands?

Talk frankly to him. If you are unsatisfied, say so. Most women find it difficult to converse with their husbands about sex, which merely protracts their frustration.

My husband had only "street" sex information and retains that attitude toward sex. This bothers me. What can I do?

*When I ask about my husband's long time (four to six weeks)
without sex, he merely says he's been too busy. Is this normal?*

Hopefully this book will help him. Once every four
to six weeks is certainly less than the average recorded
in our survey. Sex organs need to be used regularly to
function at their best. Talk to him frankly; if nothing
happens, he should get a checkup from a doctor.

*How do you make men understand that women's passions
rise and fall according to the cares and problems of the day
and that their tiredness and lack of passion are in no way a
rejection of their husbands?*

By telling them so—gently—seasoned with love.
Make sure you don't use "tiredness" as a cop-out. Do you
take a nap before your husband comes home? If you are
too tired to make love a majority of the times he desires
it, you *are* too tired. You may need a medical checkup,
vitamins, exercise, more rest, or a curtailment of some
of your activities.

*To what extent should a couple talk about previous rela-
tionships (some perverted)?*

Almost none. The Bible teaches us to forget "what
is behind" (Phil 3:13) and think of those things that are
pure (Phil. 4:8). Force your mind to think only of the
good things of life, particularly those things that relate
to love with your partner.

Counseling
Are the new sex clinics right for Christians?

That is too broad and general a question for a
precise response. A Christian should always keep in

mind when seeking any kind of counseling that non-Christians, no matter how capably trained, reflect different value systems from ours. That is what the psalm of the happy man means by saying, "Blessed is the man who does not walk in the counsel of the wicked" (Ps. 1:1). What becomes acceptable behavior to Masters and Johnson or David Reuben may prove contrary to the Scriptures. Therefore all counseling should be weighed in the light of the spiritual values of the counselor. This is not to say that his or her instruction for severe cases of a woman's lack of desire for sex, or male impotence, is not beneficial. The more you know about any problem, the better equipped you are to cope with it. Personally, we feel that a Christian couple would be better advised to obtain Dr. Wheat's set of cassettes and spend two or three weekend vacations practicing his suggestions than to get involved with some expensive form of therapy, particularly if it admittedly lacks moral values.

Sexual dysfunction clinics are in vogue now. Some clinics are staffed by competently trained personnel, but that is certainly not the case generally. We know of two former welfare recipients who maintained a nightmarish sex life, have now started their own such clinic, and are getting rich at it. Some of the advertising circulars I receive indicate that many services offer little more than a new method of sexual mating for a fee. Some of these sensitivity-group-therapy sex-dysfunction sessions reportedly end up as orgies. Obviously anyone should be advised to avoid groups of that sort, and you should investigate your state's standards for certifying such clinics and the qualifications of any counselor you seek help from.

Where can a Christian wife go for help when there is a sex problem in her marriage?

Your minister is the proper person with whom to start. Many pastors today are experienced counselors, and you can be certain that your pastor will keep your confidence. If he is unable to help you, he will probably be able to suggest another counselor.

Dating

I believe that young people need specific Christian principles to guide their sex lives before marriage. Could you please give the most important of these and tell why they are important?

Sex education coupled with moral principles should be taught discreetly by churches, but that issue is not within the scope of this book. We regularly share the following principles with our young people.

1. Your body is the temple of the Holy Spirit; it should be kept holy for Him. "Do you not know that your body is a temple of the Holy Spirit . . . ? You are not your own; you were bought at a price. Therefore glorify God with your body" (1 Cor. 6:19–20).

2. Keep your body for your life's partner. "Do you not know that your bodies are members of Christ himself? Shall I then take the members of Christ and unite them with a prostitute? Never! Do you not know that he who unites himself with a prostitute is one with her in body? For it is said, 'The two will become one flesh.' But he who unites himself with the Lord is one with him in spirit. Flee from sexual immorality. All other sins a man commits are outside his body, but he who sins sexually sins against his own body" (1 Cor. 6:15–18).

3. Date only Christians, for dating is the prelude to marriage. "Do not be yoked together with unbelievers. For what do righteousness and wickedness have in

common? Or what fellowship can light have with darkness?" (2 Cor. 6:14).

4. Always conduct yourself as if Christ were present. "Whether you eat or drink or whatever you do, do it all for the glory of God" (1 Cor. 10:31).

What about oral sex before marriage? It isn't really intercourse, is it?

Perhaps not, but it's much too intimate for unmarried people. Until they are pronounced husband and wife, they have no business handling each other's genitalia. Many a married woman suffers today from guilt feelings and shame caused by indulging in such practices before meeting her husband. "Love is blind," they say— blind to the fact that it does not always result in marriage. We know of cases in which couples had to leave their home churches after marriage because the wife couldn't face the man she was previously so intimate with before breaking their engagement.

Ejaculation
How can a man delay orgasm long enough for his wife to get aroused?

First, by delaying entrance until she is ready— well-lubricated and her labia minora (or vaginal lips) enlarged two to three times their normal size. Then after inserting the penis, by remaining motionless for one to two minutes to gain control. During this time continue to stimulate your wife's clitoris gently with your finger; this should have her on the verge of climax before you start thrusting. Avoid *deep* penetration and try to keep the glans penis between one and three inches inside the vagina to produce maximum excitement for your wife.

Fantasy

Is it wrong for a husband to fantasize as long as he doesn't commit adultery? Although I feel guilty about it, I find that it stimulates me. Three psychiatrists have told me that it's perfectly normal and everybody does it.

"Fantasizing" about a woman other than your wife is a fancy title for old-fashioned "lust," which Jesus Christ equated with adultery (Matt. 5:28). The Bible has much to say about keeping our thought lives pure (Phil. 4:8), ". . . we take captive every thought to make it obedient to Christ" (2 Cor. 10:5). The mind is the doorway to the emotions or heart. If you think evil or lustful thoughts, they will make you feel lustful—"For as he thinks within himself, so he is" (Prov. 23:7 mg). Fantasizing will often cause a person to "use" his partner rather than "love" her; it tends to overstimulate, producing a premature ejaculation, and it creates unreal expectations. Just because something is exciting doesn't make it right.

How can I learn to control my thought life?

There are six steps to gaining control of your mind.

1. Confess all evil thinking as sin—1 John 1:9.
2. Keep in step with the Spirit—Gal. 5:16–25.
3. Ask God for victory over the habit—1 John 5:14–15.
4. Whenever possible, avoid all suggestive material—i.e., most movies, questionable TV programs, and pornography.
5. If you are married, think only of your wife or husband; if single, force your mind to think pure thoughts about all other people—Phil. 4:8.

6. Repeat the above steps when your mind digs up old lustful thought patterns.

It takes from thirty to sixty days to create new thought patterns, so don't expect success overnight and don't permit your mind an exception. Gradually you will find it easier to control your thoughts, but periodically both men and women will face increased temptation in this matter.

If sex starts in the mind, should a wife try to "turn on" by thinking or imagining sexually exciting things? Like what? Are such thoughts (if not including one's own husband) sinful?

Yes and no. Yes—it is perfectly all right for a wife to visualize herself being embraced and caressed by her husband. No—a wife should not picture herself in the arms of another man; that is lust, which is expressly forbidden by our Lord. "But I tell you that anyone who looks at a woman lustfully has already committed adultery with her in his heart" (Matt. 5:28).

I love my husband and am not at all infatuated by any other man; but during sex relations I have to fantasize some illicit relations with another man (never anyone I know). I am ashamed to tell my husband this. Is this sinful for me? Is it because my husband doesn't excite me enough, or what?

You have developed a very bad mental habit. Transfer your thoughts to your husband. Visualize earlier lovemaking experiences with him, or better yet, make love in a softly lighted room, keep your eyes open, and concentrate on what you are doing.

How much sex or possible lust should be allowed to fill one's daily thinking?

None. Lust is like a disease—it will grow. Bring your mind into obedience to Christ (2 Cor. 10:5) and root out *all* evil imaginations.

Foreplay

Why are husbands always in a hurry to make love? My husband doesn't seem to understand that I need a slow buildup before I become as passionate as he is.

In talking with wives, we find this a common problem. For reasons known only to God, women and men are as different in their love timing as in their physical apparatus. Unfortunately most men just don't realize this fact. If they did, there would be far more husbands whose wives considered them great lovers, because time in buildup is probably the main difference between a husband who is mediocre in bed and one who is a fantastic lover.

Most men don't seem to realize that a woman usually prefers a long, slow burn to the instant explosion. Because a man is an instant igniter, he often makes the terrible mistake of trying to adapt his wife to himself rather than to satisfy her needs. It is a wise husband who adjusts his style to his wife's emotional pattern by beginning early in the evening to show love and affectionate tenderness, then gradually building his wife to a strong desire for lovemaking. When properly prepared, a woman's entire body becomes sensitive to his touch, and he can develop great personal enjoyment by watching her respond to his tender caressing. The old adage "Haste makes waste" certainly applies to lovemaking.

Is a woman's clitoris always the spot she desires her husband to touch to arouse her sexual tensions?

Definitely not. A woman is not a machine whose dials, levers, and buttons always produce the same effect. She is moody and cyclic, so her husband must be sensitive to her needs. When she is particularly passionate, a man can manipulate her clitoris immediately, but that is the exception, not the rule. Ordinarily she has to be kissed, caressed, and fondled in various parts of her body before she is ready for him to *gently* stroke the clitoris. Many wives complain that when their husbands learn about the clitoris, they often joggle it crudely as if it were a switch that is supposed to start their desire motor. The husband may ignite his outboard motor that way, but it won't work with his wife. Gentle tenderness is the way to arouse a woman's desire.

What about oral manipulation of breasts?

This is a common part of lovemaking with most couples. While many women enjoy it thoroughly, others do not. If it turns his wife off, a husband should find other ways to stimulate her.

Fornication

Is there a difference between adultery and fornication?

The Bible uses the terms *adultery* and *fornication* interchangeably in some places and separately in others. Some people try to distinguish between them, suggesting that adultery is infidelity on the part of married people and fornication involves intercourse between the unmarried or when one is unmarried. We can't see that it makes any difference. Both are forbidden and condemned in the Bible, which states that "those who [continually] live like this will not inherit the kingdom of God" (Gal. 5:19–21; cf. 1 Cor. 6:9).

Free Love

Why shouldn't healthy young people who have to wait several years to think about marriage practice free love as long as they are honest with each other? It is a natural way to reduce their sexual pressure.

This question is increasingly on the minds even of Christian young people today. And it is a commentary on the effectiveness of the humanistic philosophy being offered by most secular educators. We propose the following reasons for preserving sexual intercourse for marriage.

1. It will maintain your spiritual and physical health. All sexual intercourse outside marriage is condemned in the Bible; consequently you will never be a strong, growing Christian while practicing free love. Physically it is hazardous, for it leads to promiscuity if the relationship is broken. The U.S. Department of Health and Human Services has branded venereal disease the number one health hazard in the nation today for persons under twenty-four years of age. A high school principal said recently that one out of every five graduating seniors has either had or carries venereal disease. Thus free love is a risky business.

2. Sex was never intended to be an impersonal bodily exercise like swimming or football. It is an intensely emotional experience; therefore, sex without love before marriage hinders a person from pursuing sex as an expression of love after the wedding.

3. Free love usually results in the creation of unfair and unnecessary comparisons. A Don Juan may be "a great lover" but an inferior person, whereas an excellent man to marry and father your children may be somewhat lacking in bed. Some wives prefer their husbands in

every other aspect of life, but because of previous experience are dissatisfied with their lovemaking.

4. Guilt often rushes in like a flood after a person reaches thirty years of age, particularly in a woman, destroying a lifetime of wholesome love experiences.

5. It often keeps a person from finding the right mate later on. Like begets like—you won't find dedicated Christians from whom to select a life's partner amqng the free-love crowd.

6. Free love isn't free. A twenty-one-year-old young woman wrote "Dear Abby," urging her to warn young women that "free love isn't free." She admitted that she had been promiscuous since the age of fourteen and now had to undergo an operation to keep V.D. from destroying her life. "It cost me the opportunity of ever becoming a mother." The day I read that story, I couldn't help but remember the twenty-two-year-old Vietnam veteran who admitted to practicing "free love" while in the service. He wept as he said, "V.D. has left me completely sterile." There is no way in the world that a few exciting experiences in one's youth can equal a lifetime of love experiences with a married partner, not to mention the joys of being a parent.

7. Free love is wrong. God's standards are not flexible, nor does time erode them. Virtue, chastity, and modesty are still the primary building blocks of marriage. Never has a woman come to me with a guilt complex because she has entered marriage virtuously, but many have requested counseling for the opposite reason. The Devil has always been a "deceiver" of mankind; in fact, our Lord called him a liar, and the apostle Paul reminds us that "Satan . . . masquerades as an angel of light"

(2 Cor. 11:14). Free love is a lie of the Devil. Those who heed it are "not wise."

How should parents treat a son or daughter who is living with someone without marriage?

This is one of the most distressing experiences a parent can endure. As one mother exclaimed, "I would rather hear that she died!" I'm not sure she *really* felt that way, but it seemed so at the time. Such an outburst, however, does display a parent's concern.

No matter what your children do, they are still your children and in need of your love. For that reason, don't shut them out of your life. They know you don't approve of their conduct, and you may feel that you can't visit in their home without appearing to condone their actions. But we feel that you should welcome both of them into your home and avoid preaching at them or condemning them all the time—the Holy Spirit will do that. If you continue to express your love (but not your approval), then when the illicit relationship finally blows up, you will be able to help them pick up the pieces of their lives. Read the story of the prodigal son's father in Luke 15.

Please discuss "living together" before marriage. My friends feel it is unfair to both partners if they cannot try it out for a while to see if they are compatible before making a life-time commitment.

Such patently humanistic logic is expressly forbidden in the Bible. There is no guarantee that courtship or engagement will lead to marriage. Only a most unwise couple engages in premarital sex; in fact, it is the leading cause of guilt feelings after marriage.

In our survey we asked the question, "If you were getting married all over again, what one thing would you change?" The number one answer was, "I would not engage in premarital sex."

The survey also indicated that women who were virgins at the time of marriage registered a higher satisfaction level than did the promiscuous.

Frequency
How often does an average couple make love?

Most researchers and writers in the field of sexual adjustment in marriage are reluctant to publish "an average" as a norm. Obviously people are not "average," but individuals; in addition, many complex factors must be considered: What are the ages of the couple? Are they raising small children in cramped quarters? Do they enjoy bedroom privacy? Does the husband have an emotionally pressurized administrative job, or does he do hard manual labor? Does the wife work, cook meals, and keep house? Did they come from loving homes? Are they happy? What are their views of married love? Are they Christians? What temperaments do they represent?

Dr. Wheat recalls a survey on this subject involving five thousand couples. The results of the survey revealed that the average frequency was two to three times a week. Dr. Herbert J. Miles' survey of young couples indicated that the frequency was once every 3.3 days, or about twice a week. A *Parade Magazine* article on the sex life of six thousand modern executives of all ages who were confronted with the pressures of business reported an average of once a week. Our survey taken from Christians who attended our seminars indicates that about three times a week over the entire period of marriage was "average."

Actually whatever rate of frequency brings enjoyment and fulfillment to the two of you is "average" for you. A couple should not keep score on their love; they should be spontaneous, giving, sharing, and enjoying it whenever it occurs.

How much does tiredness due to extended activities affect frequency of intercourse?

Tiredness affects frequency far more than many people realize. Most people go to bed too late these days (after the eleven o'clock news); 11:30 P.M. to midnight may be great for sleeping, but it is bad timing for loving.

How can a wife have the same sexual desires as her husband?

It is not uncommon for a young wife to be aware of her husband's stronger sex drive and feel somewhat inadequate as a result. Caring for two or three preschool children can accentuate this problem because of boredom, tiredness, or both. But if she and her husband grow in love toward the Lord and each other, gradually improving their lovemaking techniques, the wife's desire for love will slowly increase through the years until she will desire him as frequently as he does her.

Does God expect a Christian wife to be compatible sexually with her husband? I feel unhappy for myself as well as my husband; I don't know what to do about it.

God intended the act of marriage to be a mutually enjoyable experience. Since the wife asked this question, she probably has not learned to achieve a satisfying orgasm regularly. If she and her husband will study this book carefully and experiment with each other accordingly, she will learn that art. Once that is achieved, her desire for the experience will increase.

According to Ephesians 5:22, wives should always submit (willingly and joyfully) to their husbands' advances. What if we are honestly tired? The times I have said no have left me feeling quite guilty, and I resent the guilt.

If you really were too tired, you shouldn't feel guilty. A loving husband can understand tiredness, even though he may be disappointed. But don't let it become a habit, and make sure it isn't an excuse. If it's just an excuse for resentment, selfishness, revenge, or something else, you will naturally feel guilty. Speak "the truth in love" (Eph. 4:15), then go to sleep with a clear conscience.

I feel I need sexual intercourse more frequently, but my wife doesn't want it. How can this be changed (we average about once every two weeks)?

First, you should analyze whether you "love" your wife or "use" her. Our survey indicates that many wives who have never experienced orgasm still enjoy lovemaking. They relish the closeness, tenderness, and endearment that always accompanies real lovemaking. But the man who is too selfish to learn the art of lovemaking and uses his wife to relieve his sexual tensions will never create desire in her for the relationship. Unless there are medical problems or deep-rooted emotional problems from their past, most married women's attitudes toward lovemaking reflect their husbands' treatment. It is a rare couple who needs sex counseling when the husband has consistently expressed genuine love for his wife, studied the art of coitus, and taken plenty of time for tenderness in foreplay and protracted cuddling after ejaculation. Consider these comments from women's responses in our sex survey:

—"Besides sexual foreplay, I feel a strong need of being cuddled and held after the orgasmic ejaculation, a soothing 'afterglow.' I feel that female orgasm in every intercourse has been overemphasized."

—"Please stress how important a husband's treatment of his wife is during the day and how it affects her sex life at the end of the day (manners, temper, etc.)."

—"Encourage the husband to tell his wife he loves her, etc., during intercourse and at other times. Even though I know my husband loves me, it's just nice to hear it often."

We are so busy in our church (meetings in evenings, etc.) that it is hard to find time to fit in a love life. How should we handle this?

When married people are too busy for love, they are too busy! Nothing should crowd that necessary part of life into disuse—even the church. God established both institutions—the church and the home. They should never be competitive; instead, He planned them to be cooperative. When the church takes excessive time at the expense of the home, your priorities are out of balance. We suggest that you evaluate your schedule, and if you're really neglecting your home and family to attend meetings night after night, it is time to cut out some activities and stay home.

As a person looks to Christ more totally, doesn't the emphasis on sex become diminished and less important as true love binds the couple?

Looking to Christ doesn't change bodily needs and functions. Since Spirit-filled Christians get hungry, thirsty, and tired, why shouldn't they maintain a desire for lovemaking? After all, it is a perfectly sacred experience between married partners. Our survey shows that Spirit-filled Christians make love more frequently on the average than other couples in today's society. Besides, "true love" looks for an opportunity to express itself; lovemaking is the God-ordained arena for love's expression.

What does a wife do whose husband does not need sex more than once or twice a month (and the wife wants it two to three times a week)?

Have a good talk with him. He may be masturbating now and then, or he may just not be aware of your desire. Check your submission; if you are an unsubmissive wife, this may be his subconscious way of getting back at you. Then try to be more seductive in the bedroom. Not many men can keep from being aroused by a sexually stimulating wife.

My wife enjoys intercourse when we have it, but how can I help her to desire it more than twice a month?

Although she may "enjoy intercourse," does she have orgasms? There is a great difference. The most exciting sensation any woman can experience is an orgasm. It is a rare woman who desires only two such exciting experiences a month. Read chapter 6, "The Art of Lovemaking," and be sure that your wife is having the real thing; you'll be amazed how her appetite for lovemaking will increase.

Frigidity, or a Lack of Desire for Sex

Are some women born frigid?

With 3.8 billion people on the earth, over half of whom are women, no doubt *some* were born physically incapable of orgasm, but their number is so small that it is most unlikely that any of them will ever read this book. Dr. David Reuben says, "There is no reason why every woman should not have regular and frequent orgasms, if she wants to."[1] To illustrate further that the problem is emotionally caused and not physically induced, he states, "No psychiatrist has ever seen a woman with this condition who was raised by loving parents in a warm, secure family environment. Most women who suffer from orgasmic impairment suffered serious emotional deprivation during childhood and after."[2]

One reason why we believe women raised in a Christian home enjoy the pleasures of lovemaking more than others (a belief verified by our sex survey) is that they are more likely to have experienced a warm father-daughter love relationship. One of the best things a father can do for his daughters is to let them run into his heart any time they like. He should avoid all selfish urges to shut them out or turn them off, no matter how busy he is. A lack of desire for sex is not usually a physical matter, but an emotional withdrawal from the opposite sex that can be well developed by the time a girl is six years old. Cold, selfish fathers are the greatest cause of cold, frigid women.

What can a man do with a wife who is sexually unresponsive? I love my wife, but I'm not sure how long I can tolerate this.

It takes a lot of tender loving care from a husband and determination from a wife to overcome this problem, but it can be done. Please study chapters 9 and 10 and carefully follow the suggestions you find there. A man displays considerable maturity when he understands that his wife's rejection of him is probably a carryover from childhood and that he must *patiently* prove to her that he is not the same kind of man as her father. Every action should be kind and tender. Never raise your voice to her, but treat her with dignity and respect in public and private; gradually she will come around. In addition to reading this book, send for Dr. Wheat's cassette tapes, listen to them with your wife, and follow his suggestions. In short, love her as your own body (Eph. 5:28).

Why does a frigid woman get married in the first place?

By no means did she deliberately set out to deceive you, for she probably never dreamed she had little or no desire for sex. In the midst of unhappiness at home and at the time of her greatest sex drive (at ages sixteen to twenty-two), she met you and fell in love. Since lovemaking at best occupies only about 1/168th of a person's time throughout marriage, she probably was thinking more about life with you, homemaking, motherhood, and the other important aspects of married life than she was about coitus when she agreed to become your wife. Like swimming, skiing, or anything else, orgasm through lovemaking is an art that must be learned. The problem is, no other function in life so combines the emotional and the physical parts of two people like coitus, and this skill demands unusually concentrated practice.

I've heard your talk on sex, and frankly I wasn't impressed. Why is it that I don't like sex and don't want to?

You are probably filled with resentment, first toward your father and now transferred to your husband. Your shell of psychological self-protection has stifled your natural flow of emotions, making you a very selfish person. Unless you seriously begin to consider your responsibilities to God and the emotional needs of your husband and children, you will destroy your marriage. Emotional self-protection doesn't really keep you from being hurt, for it wounds everyone you love and consequently you yourself. Our Lord said, "Give, and it will be given to you" (Luke 6:38)—that is particularly true of love.

One of the most rewarding experiences of a marriage counselor is to observe that women who have this problem begin to seek God's help in giving sexual love to their husbands, only to find that they simply needed a little knowledge of anatomy and a few techniques of physical stimulation to learn the exciting art of orgasmic expression. It opens a whole new dimension to their lives.

Genitalia

Is it possible for a couple to be so physically mismatched (too big or too small) that they cannot have good relations?

Many men are almost paranoid about the size of their genitalia, and women are almost as concerned with their breast size. Unfortunately ignorance usually produces ungrounded fear, and such fear proves a greater sexual deterrent than the size of their organs.

Actually, no matter how tall or short the man, his erect penis is almost always six to eight inches long, and as we previously pointed out, three inches would be adequate for propagation and wifely satisfaction. Similarly, no matter the size of the woman, her vagina will not vary more than about one inch in depth. Research indicates that very tall men married to short women have the same ratio of sexual enjoyment as two people of the same height. Extreme difference in size may make it difficult to kiss during coitus, but there is no evidence to suggest that a man may be too large or too small for a woman. God's creative design has taken care of that.

Although I enjoy it when my husband stimulates my clitoris with his fingers, why does it make me feel guilty?

We are all influenced by our backgrounds, for good or ill. Somewhere in the past you developed the idea that pleasure must be sinful, according to the saying "Everything I enjoy is either sinful, illegal, or fattening." That's ridiculous! God has given us many wonderful things in life to enjoy, and married love is one of them. Nothing in the Bible condemns clitoral stimulation between married partners. Hebrews 13:4 makes allowance for it, and the Song of Songs describes it (2:6). In fact, there is no other known purpose for the clitoris than to provide you with sexual stimulation. Your heavenly Father placed it there for your enjoyment.

To show how widely accepted this artful technique is in lovemaking, 92 percent of the Bible-believing ministers surveyed approved its use. (Keep in mind, only 17 percent of these same ministers approved self-stimulation.) We suggest that you thank God for such a tender, thoughtful husband and enjoy the experience.

Ever since I had my hysterectomy I have been unable to experience an orgasm, and I have had an increasing problem with depression.

You reflect two problems—orgasmic malfunction and depression. Both are likely to stem from the same source—fear of inadequacy. Most women fear that a hysterectomy will render them less of a woman and incapable of sexual fulfillment, but nothing could be further from the truth. While it is true that a hysterectomy will eliminate your monthly period, there is no medical reason why it should interfere with your marital pleasure. In fact, many women have indicated a greater freedom and enjoyment in lovemaking after such surgery. But you must get over the idea that because your reproductive equipment has been removed, you can no longer function normally.

The clitoris is the primary source of female stimulation, the lips around the vagina are second—a hysterectomy doesn't affect either. Besides, doctors have reported that in some of those extremely rare cases where a woman has had to have her clitoris removed, some were still able to experience an orgasm. Remember that "a woman's most important sex organ is her brain." Unless your brain has been removed, you can function normally. But you must believe it. If you convince yourself that a hysterectomy is sexually fatal, it is; so face the truth—you and your husband have many good years of enjoyment ahead of you.

Depression is another matter. Most of the time it is the emotional result of the thoughts of self-pity for having had to go through such surgery. Give thanks by faith (1 Thess. 5:18) and quit griping at God about it; you'll be amazed at how much better you will feel. If that doesn't improve conditions in a week or two, see your doctor—you may need some hormone shots. Admittedly this surgery is an emotionally jarring experience, but self-pity only complicates it and retards the healing process.

Is it right for a Christian woman to have silicone injected into her breasts?

If you have already done it and your conscience bothers you, confess it and then forget about it. If you haven't, don't bother to have it done. A foreign body unnecessarily sealed into your flesh could and sometimes does present complications. Besides, you need to accept yourself as God made you—that's your problem. Except for exercises (and it is questionable whether this helps), there is very little that can be done naturally to change the size of your breasts. Many women who have undergone a mastectomy would prefer your problem to theirs. If the truth were known, the big-breasted woman may not be so sensitive to lovemaking as her envious smaller friend. The reason? Both women have the same number of nerve endings, but those in a large breast are more likely to be spread out further and not so close to the surface of the skin.

Homosexuality

Is it a sign of perversion for a child to handle his sex organs?

Curiosity is the hallmark of every child; some have it more than others. Being curious about their genitalia and others' is natural to children, and it is a wise parent who accepts it as such. It is best not to scold, punish, or shame them for they are encountering an expected phase of growth. As they observe your relaxed attitude, they will soon get over their apparent obsession with the subject. You can use such occasions as an opportunity to talk over any questions your children may have on sex. Be sure to use, casually, accurate medical terms for the various parts of the body so they will accept sexuality as a natural part of life.

It is best for parents to study up on the subject of sexual development and plan in advance how they will answer such questions. If you let your children take you by surprise, you will be more inclined to do and say the wrongs things. (See the author's book *Against the Tide: How to Raise Sexually Pure Kids in an Impure World*.)

What should be the Christian's attitude toward homosexuality?

This problem is increasingly rampant in the world today. In California alone, one prominent gay society claims to have 100,000 members. Some ministers are homosexual and have started a whole denomination of churches for homosexuals. My associate minister and I debated two homosexual ministers on a radio program in which they sought to justify their position. It was interesting to note that they could find no Scripture to support it. The only one they tried to use was Paul's statement, "I have become all things to all men, so that by all means I might save some" (1 Cor. 9:22), a complete distortion of the apostle's meaning.

The Bible is very clear on homosexuality. It is an abnormal, deviant practice according to Romans 1:27. The children of Israel were commanded by God to stone homosexuals to death (Lev. 20:13), a severe treatment intended to keep them from spreading their philosophy. Every homosexual is potentially an evangelist of homosexuality, capable of perverting many young people to his sinful way of life.

The widespread propaganda emanating from the media, liberals in government, the entertainment industry, and secular colleges is moving society toward the acceptance of homosexuals as normal by removing all legal restraints against them. The governor of California and other state governors have signed such a law, overturning centuries of opposition to homosexuality. This has allowed their number to multiply tragically. Although Christians are commanded to love their neighbor, we should actively use whatever legal steps are available in our communities in this post-Christian culture to encourage lawmakers to enact laws against homosexuality. Christians are far too passive when it comes to using what freedoms they have to legally preserve morality and decency. Homosexuality seems to be the ultimate sin in the Bible that causes God to give men up, as He did according to Romans 1:27, and to destroy them from the earth, as He did in the days of Sodom and Gomorrah and during the Flood in the days of Noah. Even while condemning the sin of homosexuals, a Christian should bear compassion for them as individuals and whenever possible share the gospel of Christ with them. That is the only known power available today to extricate a person from this awful vice. Homosexuals need to know that there is a remedy in a genuine conversion to Christ, who can empower them to change their lifestyle. I have personally met forty-eight former homosexuals who have come out of that lifestyle, and I know of over two hundred ministries that are run by former homosexuals who now specialize in helping homosexuals come to Christ and live normal heterosexual lives.

What causes homosexuality?

There is no simple answer to this question, but this condition comes about from a combination of factors. One of the most common factors is an abnormal hatred toward the opposite sex aroused by a domineering mother, who "ruled the home," and a milk-toast father. This subconscious hatred of a boy for his mother spills over and makes it difficult for him to be attracted to girls his age. In the case of a lesbian, it is often the rejection of her father that prepares her for this life of perversion.

Rarely does a child who is raised in a wholesome atmosphere of love from his parents develop a predisposition toward deviant sexual practices.

Another cause of male homosexuality or lesbianism is an abnormal, smothering love of a child by a parent. This stifles his God-given instinctual response to the opposite sex. When a mother is not given love by her husband, she will often selfishly fill that void in her heart through an abnormal love for her son. Even though she would never think of doing anything immoral with him, such smothering affection sets up guilt complexes in the lad that stifle his normal reactions toward the opposite sex. Subconsciously he regards such feelings as a betrayal of his love for his mother. The same thing occurs when a girl is subjected to that kind of smothering love from her father, who probably does not receive sufficient love from his wife. Dr. Howard Hendricks has made the point at many of our seminars that "children need love, but they should always realize that they are number two in the heart of their parents. If they grow up thinking they are number one, they will have a difficult time adjusting normally to the opposite sex."

Normal love responses in children are most easily fostered in a warm atmosphere of love between their parents. This is so psychically normal that they feel relaxed in their attitude toward the opposite sex. Although parents should not be indiscreet in front of their children, it is good for them to see their parents embrace and display genuine affection.

Remember also that in their early teen years, as they go from childhood to adolescence, children are commonly attracted to those of their own sex. Junior boys, for example, often "hate girls." And as they begin developing sexually, they may find an unexplainable attraction to another boy or man. That is why they should be well trained in their home and church in God's standards of sexuality that boy-girl impulses are right and normal and that boy-boy sexual impulses should be rejected. Such teachings guard them through this ambivalent phase of life when even they don't know sometimes if they are "fish or fowl," after which they develop a healthy appreciation of the opposite sex.

When we moved to California, I was ill-prepared for the many homosexuals I was called upon to counsel. But every case has followed a similar pattern. A boy with a strong love need met an evangelist of homosexuality who supplied that love need, at first platonically by "going fishing with him," "weight lifting," or just spending time with him. Little did the young person realize that he was being wooed as carefully as a man courts a woman. Then, when he was emotionally hooked and the homosexual act was suggested, the first thoughts of repugnance were swept aside by fear of losing "the only person who ever loved me." Little did the lad realize he was trading a normal love relationship of a wife and probability of children in the future for the satisfaction of that immediate love need.

You may ask, "Why, if they didn't really want to do it in the first place, do they end up confirmed homosexuals?" Homosexuality is a learned behavior, and people can develop an appetite for anything if they do it often enough. Once that happens, they cultivate all kinds of mental excuses to justify it. Eventually his God-given conscience is "seared as with a hot iron," and he may become blatantly defiant in his sin; consequently another evangelist of homosexuality is walking the streets.

Can a male homosexual or a lesbian ever be cured?

The answer to this question lies in an individual's being willing to accept Jesus Christ as personal Lord and Savior. If such a person is willing, a cure is possible, but so far there is little success in any other treatment. As a prominent Los Angeles psychiatrist admitted, "Very honestly, I have never been able to cure a homosexual, and I don't know anyone else who has either." Unfortunately far too many psychiatrists, educators, and counselors don't even attempt a cure; instead they encourage the individual to accept their behavior as not being deviant but merely "another form of sexual expression."

One Bible verse is extremely encouraging to homosexuals or anyone else caught in a sinful habit: "With man this is impossible, but not with God; all things are possible with God" (Mark 10:27). We have seen several turn to Christ and by His power extricate themselves from their dilemma. It is never easy, but with God's help it is possible. The following formula we have used with several individuals:

1. Accept Christ as Lord and Savior of your life.
2. Face homosexuality or lesbianism as a sin (Rom. 1:26–27, 32).
3. Confess it as a sin (1 John 1:9).
4. Ask God to break the habit pattern (1 John 5:14–15).
5. Walk in the Spirit through daily reading of the Word of God and submit to its teachings (Gal. 5:16–25; Eph. 5:17–21; Col. 3:15–17).
6. Avoid contact with all former homosexual friends.
7. Avoid places where such people gather.

8. Cultivate wholesome thought patterns; never permit your mind to visualize deviant or immoral behavior (Phil. 4:8).
9. Find a strong Christian friend who has never had this problem, one with whom you can share your need and to whom you can turn for help when the temptation becomes strong.

One man I counseled years ago sincerely wanted to rid himself of this awful sin. He promised me he would never again go to the city park, which he had previously frequented to meet other men. As a further means of motivation he agreed that in his best interest I could ask privately, but at any time, "Have you been near the park lately?" Later he confided, "It was a real help when I was tempted to know that every now and then you would look me in the eye and ask that question." It is possible to break the habit without such a friend, but it is much easier if you have one.

Gradually the urges and temptation will diminish, but each time you do it or think about it, the habit is cultivated and becomes more difficult to overcome. Remember the sowing-reaping principle: you reap what you sow. Yet it takes time. For example, your present feelings are largely the result of your thoughts and actions of the past thirty or sixty days. If you want to reap a better crop of feelings, urges, and appetites thirty or sixty days from now, then with God's help start sowing better seeds in your mind immediately.

Will children raised by only one parent grow up with a natural attitude toward their own sex and the opposite sex?

This question is near to my heart, because I was raised by a widowed mother. I was almost ten, my sister was five, and my brother was seven weeks old when my father died. All of us developed normal relationships with the opposite sex, and we can point to three happy marriages and thirteen children among us. In fact, my brother, who never knew a father, has five children and was a first sergeant in the U.S. Air Force with 397 men under his command. Obviously he relates well to men and women.

The Bible promises that God is "a father to the fatherless" (Ps. 68:5), and we certainly found that to be true. Actually it seems that a child without one parent can make the proper adjustment to life more easily than a child raised in a home filled with parental hostility and conflict. If a widow or divorcée has to raise her children alone, there seems to be a natural acceptance of her leadership role, and unless she goes overboard and smothers them, they develop perfectly normal relationships with the opposite sex. It also helps if a mother in such circumstances simply assumes that God will provide the emotional well-being her children need. Then they are infected with the expectation of being perfectly normal, and consequently they will be.

In addition, it is always best to talk to children positively about their future. For example, never use "if" when looking ahead. "When you get married" or "when you go to college" is always a better term than "if you ever get married" or "if you ever go to college." Single Christian parents' positive attitudes, anticipating success in every phase of their children's lives, form the strongest foundation for young people, next to their heavenly Father's promise to be "a father to the fatherless."

Impotence

Is it true that male impotence is on the increase, and if so, why?

Although no survey that we are familiar with compares male impotence today with what it was thirty to fifty years ago, most active counselors will acknowledge that they face the problem much more frequently than they did twenty years ago. If, as we believe, it is on the rise, the reason is more mental and emotional than physical. Most doctors suggest that it isn't a glandular problem but is due to the emotional and mental pressures of our present society. Men get less physical exercise today than they did twenty years ago and have greater mental pressures to cope with. In addition, life in this present troubled world is less secure, and many men are less certain of their manhood than formerly. We look for this problem to increase as the woman's lib philosophy creates more conflict in the home and continues to assault the male ego.

In the early years of marriage a man's sexual drive is about 75 percent physical and 25 percent mental, but as he matures, those ratios change until by the age of fifty it is 75 percent mental and 25 percent physical. That is why we say that if a man thinks he is potent, he is, and vice versa. For a large treatment of this subject see chapter 11.

Do hormone shots help a middle-aged man's potency?

That depends on whether his problem is caused by a hormone deficiency. No amount of hormones will cure a man who thinks he is impotent. If the problem persists, he should see his doctor, because a hormone deficiency can be ascertained only after thorough medical tests.

Does vitamin E really stimulate an impotent man's sex drive?

To date, published reports are inconclusive. We know doctors who consider it a waste of money, whereas others recommend it. One doctor friend recommends 1,600 units a day for male impotence; another approves a Chinese root called *ginseng*. If you have a problem with impotence, either of these would be worth trying. If it helps, keep it up; if not, discontinue it. A one- or two-months' supply should give you an answer.

Does a vasectomy have anything to do with male potency?

This was dealt with in chapter 12, on birth control. Doctors assure us that the operation has absolutely nothing to do with a man's capability, provided he doesn't use it as an excuse to consider himself impotent. We know five doctors personally who have submitted to the surgery; you can be sure they would never have done so if it would have affected their virility.

Please give some specific ways to arouse a wife when the husband is unable to have an erection. How do couples deal with inequality of sex (e.g., when the wife is unable to respond, she can give; but when the husband is unable to respond, he cannot)?

A thoughtful husband with this problem can lovingly stimulate his wife to orgasm manually to satisfy her needs. Usually he will find this stimulating, and it may result in the erection he needs. Study chapter 11 on male impotence and remember—most male inability is caused by the brain. If you think you can, you can. A wife can also help her husband obtain an erection by gently stroking his penis.

Love

Is it possible to enjoy sex without a close, affectionate relationship the rest of the time?

Yes, such a relationship is experienced by millions of couples the world over—but that is not intercourse at its best. If such a couple have learned the art of lovemaking, they will engage in coitus on occasions, but not so frequently or so enthusiastically as lovers. Love is an emotion that must be cultivated; no Christian should endure marriage without it. The first characteristic of the Spirit-filled life is love. If you don't have such love for your partner, you should examine your spiritual condition.

Is it really selfishness on my part to want to be more than a tool for my husband's sexual happiness? Is it wrong for me to want to enjoy it too?

Certainly not! Every wife has a right to expect to be loved to orgasm. Your husband, however, may feel extremely inadequate if he is not able to satisfy you; and rather than admitting it, he may cover it up by acting as if it shouldn't matter. Talk to him, encourage him to read this book, listen to Dr. Wheat's cassettes, and consciously work on his lovemaking technique. We are convinced that any man can learn to become an exciting lover to his wife—if he is thoughtful enough to be concerned about her needs. Frequently all it takes is a little more clitoral stimulation before entrance and a little delay of his ejaculation.

Marriage Adjustment

My husband and I were mismatched. Had we been Christians when we met, we would have known we should not have married in the first place. What can we do about such a situation now that we've become Christians?

First and foremost, slam the divorce door, which is not a live option for Christians. The Bible says, "Are you married? Do not seek a divorce" (1 Cor. 7:27). Now that does not mean that you must endure misery the rest of your life. God commands you to love each other; consequently you have that capability. Now that you have become Christians, you possess a new source of love to extend to each other. We have seen some rather impossible cases transformed into love matches by the power of the Holy Spirit. Learn to love each other. We suggest that you get a copy of our book *How to Be Happy Though Married* and put its principles into practice.

Masturbation

Is it wrong for a Christian to masturbate?

There is probably no more controversial question in the field of sex than this. A few years ago every Christian would have answered this question with an unqualified yes, but that was before the sexual revolution and before doctors declared that the practice is not harmful to health. No longer can a father honestly warn his son that it will cause "brain damage, weakness, baldness, blindness, epilepsy, or insanity." Some still refer to it as "self-abuse" and "sinful behavior"; others advocate it as a necessary relief to the single man and a help for the married man whose wife is pregnant or whose business forces him to be away from home for long periods of time.

To show the influence of humanism on people's decisions, we found it interesting that in our survey of twenty-five Christian doctors, 72 percent approved of masturbation and 28 percent felt it is wrong. By contrast, among pastors (whose graduate-school training was in seminary and undergraduate education often in a Christian college) only 13 percent approved of self-manipulation and 83 percent considered it wrong. In most cases, ministers are not uninformed on the subject; they probably have to cope with it in the counseling room more than doctors. Certainly they deal with it among single men through their camp and youth programs. Among those who took our survey, 52 percent of the men and 84 percent of the women declared they had never or seldom practiced masturbation; 17 percent of men and 4 percent of women indicated they had practiced masturbation frequently or regularly. Many of these stated specifically they no longer did so since becoming a Christian.

Unfortunately the Bible is silent on this subject; therefore it is dangerous to be dogmatic. Although we are sympathetic with those who would remove the time-honored taboos against the practice, we would like to suggest the following reasons why we do not feel it is an acceptable practice for Christians:

1. Fantasizing and lustful thinking are usually involved in masturbation, and the Bible clearly condemns such thoughts (Matt. 5:28).

2. Sexual expression was designed by God to be performed jointly by two people of the opposite sex, resulting in a necessary and healthy dependence on each other for the experience. Masturbation frustrates that designed dependence.

3. Feelings of guilt are a nearly universal aftermath of masturbation unless one has been brainwashed by the humanistic philosophy that does not hold to a God-given conscience or, in many cases, right and wrong. Such guilt feelings interfere with spiritual growth and produce defeat in single young people particularly. To them it is usually a self-discipline hurdle they must scale in order to grow in Christ and walk in the Spirit.

4. It violates 1 Corinthians 7:9: "It is better to marry than to burn with passion." If a young man practices masturbation, it tends to nullify a necessary and important motivation for marriage. There are already enough social, educational, and financial demotivators hampering young men now; they don't need this one.

5. It creates a habit before marriage that can easily be resorted to afterward as a cop-out when a husband and wife have sexual or other conflicts that make coitus difficult.

6. It defrauds a wife (1 Cor. 7:3–5). No married man should relieve his mounting, God-given desire for his wife except through coitus. She will feel unloved and insecure, and many little problems will unnecessarily be magnified by this artificial draining of his sex drive. This becomes increasingly true as a couple reach middle age.

As a divorcée, I have sexual needs that require fulfillment. Is it better to use a vibrator than become promiscuous?

Both alternatives are wrong and harmful. Other alternatives should be considered. The use of special vibrators is not only acceptable to, but is advocated by, humanists who regard man as another form of animal; many popular sex writers recommend these devices today. However, we feel they are dangerous and harmful to the psyche. The sex urge is basic in both men and women.

It should be cultivated in marriage but de-emphasized by singles until marriage.

God put the sex drive in human beings to inspire them to mate throughout marriage. If a single person satisfies that drive with a vibrator or other such means, his or her major motivation to marry is destroyed. It is also dangerous because it creates an erotic sensation that no human on earth can equal; if the person remarries, there will be a natural temptation to resort to this same practice because the human partner cannot match that sensation. This is "defrauding" the partner.

If it is wrong to masturbate, what can a widowed or divorced person do to control his sex drive?

We were confronted with this question by a lovely young woman whose husband had been killed in an auto accident. She asked, "What does a woman who is used to as many as ten orgasms a week do when she suddenly has no husband?" Admittedly she had a problem. She needed to know that (1) God's grace is sufficient for even her need (2 Cor. 12:9); (2) her stimulated desire would ease considerably in time with disuse; (3) she must guard her thought life carefully by Bible reading and prayer; (4) she must avoid all suggestive or compromising situations with the opposite sex; (5) she should become active in a local church and trust God to (a) supply another person with whom she can share her love need or (b) give her the self-control to cope with her problem (1 Cor. 10:13); and (6) she could ask God to take away the craving (1 John 5:14–15).

Fortunately this young widow was a deeply spiritual person, and God supplied her need. Two years later she remarried, and she testifies today that God is able to supply *all* needs as He promised in Philippians 4:19.

A close friend of ours lost his wife of seventeen years and confessed to a severe problem at first. He finally prayed earnestly that God would help him, and God removed that strong drive for six years. When he met another woman who later became his wife, his normal appetite for lovemaking was quickly revived.

If my husband fails to bring me to orgasm, should I induce orgasm myself when he's asleep?

As a couple develops the kind of relationship that encourages open communication, the wife can make her needs known to her husband. A thoughtful husband who can't control his ejaculation long enough to bring his wife to orgasm can at least lovingly caress her clitoris until she shares his experience. The wife can help in this regard by faithful practice of the Kegel exercises described in chapter 10. Many women develop such powerful muscle tone around the vagina that they can actually squeeze the shaft of the inserted penis enough times to bring on orgasm even before the husband starts deep thrusting. Those who have developed this art report that it introduces a dimension to the act of marriage they never previously dreamed possible. In fact, several women who had no difficulty reaching orgasm reported that even their sensations were improved by these exercises.

Is clitoral stimulation by squeezing the legs together prior to intercourse termed "masturbation"?

This technique is not well known, probably because not all women are able to do it, depending on the location of their clitoris, their body size, and other factors, We would suggest that if it is done to heighten sexual tension in anticipation of lovemaking, it could be labeled a form of foreplay. If practiced without a husband, it is masturbation.

Menopause

What is menopause, and what causes it?

Menopause, or "the change of life," as it is frequently called, is actually the gradual decrease of ovarian activity. Although there is great variability, irregular menstrual periods begin in the forties for most women, but complete cessation of the menses may not occur until they are well into their fifties. As a woman ages, her supply of estrogen, responsible for ovum production, begins to diminish; she will experience some changes in the lining of the uterus, producing irregularity. In some extreme cases, a woman in the menopausal period may notice a sagging of the breasts, a broadening of the hips, and an increasing weight problem. Some women complain of hot flashes, whereas others become depressed, weepy, and irritable. Any woman with these symptoms should see her doctor, as many of these symptoms may be controlled by taking estrogen. In most cases it can be administered in convenient pill form.

Why do some women have more problems during the menopause?

All women are different in temperament, mental attitudes, glandular functions, and body chemistry. The two biggest problems are:

1. A decrease in estrogen. Only a doctor can help alleviate this problem; many women testify that

medically prescribed estrogen transformed them during this period of life.

2. One's mental attitude, which is more significant than most people realize. The woman who expects menopause to "wipe her out" will usually not be disappointed; the busy, motivated woman who expects to take it in stride usually does.

Does menopause reduce a woman's sex drive?

That depends on the woman and her husband. Menopause certainly may create a problem within an already strained marital situation; in a few cases it may even overtax a healthy marriage. Some women, however, find their inhibitions vanish as their menstruation diminishes. Current research indicates that many become more interested in sexual relations after forty than they were before. Much depends on whether or not the woman fears that discontinuance of periods will begin a loss in her femininity. Once she realizes that femininity is not dependent on having a monthly period, she can go on to many years of married love.

After menopause, intercourse may be painful for some women because the lower hormone levels cause the vaginal walls to become thin and less elastic, making it somewhat easier for them to become irritated by coitus. This can usually be avoided by taking sufficient estrogen or by using a vaginal cream locally that contains estrogen, which is absorbed there through the skin. Also, there may be a need for more artificial lubricant such as K-Y jelly.

It has been conclusively shown that women who have satisfying sexual intercourse once or twice a week all through the menopausal years have fewer symptoms of hot flashes, irritability, and nervousness, and much less change in the vaginal walls even with little or no hormone replacement.

Can a woman get pregnant during her menopause?

Yes, it is possible. That is the source of the term "change-of-life baby." Many women erroneously conclude that because they skip a few periods, they can discontinue using birth-control pills. A woman can ovulate each month even without menstruating, and this is when she is vulnerable to pregnancy. Only a small percentage of women are likely to become pregnant during this stage, but there is no way of identifying them. Some doctors recommend that a woman continue using her birth-control measures at least one year after her last period. After that length of time, it is safe to assume that the ovaries will no longer function.

What can a husband do when his wife is going through the menopause?

On his wedding day he promised to love her "for better or for worse." Even if he may consider this to be the worst phase of his marriage, God expects him to love his wife anyway. Some women may feel insecure at this time and need to be reassured of their husband's love and their own feminine appeal. Her husband is the only one who can adequately give her what she needs: love, patience, kindness, long-suffering, and understanding. A husband should remember that God never required what He will not supply; He will certainly provide him with the kind of love his wife needs if he is really interested in loving and helping her. She will respond warmly to such a husband and be appreciative when the menopausal stage is over. It is only a temporary period, and the years that follow can be long and full of tenderness for the understanding couple.

A husband can also help his wife at this time by seeking her companionship and including her in as many of his activities as possible. At this age the children usually no longer require her constant attention. With this lack of responsibility and extra time on her hands, she needs to feel wanted and needed by someone. A good church can be especially helpful to both husband and wife; fellowship with other people their own age and having a place of Christian service can be rewarding.

Menstruation

Is intercourse during menstruation medically approved?

Most modern medical authorities indicate that intercourse during the time a woman is menstruating is not harmful. It is untidy and should usually not be prolonged because the female organs are sometimes tender at that time and can easily become irritated. A woman may go from a warm, amorous mood to a chilly feeling suddenly. Interestingly enough, however, this is one of the times when her sexual interest may easily be aroused.

Does the Bible condemn intercourse during menstruation?

The ceremonial laws of the Old Testament required that a woman go through a period of "uncleanness" for seven days as a result of menstruation, and intercourse was forbidden (Lev. 15:19). Usually the ceremonial laws were for hygienic reasons as well as spiritual. But those laws were given thirty-five hundred years ago, before showers and baths were so convenient, before tampons, disinfectants, and other improved means of sanitation had been invented. The death of Christ, "once for all," has done away with the ceremonial laws, rituals, and ordinances (Heb. 9:1–10:25); therefore we are no longer bound by them. We do not believe that intercourse during menstruation is sinful, but it should probably be avoided during the first three days of a wife's flow of blood and should be initiated only by the wife.

Oral Sex
What is oral sex?

Two words are used to describe oral sex. In *fellatio* the woman receives the male penis into her mouth in order to stimulate the glans penis with her lips and tongue; *cunnilingus* is the act of the male stimulating the woman with his mouth over her vulva area, usually with his tongue on her clitoris. Both forms of oral sex can bring an orgasm if prolonged.

Is it right for Christians to practice oral sex?

Almost every week we receive this question by letter or in the counseling room, especially during the last few years. Husbands tend to desire this experience more than wives, but recently because of the many sex books on the market, there seems to be increasing curiosity on the part of women in this form of sexual excitement. Doubtless the practice is increasing. One author suggests that as many as 80 percent of couples have tried it. Although they may find it pleasurable, many feel guilty about it.

The Bible is completely silent on this subject, and we have encountered a wide variety of opinions. Of the Christian doctors we surveyed, 73 percent felt it was acceptable for a Christian couple as long as both partners enjoyed it; 27 percent did not approve of it. To our amazement, 77 percent of the ministers felt it was acceptable, and 23 percent did not. It is strange that many people who approach us for our opinion indicate they have already counseled with a minister who opposed it. We almost wonder if many ministers who express opposition to it to counselees (perhaps because they consider it the stand they should take) adopt a different position when reporting in an anonymous survey.

Usually one encounters strong opposition when discussing the subject; very few seem to advocate it, but who knows what people do in the privacy of their bedrooms? Some object to the practice probably because of personal prejudice for what they feel are hygienic or spiritual reasons; but doctors say it is not unhealthy, and the Bible is silent on the subject. Therefore each couple must make their own decision on the matter.

We do not personally recommend or advocate it, but we have no biblical grounds for censuring two married people who mutually enjoy it. We do not think, moreover, that it should be used as a substitute for coitus; if it has a place in marriage, we would suggest it be limited to foreplay. A warning, however, should be sounded: Love requires that one partner *never demand* the experience from the other if he or she does not enjoy it or feels guilty or uncomfortable about it.

Why is oral sex on the increase?

Many factors contribute to the currently widespread discussion of oral sex: (1) the sex revolution has led to more sexual experimentation; (2) secular authorities and writers have popularized it in the recent rash of sex books on the current best-seller lists; (3) many young people are reported to be using oral sex as a substitute today for intercourse to avoid pregnancy and loss of virginity; consequently they marry with an appetite for the experience. Some women find it harder to reach orgasm in marriage by the conventional method after they have had this premarital experience; (4) it seems to be the sex fad of the twentieth century, though it has doubtlessly been practiced privately for centuries.

Are there hygienic factors related to oral sex?

The current craze for oral sex may yet prove to be far more harmful than its exponents imagine. Some medical researchers are inclined to believe it is possible to transmit herpetic diseases through oral sex, leading in some cases even to cancer of the cervix. The following letter to columnist Ann Landers from Dr. Louis Berman, a counselor of students at the University of Illinois, is extremely informative:

> Dear Miss Landers:
>
> In a recent column, you warned of a little-known but not-so-rare disease called herpes simplex II, which has been linked with sterility and cancer.
>
> I am not a physician, I'm a college counselor who became acquainted with herpes through the sad experience of a bright, handsome college student, who picked up the infection during a holiday break when he renewed an acquaintance with a former girlfriend. During our discussion he remembered his girlfriend had been intimate with a man who had frequent cold sores.

Herpes is a cold-sore virus that is rapidly becoming a venereal disease because of the increasing incidence of oral-genital sex. Pornographic movies and "art" have popularized oral sex in a way that was unheard of even five years ago.

As a counselor, I can tell you many of my colleagues (as well as sexologists) are directly or indirectly encouraging oral sex play. I think it is only fair that the public be made aware of the risks that accompany this sort of activity.

I have seen many articles on herpes in newspapers and popular magazines, but I have never seen any mention of the connection between herpes and oral sex. Maybe the writers are too gutless to tell it like it is. How about you, Ann Landers?

It may well be that additional research will confirm some of these serious possibilities and expose oral sex, which some already find repugnant, as being extremely dangerous to the health.

Orgasm

We experience simultaneous orgasms most of the time, but can't understand why we don't every time.

Nothing is more intricate than a human being. When the success of a bodily function is dependent on two very different human beings, it is unreal to expect 100 percent performance. When you consider that lovemaking is contingent upon two different brains, emotional systems, spiritual conditions, mood swings, fatigue levels, physical conditions, and reproductive mechanisms, you will realize that utopia every time is impossible to achieve. In addition, there are different levels of satisfaction. Admittedly orgasm is without doubt the most exciting single experience in life, but even when it is not achieved, there is a degree of satisfaction in sharing yourself intimately with the person you love.

It has long been interesting to us that professional baseball players are considered outstanding if they maintain a batting average of .333. That signals success even though they fail to hit two out of three times. Of course, hitting and pitching suggest competition, whereas love-making features two people in cooperation; consequently you can expect a much higher "batting average" from lovers. In all probability, an excellent love life consists of a very exciting orgasm 60 to 70 percent of the time.

Do some women consistently experience greater sexual satisfaction through direct stimulation than through intercourse alone?

This is frequently the case, because it is easier to direct the hand and fingers to exactly the right spot than it is the penis. In addition, the vagina may be sagging and weak in muscle tone from childbirth; consequently it does not respond to the penis as it should. This can be corrected through exercise, and stimulation during intercourse can be enhanced through practice. It is very common for a wife to experience her first orgasm through direct stimulation, then graduate to simultaneous orgasm with her husband. Some women take longer to graduate than others, and some never do. Practice makes perfect, so keep practicing.

Do most women feel it is necessary to reach an orgasm for a sexual experience to be satisfying?

Most women want to experience orgasm—it is the ultimate sexual enjoyment, so why shouldn't they? God gave them that capability, and we think they should learn to experience it. However, millions of women never have the experience, yet indicate they enjoy lovemaking. We were amazed to note how many women who had never enjoyed orgasm reported that on a scale of 0–100 they would rate their sex lives 75–85.

Is there something wrong with a woman who seldom reaches an orgasm and yet is satisfied with sex?

No! Hopefully she is as easily satisfied in other things also. Then again, perhaps she doesn't know what she's missing. If she would have one exciting, exploding orgasm, we suspect she would no longer be so fully "satisfied with sex" without it.

Do most women really enjoy sex or submit to it only because they know they should because the Scriptures teach submission? Why do women enjoy it?

This question could not possibly be asked by a wife who experiences fulfilling orgasm. The woman who enjoys lovemaking and finds it her most exciting single experience usually desires it on an average of two to three times a week.

Orgasmic Failure

How does one deal with disappointment over failure to find pleasure or orgasm in sex after seventeen years?

By making orgasmic fulfillment a prayerful quest. Study chapters 9 and 10, "The Unfulfilled Woman" and "The Key to Feminine Response," and carefully exercise your P.C. muscle as described by Dr. Kegel. Remember that 85 percent of the nonorgasmic wives so counseled have learned how to achieve regular orgasm this way. We believe no married woman should accept orgasmic failure.

If four out of ten women are nonorgasmic, how do they cope with this problem (to avoid the feeling of marriage failure and guilt)?

Don't cope with it. Follow the suggestions given above to a whole new dimension of lovemaking enjoyment.

How important is it that women experience orgasm during intercourse?

It depends on whether or not you are accustomed to settling for "good" or "best." If you can experience orgasm through your husband's manual stimulation, you can learn to climax your lovemaking with simultaneous orgasms—which is the ultimate, but it is an art that takes practice. Perhaps your husband inserts his penis too soon, or possibly he discontinues manual stimulation after entrance. You're almost there—keep working on it.

How does a wife reach orgasm with the penis in the vagina?

By waiting until she is sufficiently aroused before the husband inserts his penis. The telltale sign for the husband is not secretion of sufficient lubrication, but the enlargement of the inner lips of his wife's vagina. It is also important that he continue the manual stimulation of her clitoris for a few moments after entrance and that he learn to retard his ejaculation. He will likewise expedite the process if he avoids deep thrusting, but concentrates on keeping the enlarged head of his penis nearer the entrance to her vagina. Deep thrusting, which men tend to do instinctively, places the largest part of the penis in the least responsive part of the wife's vagina. Keep in mind that most of her nerve endings are within the first two inches of her vagina.

Petting
What is petting?

Someone has suggested that "necking" is what goes on above the neck between two unmarried people of the opposite sex, and "petting" is what occurs below the neck. Actually petting is just a sophisticated term describing illicit foreplay by the unmarried, and it is dangerous. Almost all consenting girls who become pregnant out of wedlock engage in heavy petting before they are swept into intercourse. Petting is intended to stimulate passions in preparation for intercourse; consequently it should be practiced only by married partners. The price of petting should always be a marriage license. Most single girls do not realize that the time of the month when they are most amorous coincides with the time when they are most fertile and least able to control their passions; consequently it is the most dangerous for them when it is the most appealing.

Because petting is really "foreplay," it must be reserved for marriage. Among married couples it is usually considered their most exciting pastime.

Is heavy petting before marriage damaging to the initiation of a good sexual adjustment in early marriage? (It was to ours because of guilt.)

Most counselors will agree that your experience is common.

Positions

Should married couples always have intercourse in bed? What other places are acceptable?

For most people the bed is the most convenient place to make love, but it certainly isn't the only place. Statistics indicate that at least 90 percent of married love occurs in bed, but almost all couples experiment with other places and positions when the mood suggests something new. It is wise to be creative and experimental at times. Any place that is mutually agreeable and does not betray your privacy is acceptable.

Privacy

How can a couple with young children at home really have the privacy to do anything they want in their sex life?

Put a lock on the bedroom door. Children should be taught to respect their parents' privacy; it's a necessary part of their training in recognizing the need to honor the rights of others. Besides, their parents will be better parents if they can freely and frequently express married love without distractions or inhibitions.

What do you do about lack of privacy with a teenager in the house? When do you relax and make love when you are afraid of being heard?

All couples should have a lock on their bedroom door, and children should be taught to stay out of their parents' bedroom. Locate children's bedrooms so that they cannot hear every noise that comes from the parents' room. Finally, relax—children are usually sound sleepers.

Should Christian parents expose their bodies to their children (as in bathing or dressing)? Doesn't supermodesty help to breed sex consciousness?

One of the harmful fads of humanism during the past fifty years is the encouragement of parents to let their children see them naked. This is expressly forbidden in the Scriptures and is unnecessary for child development.

"Supermodesty" is almost a thing of the past; we could do with more modesty today. Children should not be taught to fear seeing their parents naked but, out of respect for them, avoid doing so.

Romance

Most sex manuals advise couples to get away occasionally for an overnight honeymoon, but how can a pastor on a very tight budget afford such a luxury?

The first thing he should do is prayerfully examine whether his salary is too small in relation to the total church budget. If it is, and the church could afford to give him a raise, he should prayerfully consider having a talk with the budget committee when the annual budget is being prepared, forthrightly advise them that he is finding it difficult to live on his salary, and request a substantial raise. At issue is Matthew 6:33; if your first objective is to seek the kingdom of God, there is nothing wrong with your third or fourth objective being a decent salary to live on. You owe that to your family.

Asking your church for a raise, however, doesn't guarantee that you will receive it (though at least they will know how you honestly feel). Consequently you had better be equipped with "plan B." For that we suggest that you make your desire a special matter of prayer, for God will provide some extra work or a thoughtful gift from some member or in some other way make it possible. "Ask and it will be given to you" (Matt. 7:7). It boils down to moving that "overnight honeymoon" higher up on your priority list—you and your wife need it!

We will never forget the thoughtful couple who rented a motel in Palm Springs for us for one week back in the days when we didn't have two nickels to rub together. I can only wish that more church members would provide so bountifully for their minister and his wife.

You might also save the honorariums received from weddings and use them to improve your marriage by getting away for occasional "overnight honeymoons." Moreover, it isn't only ministers who need to get away from the children and household chores once in a while; every marriage will profit from such therapy. Even if you have to skimp and save, it is worth the investment.

September Sex
At what age do couples stop making love?

While writing this book, we had lunch with two very close friends of many years. He is seventy-six, she is three or four years younger. We have long treasured their friendship and the sight of the beautiful relationship they share. When informed of our subject, he jokingly said, "I could tell you a lot to put in that book." Somehow I got the courage to ask him how often he and his wife make love at their age. He smilingly replied, "At least three times a week!" Then he added, "Now that I'm retired we have more time for that sort of thing." Obviously he didn't know that he was supposed to slow down, so he didn't! And that's the way it should be. Two healthy people should be able to make love into their eighties. We know several who claim that they celebrated their golden wedding anniversary by making love.

As people grow older, the various parts of their body begin to wear out. But the process is as unpredictable as the people involved. Consequently some experience one malfunction, some another. When vital energies begin to run down in our maturity, many activities of our youth are pursued less energetically and frequently. It is not uncommon for senior citizens, particularly men, to experience occasional malfunctions in lovemaking. Unfortunately they jump to the conclusion that "it's all over" after a few nonorgasmic experiences. If they were to analyze their situation more carefully, they would notice something that gives hope and inspiration to try again.

Contrary to masculine obsession, a man does not have to ejaculate to enjoy coitus. Upon arousal, he can have a substantial erection, enter his wife, experience many minutes of exciting stimulation, bring her to orgasm, and gradually lose his ejaculatory drive. Instead of the usual high peak, his feeling just seems to pass without the customary explosion. Although it is not as satisfying as the ejaculatory climax he so enjoys, it does satisfy both his sex drive and his wife's. If he learns to settle for this lessened experience, he will still occasionally ejaculate, and as his confidence returns, so will the frequency of his success. Many, however, erroneously short-circuit their long-range capabilities by *thinking* that it is all over when actual experience would dictate otherwise.

What would you suggest for older couples who have had very little sex education?

Basically the same things work for them that inexperienced couples must learn, except that they must unlearn the faulty concepts and practices that may have hindered their love lives. Our counseling experience indicates that one is never too old to learn something new about lovemaking, and no couple should be closed to the possibility that perhaps something they are doing is not in the best interest of one of the partners. Hopefully the concepts in this book will encourage many such couples to new lovemaking joys.

When one reaches middle age and feels too tired for intercourse, how can life be meaningful and exciting?

A person's sex drive parallels his other bodily drives. They decline together. Middle-aged people who are as tired as this person should see a doctor, examine their eating habits to see if they are destroying their vital energies with the wrong kinds of foods, or investigate potential vitamin deficiencies. We know of tired folks in their fifties who solved this problem by regularly going to bed one hour earlier. This gave them more zest. A number of people in our church have found that eating a large breakfast, a moderate lunch, and a skimpy dinner without an evening snack not only rids them of unwanted fat, but produces renewed energy. An increased sex drive will naturally follow and improve with an increase of vital energies.

Why does the desire for lovemaking fade as we get older?

Aging tends to reduce the intensity of most human drives, including sex, but by no means should they cease entirely. For forty years I enjoyed 20–20 vision, but for the past few years I've had to learn to live with glasses. And that's only one of many normal adjustments we all must make as we grow more "mature." Because people live longer today than they once did, such symptoms are more noticeable, and because we don't get as much exercise as we should, we compound the problem. Most of all, a person's mental attitude is extremely important. If you think your sex drive is fading, it will fade. Most middle-aged couples are still enjoying all the coitus they want—they just don't want as much as they once did. Our research, however, has indicated that many such couples have learned to love better and enjoy enriched love lives through the years, even though sexual experiences have decreased in number.

Men in their late sixties and older should consult a nutritionist to see if vitamin E, zinc supplements, prostada, and other natural helps can reignite their virility. Many have found it beneficial to visit their health-food store for this purpose.

Sex Drive

How do I cope with my husband's indifference to our sex life?

Have a frank talk with him—perhaps you are doing something that turns him off. Then try to ignite his interest by showing affection, displaying provocative attire in the bedroom (or elsewhere when no one else is around), and massaging his penis. Even the most reluctant penis can hardly ignore wifely stroking.

Is it wrong for a woman to have a stronger sex drive than a man?

No, your temperament, background, and general energy level will account for some of the difference. If you both approve your being the aggressor, enjoy it; never feel guilty about it. Many men are so mentally pressured by work and responsibilities that their sex drive is lessened until a loving wife stirs their attention.

What can a woman do to increase her sex drive?

She can change her mental attitude toward sex in general and work toward experiencing an orgasm. That usually increases a woman's appetite; repeated frustration often thwarts it.

Sex During Pregnancy

I am pregnant (first child), and my husband is overly concerned about hurting me or our baby. This has greatly hampered our sex life. Is this normal?

You are fortunate to have such a thoughtful, considerate husband. However, his groundless fears are cheating you both out of many exciting opportunities to express your love for each other. Most doctors indicate that love relations are perfectly safe until about six weeks prior to the expected birth of your child. Urge your husband to have a talk with your doctor; he or she is the best one to correct his thinking on the subject.

Stimulation

Should a wife stimulate herself prior to intercourse to get into the mood? (This seems wrong to me, but some sex clinics teach this.)

We see nothing wrong with this, but it would be better if the husband stimulated you through adequate foreplay. Self-stimulation is never as exciting as being stimulated by the person you love.

For a woman, so much of sex starts before the actual act. Women read books and seek help, but men usually don't. How do men get this education? What can a woman do to help her response when this area is lacking?

One of the reasons we are writing this book is to help such men. If your husband is not much of a reader, perhaps he will listen to Dr. Wheat's cassettes referred to on page 133, n.1.

Is it acceptable to use "playthings" for stimulation during lovemaking?

By "playthings" you probably mean vibrators to heighten stimulation. Those might be helpful in cases of male impotence or failure of a woman to respond to clitoral stimulation, but otherwise they should be unnecessary. In fact, to those who respond normally but use them as a lark, they might prove dangerous in over-stimulating and establishing an appetite for a level of stimulation their partner could not provide naturally.

How many women get "turned on" by the sight of a man's body as men do from seeing women?

Not many. Women must cultivate the problem of visual lust, whereas men almost universally must cope with the problem just because they are men. Many wives indicate that at times they get excited by seeing their husbands undress, but that is more in response to the pleasure they anticipate than in what they see.

How can a phlegmatic wife be stimulated to an orgasm more often than rarely? My wife enjoys our sexual relations, but manipulation does not bring her to orgasm.

Perhaps you're not doing it right. If you don't get sufficient lubrication on your fingers, either artificially with K-Y jelly or the natural lubrication of her vagina, you may be irritating her instead of exciting her. Start out slowly and lovingly, then gradually increase your movement as her excitement intensifies. Discuss it with her frankly to learn what she enjoys best.

Television

I've heard of a medical doctor who advises young couples not to buy a TV set until after one year of marriage. Do you agree?

You are probably referring to my friend Dr. Wheat, who has proved most helpful in the preparation of this manuscript. He makes that observation quite clearly in his sex education cassettes referred to earlier. Yes, we do agree with him, not only for newlyweds, but others also. Because of the busy pace and complex schedule most people are forced to keep these days, they have little enough time together. The hours they do spend in the privacy of their homes or apartments should be utilized in learning to communicate with each other on every level, not permitting the TV to absorb their prime time from after dinner until bedtime. Instead of talking, teasing, loving, and expressing themselves freely, they often spend the evening being entertained and consequently forfeit the much-needed sharing. This is particularly true in the first year of marriage. Dr. Wheat reports that after their first year together many couples have thanked him for that piece of advice. We noticed that our two married children apparently made exceptionally good adjustments early in their marriages; since neither of them could afford a TV while going to seminary and college, we concluded that a definite relationship existed.

TV is a thief of love, not just for newlyweds, but for most married couples. Wives with small children look forward to their husbands' coming home for an evening of fellowship, then become resentful when hubby can muster only a few grunts and nods between commercials. In addition, TV-watching tends to become a habit each evening until after the eleven o'clock news. Consequently, at least one of the partners is just too exhausted to make love enthusiastically. We suggest that shutting off the TV or at least cutting down on its use and developing the habit of going to bed regularly at or before 10 P.M. would increase the frequency of love-making for almost any couple. It would probably increase the quality of the experience also. When measured in that light—TV just can't be that good!

Temperament

Does one's predominant temperament also affect his attitudes and feelings about sexual relationship?

The people with more aggressive temperaments will usually be more aggressive about love; conversely those who are more passive will desire it less. Our survey indicated that sanguine people are very responsive to lovemaking. Choleric men are "quick" lovers and may not satisfy their wives; choleric women fall into two categories: (1) those who learn orgasm early—they will often initiate lovemaking; (2) those who do not—they will develop a distaste for it. Melancholic people have a sensitive nature and can be good lovers, provided they don't develop the deplorable habit of letting their perfectionistic tendencies cause them to make a mental "checklist" of duties that must be fulfilled before they parcel out their lovemaking favors.

It was particularly interesting to us to find that phlegmatic women registered a higher frequency of satisfaction than phlegmatic men; but this is probably because a phlegmatic wife is more inclined to go along with her husband's desires.

Nevertheless, temperament is not the only factor that influences those responses. There are others—such as training, childhood experiences, and proper sexual understanding. However, in our opinion, the most important factor that produces happiness in a couple's love life is not their temperaments but their ability to be unselfish toward each other. Selfishness is the enemy of love; unselfishness produces love.

Miscellaneous

Do people shower or clean up after sex?

This is a subject we failed to include in our survey. Dr. Miles, however, did ask this question, with these results: 58.8 percent got up immediately and washed; 41.2 percent enjoyed an endearing conversation for a few minutes. Sometimes couples fall asleep in each other's arms. Usually the man can sleep all night without washing up, but, because of the drainage of seminal fluid, the wife usually cannot.

Do questions 27 and 28 of your survey referring to clitoral manipulation mean other than with the penis?

Yes, with the finger. This is a necessary part of the art of love. Almost all wives can experience an orgasm with proper clitoral stimulation.

Why does a woman use sex as a weapon?

Because it is usually the last "weapon" she has— but why do lovers need "weapons"? When a woman uses sex as a weapon, she is grasping at straws, and unfortunately it leads to sexual suicide. Evidently she feels insecure in her husband's love. A man whose wife does this ought to respond in two ways: (1) talk to her lovingly and point out how it appears to him and (2) check his treatment of her—perhaps this dangerous practice is her frantic cry for help, and what she really needs is more love, tenderness, and consideration. Those attributes will automatically lead to a better relationship and more exciting lovemaking.

Is it ever wrong to resist a husband's advances? Is it harmful if done nicely with an explanation?

All spouses at some time have to resist the advances of a partner because of tiredness, preoccupation, mood, or for other reasons. It should not be done often (1 Cor. 7:1–5) and should always be accompanied by a reason and an assurance of love so that the partner knows it is not a personal rejection, but a human limitation. This really should be no problem for two people who are so much in love that they are sensitive to each other's needs and desires.

My husband always wants me to be the initiator and him the responder. How can I encourage him to take the lead in the marriage act?

Have a frank talk with him and explain your needs for his expression of love. Your temperaments may be the cause—he probably has a phlegmatic temperament and you are probably aggressive in most things. If so, accept it and do your best; look on it as a challenge to turn him on—you'll both be winners!

How can the sexual relationship be a spiritual experience also?

Everything a Christ-controlled Christian does is spiritual. That includes eating, elimination, spanking children, or emptying the trash. Why isolate sex in marriage as if it were in a category all by itself? Many spiritual Christians pray before going to bed, then in a matter of minutes engage each other in foreplay, stimulation, coitus, and finally orgasm. Why isn't that just as spiritual as anything else couples do? In fact, we believe the more truly spiritual they are, the more loving and affectionate they will be with each other and consequently the more frequently they will make love. Actually, coitus should be the ultimate expression of a rich spiritual experience that continues to enrich the couple's relationship.

Notes

1. David Reuben, *Everything You Always Wanted to Know About Sex* (New York: David McKay, 1969), 141.

2. Ibid., 127.

Bibliography

Andelin, Aubrey P. *Man of Steel and Velvet*. Santa Barbara, Calif.: Pacific Press Santa Barbara, 1972.

Anthony, Catherine Parker. *Textbook of Anatomy and Physiology*. St. Louis: Mosby, 1963.

Bird, Lewis P., and Christopher T. Reilly. *Learning to Love*. Waco, Tex.: Word, 1971.

Caprio, Frank S. *Sex and Love*. New York: Citadel, 1965.

_____. *The Sexually Adequate Male*. Greenwich, Conn.: Fawcett Publications, 1952.

Chandler, Sandra S. *The Sensitive Woman*. Pasadena: Compass, 1972.

Clark, LeMon. *101 Intimate Sexual Problems Answered*. New York: New American Library, 1968.

Cooke, Charles E., and Eleanore Ross. *Sex Can Be an Art!* Los Angeles: Sherbourne, 1964.

Curtis, Lindsay R. *Sensible Sex* (A Guide for Newlyweds). San Juan, Puerto Rico: Searle & Co., 1971.

Deutsch, Ronald M. *The Key to Feminine Response in Marriage*. New York: Random House, 1968.

Drakeford, John W. *The Great Sex Swindle*. Nashville: Broadman, 1966.

Ellzey, W. Clark. *How to Keep Romance in Your Marriage*. New York: Association, 1965.

Florio, Anthony. *Two to Get Ready*. Old Tappan, N.J.: Revell, 1974.

Greenblat, Bernard R. *A Doctor's Marital Guide for Patients*. Chicago: Budlong, 1964.

Hamilton, Eleanor. *Sex Before Marriage*. New York: Meredith, 1969.

Jones, H. Kimball. *Toward a Christian Understanding of the Homosexual*. New York: Association, 1966.

LaHaye, Timothy, and Beverly LaHaye. *Against the Tide: How to Raise Pure Kids in an "Anything Goes" World*. Portland, Ore.: Multnomah Press, 1993.

Levin, Robert, and Amy Levin. "Sexual Pleasure: The Surprising Preferences in 100,000 Women." *Redbook* 145 (September 1970).

Masters, William H., and Virginia E. Johnson. *Human Sexual Response*. Boston: Little, Brown and Co., 1966.

Miles, Herbert J. *Sexual Happiness in Marriage*. Grand Rapids: Zondervan, 1967.

Mumford, Bob. *Living Happily Ever After*. Old Tappan, N.J.: Revell, 1973.

Petersen, J. Allan, ed. *The Marriage Affair*. Wheaton, Ill.: Tyndale House, 1971.

Piper, Otto A. *The Biblical View of Sex and Marriage*. New York: Scribner, 1960.

Rainer, Jerome, and Julia Rainer. *Sexual Pleasure in Marriage*. New York: Pocket Books, 1959.

Reuben, David. *Any Woman Can!* New York: David McKay, 1971.

_____. *Everything You Always Wanted to Know About Sex*. New York: David McKay, 1969.

_____. *How to Get More Out of Sex*. New York: David McKay, 1974.

Rice, Shirley. *The Christian Home: A Woman's View*. Norfolk: Norfolk Christian Schools, 1965.

_____. *Physical Unity in Marriage: A Woman's View*. Norfolk: Norfolk Christian Schools, 1973.

Robinson, Marie N. *The Power of Sexual Surrender*. New York: New American Library, 1962.

Scanzoni, Letha. *Sex and the Single Eye*. Grand Rapids: Zondervan, 1968.

_____. *Sex Is a Parent Affair*. Glendale, Calif.: Gospel Light Publications, 1973.

Sheridan, Edward P., and Kathleen Sheridan, eds. *28 Experts View the Sexual Marriage*. Huntington, Ind.: Our Sunday Visitor, 1974.

Smith, Bob. *Love Story . . . the Real Thing*. Staff research at Peninsula Bible Church, Palo Alto, Calif., 1974.

Strong, James. "Dictionary of the Words in the Greek Testament" in *Strong's Exhaustive Concordance of Words in the Greek Testament*. New York: Abingdon-Cokesbury, 1890.

Subak-Sharpe, Genell J. "Is Your Sex Life Going Up in Smoke?" *Reader's Digest*, 106 (January 1975).

Thayer, Joseph Henry. *Thayer's Greek-English Lexicon of the New Testament*. Marshalltown, Del.: National Foundation for Christian Education, 1885, rev. ed., 1889.

Timmons, Tim. *One Plus One*. Washington, D.C.: Canon, 1974.

Vincent, M.O. *God, Sex and You*. Philadelphia: Lippincott, 1970.

Printed in the USA
CPSIA information can be obtained
at www.ICGtesting.com
LVHW051531210724
785408LV00008B/54